Frank Keating spent the early part of his career as a regional journalist and an Independent Television producer but for the last two decades has devoted himself to full-time sportswriting. He has already won eight Fleet Street awards for work as a staffer on the *Guardian*, and also for his pieces in *The Spectator* and *Punch*. He is the author of several books including, most recently, his autobiography *Half-Time Whistle* which was the runner-up in the William Hill Sports Book of the Year award. He is married and lives in Hertfordshire.

Also by Frank Keating

ANOTHER BLOODY DAY IN PARADISE
(DEUTSCH, 1981)

UP AND UNDER – A RUGBY JOURNAL
(HODDER & STOUGHTON, 1983)

HIGH, WIDE AND HANDSOME – A BIOGRAPHY OF
IAN BOTHAM (COLLINS, 1985)

HALF-TIME WHISTLE – AN AUTOBIOGRAPHY
(ROBSON, 1992)

THE GREAT
NUMBER TENS

Frank Keating

Foreword by Barry John

CORGI BOOKS

THE GREAT NUMBER TENS
A CORGI BOOK : 0 552 14688 9

Originally published in Great Britain by Partridge Press,
a division of Transworld Publishers Ltd

PRINTING HISTORY
Partridge Press edition published 1993
Corgi edition published 1999

Set in 11/12pt Sabon by Falcon Oast Graphic Art

Corgi Books are published by Transworld Publishers Ltd,
61–63 Uxbridge Road, London W5 5SA,
in Australia by Transworld Publishers,
c/o Random House Australia Pty Ltd,
20 Alfred Street, Milsons Point, NSW 2061,
in New Zealand by Transworld Publishers,
c/o Random House New Zealand,
18 Poland Road, Glenfield, Auckland
and in South Africa by Transworld Publishers,
c/o Random House (Pty) Ltd,
Endulini, 5a Jubilee Road, Parktown 2193.

Reproduced, printed and bound in Great Britain by
Cox & Wyman Ltd, Reading, Berks.

*To Patrick and Tess, who
say they like history*

Contents

Foreword by Barry John

It was a memorable and long late-night session in a favourite Chinese restaurant in Cardiff's Tiger Bay – FK and BJ chewing the sporting fat into the early hours, and all the while being serenaded by Shirley Bassey (if only on the jukebox!). *Perfick*.

FK moves deftly into his stride of utter certainties (as he does past midnight) and even begins to pick holes in the coaching techniques of our beloved Carwyn James. 'Not only that,' he insists, 'but I was the only person to spot the early weaknesses in Phil Bennett's game . . . and as for that Jonathan Davies . . .'

Well, as far as I was concerned, such relishing enthusiasms ensure FK's undeniable references to undertake the task of such a special book as this, on the complex issue of the outside-half's position; its requirements; and the skills or otherwise of those who have worn the No. 10 jersey for a century now and from every point on the globe.

Mind you, that evening my eyelids did flicker with more than the slightest of double-takes when FK added solemnly, 'And as for you, BJ, I always reckoned that *tackling* was your strongest point.' Ah, well.

FK is a sportsman through and through. His writing cherishes the fact. I realize that his first love was cricket, and that to witness and then describe an effortless David Gower cover-drive gently caressing the ropes on a sunlit day was absolute heaven to him; as was, in the winters, a super-special by Greaves or Best when both seemed to run in a straight line at defenders who, courteously it seemed, would fall to one side as they went for the whites of the goalkeeper's eyes and the kill.

This is FK to perfection – the true romantic, always hoping for and seeking that priceless moment in sport

9

which first transforms and then even lifts the momentous passage into another stratosphere.

It is the reason why, I am certain, he has now decided to study and interrogate rugby's No. 10s. Fly-half play, in all its aspects, has tickled FK's palate. He has loved what they try to do – and needed then to explore the question *What makes them tick?*

Born in Hereford and brought up in Glos., he would have been intrigued and fascinated through his boyhood at hearing the crunch and the thunderous roars, the songs and the sweet smells of liniment that wafted across the border from Wales. So I suppose it was inevitable that rugby would catch up with him in the end.

He is now a dedicated and devout rugby man who totally understands the game – and he will even sagely tell you that he knows through bitter experience exactly what a late tackle feels like!

I believe it is his unique understanding of other sports, personalities and occasions and dramas – plus his massive mental library and detail for fact – which contributes as much as anything to making this book such a joy to read.

The fly-half's job is complex, it is a jigsaw where cunning, skill, awareness, daring, courage, and more than a little bit of arrogance are all part of the make-up – and each attribute must be put exactly in place to conjure up a command performance.

FK has captured all this and more in a truly illuminating, lively and humorous manner. This is history come to vibrant life – and it has been a privilege for me to write this foreword to a book I can only describe as *Perfick*.

Barry John
Cardiff, June 1993

Preface

It is a myth that Rugby Union has been poorly served by its celebrating, or even sarky, writers down the century. But, secure in its own freemasonry behind the clubhouse door, the game as a whole has never bothered much either way about adjectival fripperies – and most certainly not about the nuts and bolts of hard facts and stats in the way cricket, for instance, has created its own thriving swots' cottage-industry which is inevitably sliderule-exact to the fourth decimal point. In which respect, even less than ten years ago this rugby book could have been no more than a hit-or-miss mass of airyfairy guesses and inexactitudes. So my first indebtedness must be to the recent diligent pathfinding by two friends and meticulous students of the small print – John Griffiths, especially for his microscopically detailed *Phoenix Book of International Rugby Records* (1987) as well as his annual triumph with the Rothmans *Yearbook,* and Terry Godwin (and his researcher John Jenkins) for the scrupulous *Who's Who of International Rugby* (Blandford, 1987). Their work has laid down markers for which the world game's still often hopelessly insular, red-nosed establishment burghers should be truly grateful.

Keith Quinn's love's labour *The Encyclopaedia of World Rugby* (Lochar, 1991) was never far from my elbow when it came to checking a fact; nor, to bring down to earth any pretentious sporting-social historian, was the stupendous epic by David Smith and Gareth Williams, *Fields of Praise* (University of Wales Press, 1980), surely the best book of its type on any sport, C. L. R. James notwithstanding. The writings of another James, the late Carwyn, in the *Guardian* inspired me at the time, and it was rewarding to go back to them. That compact romance *A Touch of Glory*, by dear Carwyn's Boswell, Alun Richards, was also a touchstone.

But what gave me the warmest buzz as I settled to the candle-burning task after Jane had poured me yet another late-night whisky was the regularly enchanting eye-openers provided by unsung and forgotten workaday journos like myself who, as this book took on a life of its own (as they always do), steadily became as much my newly discovered and shining heroes as any of rugby's grandest No. 10s of the chronicle – Quink-ink, nicotine-stained men in homburg hats, now totally unconsidered and keeping company only in fusty, musty newspaper files, but whose scintillating stuff (when dusted down between sneezes) really does live again – indeed dances and sparkles and illuminates like light through a prism. It was truly a pleasure to dawdle through the library cuttings of such pen-pushing pioneers as E. H. D. Sewell of the London *Evening Standard* and W. J. Townsend Collins of the *South Wales Argus*. A. A. Thomson, of *The Times* and *Punch et al.* (whom I knew of from cricket), was another unrealized delight on rugby. All were prolific old-timers who logged the development of the game out of its prehistory with a fidelity and fondness and lightness of touch quite above the call of daily deadline duties.

Likewise more already lauded and lofty archive names in the game who so readily took it upon themselves – doubtless with no thanks from their respective Unions' officials – to log their particular country's rugby progress down the century: journalists like South Africa's 'Ace', A. C. Parker of the *Cape Argus*; Terry McLean of the New Zealand *Herald;* Vivian Jenkins of London's *Sunday Times*; and, it goes without saying, the prolific rugby zealot J. B. G. 'Bryn' Thomas of the *Western Mail*. They have been guiding lights – and the latter trio, in their celebrated dotage, have been werry, werry kind to a tyro like me. As have my present mates in the press box. Their convivial comradeship is even more valued than their cribs – many of which, nevertheless, have helped put most of the professional insights and gloss on the following pages and for which my thanks far outweigh the passing acknowledgements to them which speckle the text.

Gratitude in abundance to those superduper stars of the book itself – the heroes in the No. 10 jersey – who so freely and uncomplainingly gave up their time to be interviewed. It is rewarding to have the all-time elite guard pinned down at last between hard covers. But if the finished job has failed to put them collectively where they deserve, on the topmost plinth in the game's pantheon, then it is my fault alone.

For the last twenty years or so, I have enjoyed with relish 'noting the nannies' and getting in the snorts for the *Guardian*'s two different but outstanding Rugby Union correspondents, David Frost and Robert Armstrong. Applause to them – and also to the Faringdon Road sports desk and our editor, Mike Averis, a devout rugby buff with the enthusiasm and encouragement of the very best of scrum-half skippers.

The super and simple idea to chronicle a history through the succession of reigning monarchs was Dick Douglas-Boyd's. He pestered eagerly, and once Debbie Beckerman added her resolve and an expert team from Partridge, the project was irresistible. All that was needed then was whisky enough to keep priming Lindy Glover's word-processor and ask, who else? the onliest Barry John, if he would seal his imprimatur on the wheeze and then launch it with an inimitable kick-off.

F.K., Hereford, June 1993

1

Hat-hurling hooraymanship

Any half-decent sport has to be a sucker for nostalgia. That makes two of us – for there is a glistening purity about one's fondness for, and recollection of, the boyhood heroes of the sports fields.

Rugby Union at fifteen a side, uniquely in any of the world's leading team games, cuts down the romantic's options. Well, for the spectator not many sprinklings of magical fairy dust pervade the dark and dingy recesses of the scrum. Two distinct and basic strategies by men of different build and character make up a team at rugby. Eight footslogging forwards picked for brawn and height and strength and stamina perspire manfully as a collective, at the coalface as it were, to provide the ball – and, with it, sunshine and light and fresh, open spaces – for seven high-steppers outside them who fancy themselves as free-as-air dandies and darters and dodgers. The men who do not just sniff the wind but create it. The men who warm the cockles, riddle the spine – and make you thankfully pleased that you were there.

No offence, but for the sake of the matter in hand let's leave those eightsome reelers of the scrum at their private dance for consenting adults. They prefer it that way, too, and are well aware that a treatise on how they go about their pulling and pushing, shoeing and shoving, would not have much light shed upon it by an advanced PhD scholar with a Davy lamp and a First in Furniture Removing and

15

Applied Muscular Physics. What concerns us here is only that they get the ruddy ball back to their scrum-half. We will presume that they do – every single time we want it. Thank you, gentlemen . . . now back down in your cage to the coalface.

My first rugby hero was a wing-threequarter, my second a full-back. This juvenile idolater bought their dummy both times, as one so often does with un-considered hero worship, I'm afraid. I was brought up near Gloucester, in a sprawling railway village called Stonehouse, which was solemnly plonked, like an after-thought, below the western rim of the last of Stroud's sublime golden valleys. But it still made for pastoral, butterfly-bobbing summers at cricket on a myriad of hillocky village fields or lovingly tended factory paddocks which speckled the length of the disused, green-slimed Stroudwater Canal. In those dozy, sun-baked summers, it was all peace and quiet and cricket.

But in the ice-armoured winters, it was sport and noise of a very different clatter and hue and texture. For this was very business-like rugby country. Soccer was second-place. Stroud had a grand rugger team; Cainscross and Painswick too; then there were the Nomads and Stragglers, and no end of factory sides, each in regular, rollicking rivalry, with no holds barred. When they were not amiably kicking bruises into each other, they travelled the ten miles or so on other Saturdays for ditto fun against the umpteen local city sides in Gloucester, a rugby bastion famed round the world for its proud and insular hard-headedness, with its home at Kingsholm even more celebrated a shrine, to some, than the mellow, honeyed-grey Norman tower of the Cathedral, a few hundred yards away, which has kept sentinel to the old city for eight centuries.

Kingsholm is where I first saw John Vincent Smith, playing on the wing for Stroud against Gloucester in an evening match in the autumn. He was a tiny man, but when given the ball he ran like a hare startled out of a hedge. His family were corn merchants in Ebley, just down the road from us. The whole district knew him simply by his initials. He was 'our JV'. He left the local grammar school, Marling, and went up to Cambridge. I was in my last year at a prep school in Hereford, Belmont Abbey, run by the black-cowled Benedictines. JV was picked on the wing for Cambridge in the 1949 University Match at Twickenham, and I spent a week pleading with Father Fabian if we could be excused games that first Tuesday afternoon of December to listen to the BBC commentary on the match winging down through the crackle and static right into, and out of, that old, fluted, faked walnut wireless set in the corner of the Common Room.

The dear chap agreed, so I doubled my bets on how many Cambridge would win by and how many tries my JV, Stroud's very own world-class full-pelter, would get. The lads scoffed and doubled their stakes with urchins' bravado and confidence. He would not even get one single try, they chided. I took the bets, and prayed to St Francis, St John and St Vincent.

We huddled round the wireless. The scoffs gradually turned to sneers. It was obviously a turgid, ground-out yawn at Twickenham in the mud. For an hour and more, the only occasional mention my hero had from the commentator was when he tossed the ball into the lineout. Oxford scored an early try and then closed the game down. I was mortified – and more than being on the verge of pocket-money bankruptcy was the shame of it. JV had blatantly double-crossed his worshipper.

I was done for. They were into injury time now. In the wintery, teatime gloaming, the commentator said he could hardly see.

But then he suddenly launched into a banshee shriek . . .

'Cambridge have it . . . Scrum-half Dorward blindside, to Smith . . . He dummies his wing, and beats him . . . Small, the Oxford flanker, is there . . . No, Smith swerves outside him . . . He's up to the halfway line now . . . J. V. Smith is clear . . . Curtis and Rittson-Thomas thunder across to cover . . . Smith, gloriously, has the legs of them

17

both . . . He's racing up to the twenty-five now, with only the retreating Hofmeyr, the Oxford full-back, to beat . . . Smith rounds him disdainfully, and he's on like a whippet . . . No-one can touch him now . . . The line is at his mercy – Smith must score one of Twickenham's most superlative individual tries in history . . .'

At which the bawling crescendo died like a fierce breaker on the sea-wall . . .

'Oh, no – what's this? Who's this? Smith's been hurled into touch just a foot from the line. Oh, what a tackle! Just where did Kendall-Carpenter come from . . . ?'

I was ditched too. Double-crossed by a ruddy double-barrel. My mates chortled. I bitterly passed round exorbitant IOUs, for many of which I was still being called to account in the next summer's term. The awful price of hero worship betrayed.

Many years later, J. V. Smith and John Kendall-Carpenter would both become presidents of the Rugby Union itself. Once, at a black-tied club dinner, I sat between them. 'C'mon, gents,' I said, 'the truth about that childhood trauma of mine?'

Said 'Carps' (who was to die of a heart attack in 1990): 'JV was fast all right, but like most great wingers he only needed to be over twenty or thirty yards. I was meant to be a lumbering forward, but I knew I could always gobble him up over the full length of the pitch. When he got clear that day, with just a few strides left as I came across at him, he should have dived like a bullet for the line. Instead, he turned and glanced at me. Our eyes met, and I saw a hunted look in him – and I knew I'd captured my prey, and I took off and bombed him into touch just a couple of ruler-lengths from the line.'

Said JV: 'The whole point is – where did "Carps" come from? It was so murky, nobody could see much. I still think he'd been kneeling on the twenty-five doing up his bootlaces from the previous scrum – so when I came past, he just got up and ambled across to tackle me. A try would have drawn the match for us, but a conversion would have won it, so I had in my mind to attempt to get near the posts. I forgot that when I saw him coming at me, and reckoned in the split second that my best option was to dive for the line but to let him tackle me hard and so allow the momentum to carry me over. Alas, with his weight and the angle he came at me, when he hit me amidships it crashed me into touch.'

In the year after that match, JV played four games for England on the wing – and scored four splendid tries. But for me the romance had died that dingy December day. My first lesson that heroes can turn to clay.

A year later, the second rugby giant of my youth also, and mortifyingly, bit the dust. Bill Hook was Gloucester's full-back, a stately, unsupple man with a Sar'nt Major's mien, and a greased head of black hair with a signwriter-straight middle parting. His two attributes were a safe pair of hands and a kick like a Bisley mule from both hand and ground. Bill kept a sports goods shop in Westgate Street. In the Christmas holidays of 1951 we would gawp at him through the shop window, or dare each other to enter and buy a ping-pong ball, just so the most famous man in Gloucestershire would utter a word to us. For England had picked him to play full-back at Twickenham in January – twice: first against mighty South Africa, and, just a fortnight later, against Wales. Barring injuries, the England team would remain intact for both games.

Old Bert Cole, a friend of my father's, had installed in his village-green cottage next to the Crown and Anchor a wondrous, new-fangled television set. The tiny monochrome figures flittered, fuzzily, to and fro across the minuscule screen. England could well have beaten the gargantuan Springboks, who won by only 8–3. In fact, our Bill Hook it was who did the very deed. He missed two totally easy-peasy penalty pots at goal, through nerves, and then he allowed a South African to as good as vault over his creaking geriatric semblance of a tackle and post the winning try. The whole county could not think where to look.

At least Bill could not do worse in the Welsh match? Sad to say, he did. Wales played with fourteen men almost throughout. England scored two early tries. Both conversion attempts by Bill would have sailed sumptuously over at Gloucester had he been blindfold and wearing his slippers. Here he muffed them miserably. Still, England seemed to have the match quite comfortably in the bag. Depleted, brave, Wales manfully mounted a last-gasp throw – and twice despairingly worked the ball out to their Olympic relay sprinter on the wing, Ken Jones. Both times, with no other choices, Jones ran straight through Bill as if he were a spectre.

Look it up – Twickenham, 19 January 1952: England 6, Wales 8. CORRECTION: England 6, Hook 8.

The sales of ping-pong balls in his little Westgate Street sports shop took a dramatic dive. As dramatic, anyway, as Bill's dying-swan tackles.

I reverted to cricket's much safer and rewarding giants, who actually brought home the bacon – and kept any likely rugby heroes locked firmly in the deep recesses of my boyhood breast till a long time later.

And so it was that, in the contrary way of man's seven ages, the older I've become, the far more contentedly susceptible to romance. Is it a shaming admission for a middle-aged adult to say that he has found himself increasingly on tiptoe, and hollering hoorays and hurling his hats up and away, in grandstands and press boxes round the world as the pageant moved inexorably on and yet another true-great passed by into the pantheon's all-time hall of fame?

I was there, for instance, in the ancient, now dolled-up but still palpitating amphitheatre at the Arms Park less than a winter ago when the whole of history's most opulent one-off wizard of a wing-threequarter, David Campese of Australia, signed off in an international match. Even if 'Campo's' farewell performances to Test rugby had been almost as numerous as his compatriot Dame Nellie Melba's had been to the concert stage, all of us in the vast throng sensed this really was a goodbye to utter grandeur.

Tony O'Reilly, no mean touchline trampler himself,

once spoke of rugby's joy in the wing-threequarter – 'for there is hardly a more stirring sight than the lonely foray of a solitary figure striding to death or glory into the gathering gloom of a winter's evening'. Such was the sight of Campese in Cardiff that Saturday against Wales – a sixty-yarder in the final minute to ice the cake. It had the vast throng in the famous old stadium on their feet, to a man, garlanding the Australian with a din of acclamation throughout his almost sheepish trot back to the halfway line.

An hour later I gawped, like the groupie I am, with a jostle of Welsh autograph urchins as the Australian squad embarked on their hotel coach. All but one of them were dressed in badged green regulation blazers and free-issue outback brogues. The onliest 'Campo' carried his blazer, as well as a beautifully cut Italian raincoat; his shoes, slacks and haircut obviously bespoke Milan. He likes to chew a toothpick, as young Italian dandies do.

His game has the flamboyance of the Latin-Celt. Which he is. His mother is a Murphy, whose family sailed from Kinsale to New South Wales at the turn of the century. His father, a carpenter, was born at Montecchio, a village between Venice and 'fair Padua, nursery of the arts', who left for Australia the day after his twenty-first birthday. David was born at Queanbeyan, NSW, thirty Octobers ago.

Wingers, in my lifetime anyway, have come in all shapes and sizes – and from every segment of the speedometer. There have been explosive, straight-track sprinters with delicate frames and ankles, such as Ken Jones, Pat Lagisquet or J. J. Williams. Or thunderous, scary, ground-rumblers, like Doug Smith, Ted Woodward, B. G. Williams or John Bevan. Or full-shouldered, full-pelt, wings-on-their-heels swervers such as Grant Batty and Rory Underwood. Or red-hot all-rounders with rugby 'brains', like Mike Slemen, Stu Wilson or John Kirwan. There have been solid, speedy enough toughies, like all those recent Scots, or Western Samoans, or Ireland's teaky Trevor Ringland. And a handful of unclassifiable one-offers like Chris Oti, Roger Baird, Simon Geoghegan or Rodney Webb, and good ol' O'Reilly himself. I never saw, of course, those two famed rockets of the 1950s on the veldt – Tom Vollenhoven and Theunis Briers, both bullet-heads and bullet-speed – but I did see their successor, Gerry Germishuys, scorch the Lions' tail in 1980 with endless tries.

For England, times without number, we waited and waited for David Duckham to be given a decent pass. So did David. But the Lions understood his famine – and he must have pinched himself for dreaming when he scored those six in a game for the 1971 Lions or that scintillating try against North Auckland on the same scintillating tour. I remember Duckham's first vivid score at Twickenham. Another daring pass and loop in his first Calcutta Cup game. In the next season came his, mine and everyone's favourite of all – that coruscating sprint against the dreaded Springboks at Twickenham, fair hair streaming like a pre-Raphaelite angel, winged boots never more than an inch from the left, Royal Box touchline till he ducked inside the murderous tackler, De Villiers, with no more than a shrug of a hip. From ten yards away, Mervyn Davies once told me, 'David's side-step looked obvious and predictable, but when you were confronted with it in close-up it had you stranded and leaden-footed.' Mervyn complimented very few Englishmen.

And then the Nijinskys – the darters, the dancers, the side-steppers, the intricate top-lick weavers of spells: Peter Jackson and Gerald Davies . . . ah, Gerald, frail-looking, pale and lonely on his touchline, scarlet shirt buttoned to the neck, fingers picking at his 'tash, or arms crossed as he warmed both hands in his armpits, till the ball was delivered and he'd pin his ears back and go at and through the slithering, cursing cover like an electric eel with brand new batteries. Now, in the press box, Gerald and I might giggle together as he passes the half-time peppermints, and as I blush at the wonder of little me sitting next to a legend, I think, 'Don't worry so: the greater the one-time hero, the greater the man.' At my birthday party last year

Gerald turned up with a bottle of bubbly. I didn't open it; I haven't opened it; well, you 'lay down' the vintage stuff, don't you? And if Gerald Davies gave it and wrote on the label to prove it, well, it's a vintage by definition, ain't it?

Campissimo has most affinity with the Nijinskys. But the nonpareil also carries in his kitbag of tricks a slice of every other style and facet and quality. And opponents never know which rabbit he is going to pull out next. On which zoological metaphor the great O'Reilly expands: 'Wingers can be lion or leprechaun, greyhound or tortoise, prancing circus horse or pampas bull.' What is Campese? 'I've no idea,' drawls the Australian marvel himself. 'I'm just me, I guess.'

Campese occasionally played full-back for Australia – doubtless with a mind to suss out every aspect and ploy of the position and those No. 15s he would be taunting again soon enough. Duckham and Davies both began their careers at centre-threequarter, at the core of the midfield. Carwyn James, that prince of coaches from Wales, who plotted the grand 1971 Lions victory against New Zealand – with Duckham and Davies on either wing – once told me, 'If Rugby Union was a professional game and I was entrusted with running a club and given a pot of gold, I would pay out the treasure trove for that rarest of species if I could find him – a real, genuine, copper-bottomed centre-threequarter.'

Carwyn knew the value of the un-soft centre. He played with and against such lustrous midfielders as Bleddyn Williams and Lewis Jones, two in the direct Welsh lineage founded by their Welsh compatriot, the acknowledged 'inventor' of centre play at the turn of the century, Arthur 'Monkey' Gould. I never saw Jones or Williams play – seven of the latter's brothers also played for the Cardiff club and their father was once asked the family secret: 'Two huge platefuls of beef stew every day, and rugby discussion in the evenings.' I did, however, revel in the calm arts and sciences of John Dawes, captain and centre of Carwyn's 1971 Lions and another notable heir of Gould.

A pair of centres used occasionally to play 'left and

right'. Now, invariably, they are 'inside' (next to the fly-half) and 'outside' (the direct link with the winger). In New Zealand, of course, the inside-centre – usually the more bludgeoning runner of the two, being nearer the predatory forwards – is called 'second five-eighth' (the 'first' being everyone else's fly-half). This second five-eighth and his single centre partner have provided New Zealand with some thundering good duos all down the years. I remember wincing in the grandstand almost as much as their red-shirted markers must have when Pokere and Fraser corralled the Lions in 1983. Osborne was another All Black five-eighth to put his weight around in midfield, thrillingly, in contrast to such quicksilver attackers with nous as Bruce Robertson and Joe Stanley. Three years previously, on the last Lions tour to South Africa before the republic's banishment by Britain, Smith and Du Plessis were a formidable pair in tandem. It was on that tour that we had our first view of a youthful Gerber in the centre. How famed would he have been round the world but for the apartheid ban.

In my memory, France have seldom failed to field one-off centres to riddle the spine: Codorniou, Bertranne, Sella – but who ever better than Maso? For Scotland, I remember that diminutive terrier Renwick tearing Wales apart on his own at Cardiff one day. Scott Hastings, brother of a true great, Gavin, at full-back, was another favourite centre with the thistle at his breast. At school in the 1950s, when Douai took on Wimbledon College I played two or three times against Joe McPartlin, who went on to captain Oxford and play in the centre for Scotland. A real card was Joe. He offered a new slant on old dogs changing positions and reverting to new positions on the field, especially on those occasions when the fifteen-man game resorts to 'sevens'. Joe also captained the Harlequins, and at one Middlesex sevens in the late 1950s he dreamed up the wheeze of putting that uncompromising international forward toughie Vic Marriott inside him at scrum-half. When they came up against their first elite side in the quarter-finals, Harlequins were well and truly stuffed. I asked Joe afterwards whether the experiment of playing doughty Vic at scrum-half had been a determining factor.

'You could say that,' he answered. 'Not that I minded too much about getting the ball along the ground every time. Or even having to fall on it. But the thing that was slightly worrying throughout the game (and it only lasted for fourteen minutes, of course) was that each of the dozen times I did have to go down on the ball, it was always Marriott who was first there to kick me in the back!' Happy days.

Think of one centre and you often think of two – like opening batsmen at cricket, or Marshall & Snelgrove in the high street. If the two most enduring partnerships for England at cricket in my time have been Hutton & Washbrook and Boycott & Edrich, the three centre-threequarter partners to come most trippingly off an Englishman's tongue have been Davies & Butterfield, Spencer & Duckham (before he was 'winged') and Guscott & Carling. Each complemented the other – Davies, Spencer and Carling had power and strength, Butterfield, Duckham and Guscott were each more fluid runners, almost pouring themselves through the gaps, it seemed. At the time of writing, I would say only the vibrant and gloriously competitive Australian centres Horan and Little would keep Carling and Guscott out of any World XV. With luck and (as always) barring accidents or Rugby League, all four are young enough to face each other again in the 1995 World Cup. Horan and Little are particularly merciless in the tackle. Since the 1991 World Cup, Carling has become almost a cult figure to an England newly exposed to the hitherto closed-shop freemasonry of Rugby Union. Carling suddenly represented the most marketable and recognizable gleaming white face for the hoardings. You do not have to know how many make up a rugger team to recognize the fizzog – cleft chin by Cary Grant, quiff by James Dean, shoulders by Stallone and, when cued, grin by Colgate. Almost by the way is he one of the world's most outstanding all-round centre-threequarters. He has pace and panache; he is brave, bold and rippingly strong off the front and back foot; few centres have ever 'presented' a pass to a confrère more securely (although quite a few have presented them more often). He has never allowed the teak-hardness of his play to spill into any snide or bullying dirtiness. Compared with some around him, he plays chivalrously and honours the foe, yet he is the despised demon king whose seeming swank, strut and swagger as chairman and chief executive of W. Carling plc must be brought down a peg, and the more viciously the better. Scottish (especially), Australian and Welsh crowds vie to jeer him most. Prep school, public school, university, British Army and England captain at twenty-two without having got his knees dirty: that is what, deep down, riles to distraction the Celts and colonials. How they cheered when he failed to make the Lions Test team in 1993.

Carling was at Sedbergh, the Lake District public school which, amazingly, has produced twenty-eight rugby internationals down the years for England (eleven), Scotland (fifteen) and Ireland (two). A predecessor of Will's in the centre both for Sedbergh and for England was John Spencer. The old rugby master at the school, Brooke Douse, once recalled in the *Guardian* his two famous centres: 'John and William were very different; John was physically bigger, for a start. But both had this thing you can't coach: the ability to time a pass.' Douse's earliest memory of Carling was from a match in his first senior season against Blackrock College when he broke clean through a midfield which included Brendan Mullin. 'I said, "That chap will go far. I haven't seen anything like that since John Spencer."'

Spencer, too, has an early recollection from an old boys' match. 'I remember Will's father asking, just before he went up to Durham University, if I thought he would make it. I said there was no reason why he shouldn't; he'd got the pace, he'd got everything. But even as I said it, I didn't really think he would. At that time there was quite a lot of talent about that never really came to fruition. In some ways he was a bit lucky to get in at the start, but he's certainly well worth his place now.'

In these off-hand, cursory and personal recollections, setting the scene, a couple of my own favourites – by no means the very best in the world game, but good, very – nudge me for a mention. Both were fine enough centres to play for the British Lions; both had that singular personality off the field that set them apart. David Hewitt was an Ulsterman, Ray Gravell a West Walian. Tony O'Reilly tells the story of playing outside Hewitt on the Lions tour to New Zealand in 1959: 'We had been beaten late in the first and second tests, had lost the third comprehensively, but led 9–6 going into the final few minutes of the last. We were well on top, but strange refereeing decisions had conspired to give them penalty chances. As they attacked, I stood on the goal line, deep in thought and thinking what my opposite number would do if he got the ball.

'Suddenly Dave Hewitt moved out towards me and with the crowd going crazy for an All Black score, says in a Northern Ireland accent: "Have you seen that cloud formation up there? Why, that's a very interesting and beautiful sky. I'm going to take a picture of that when this game is over." I said to myself, "My God, here is a man who is committed passionately to the game of rugby football!"'

Ray Gravell was a similar dreamer of passion. Dear Ray. He was a centre for the Lions in South Africa in 1980. In a span of ten years for Wales – a man of flint and pitch, unceremoniously knocking down trespassers and preparing the canvas for Dylan's 'boys of summer' inside and outside his darling Wales' last golden age – Ray was twice dropped from the national side. He found it unbearable both times he read 'RAY AXED' in the *Carmarthen Guardian*. Finally, after twenty-three matches proudly wearing the red he wrote to the selectors, asking not to be considered ever again: the joy of being selected could not match the pain of being discarded. 'It was the country, you see. Dropped, I felt unclean, I felt I had a stigma. I could risk it no longer.'

Gravell's father, a miner injured in a rock-fall at the

face, would take his only son down on Eynon's bus of a Saturday and they would stand, hand in hand, on Stradey's 'tanner-bank' and watch Llanelli's Scarlets play. Dad died before he could know Ray was to captain Llanelli – and even get a tasselled cap for the national team. 'I remember, too, when I ran out for my first game for Wales against France at Paris in 1975. It wasn't so much that I had to think of Dad then, I knew he was just there, all around. Then they played *Land of My Fathers*. "Over freedom they lost their blood, The struggle still goes on . . ." Yes, it was a natural reaction to cry. I was giving my allegiance, you see. And to my father.'

The boy's beard was damp that day. He had the dressing-room telegrams from the village, and from his wife, the local golden girl called Aurona, and then his mother's: 'Chi'n gwbod pwy yw Toodles bois. Y gath!' ('Best wishes to my son, all my love from Mam and Toodles'). 'Do you know who Toodles is, boys? The effin' cat! The effin' cat sent us a telegram!' They all cried too, led by the coach Clive Rowlands. To Carwyn James, Ray was the true and living, pre-medieval Prince of Wales, Llewellyn, killed by the English in 1282.

Then what about the scrum-halves? Jeeps, the mudlark; Ken Catchpole, possibly the finest ever for purity of pass . . . as Gareth was for everything else; there was Steve Smith's smile, and Sid Going's heroic industry, tenacity and drive; Terry Holmes and Robert Jones, who both had to carry all of Wales on their shoulders; Jerome Gallion, of France, and his confrère Jacques Fouroux, most unlikely and ungainly little Gauloise stub; the beaver and burrower, Roy Laidlaw, and his shining apprentice Gary Armstrong . . . not, ever, to forget D. O. Brace, of Oxford and Wales, another to mesmerize a schoolboy; nor the man himself, Andy Mulligan, who once went up for a job from Dublin to Belfast and his prospective boss asked him: 'What religion are you, Mulligan?' Replied Andy, 'What religion did you have in mind, sir?'

And on and on . . . Chris Laidlaw, and Loveridge, and Dawie de Villiers. Not forgetting Farr-Jones, after

28

Catchpole and Edwards probably the most 'complete' of all the scrum-halves I've seen. Catchpole's secret, I fancy, was that while you gasped at the speed of his hands whipping the ball away, it was in fact the correct position of his feet which allowed him such a balanced, geometrically exact pass off either side.

Edward's last match for Wales was at Cardiff against France in 1978. At the final whistle that day, Edwards's gallant friend and foe Jean-Pierre Rives sought him out and embraced him. 'Gareth, *mon ami, magnifique*, you old fox!' He smiled. 'See you next year, eh?'

'Yes,' said Edwards, 'you bet.' But deep down he had made up his mind; he was going to begin the second half of his life. 'I always adored the French match. Over the years, opponents would fall into set categories. Like you always wanted to beat the All Blacks, but even more desperately had to beat the English. Scotland and Ireland always looked to spoil, to stop us playing. But France always came out to beat you, and us to beat them. It was the team to beat – and then retire, content.' Just like that.

From that day to this, Edwards played only one more game of rugby. 'Just once, all of ten years later, did I pull on a rugby shirt. In France again, too. In Toulouse. For an Invitation XV against the reassembled French Grand Slam side of 1977.

'It was truly glorious, reliving everything. I thought I'd last five minutes; I lasted an hour; what fabulous comradeship and true warmth. Phil [Bennett], seemingly fitter than ever, really turning it on, scurrying footwork and all; Jo Maso full of all his old magical, weaving patterns. I was so elated to be involved, I can hardly describe it. An excited crowd, full to capacity, and all of us seeming to play just like we used to, like people said we had played. So unreal, so fulfilling – unless we all saw it through tinted glasses on account of the wines we had drunk.

'Near the end of the game I had a run. Just like the old days. I got it around our twenty-two. Suddenly I was through, and going for the line; thirty yards, forty, fifty.

Would they catch me? The crowd going mad. Maureen was up in the stand. Suddenly she was on her feet, apparently, pleading with me: "Stop! Stop!" She thought her old man was going to kill himself. Funny, a dozen years earlier, she'd have been on her feet bellowing "Go on, go on", wouldn't she?

'That's what growing older means, at the end of the day, I suppose.' And he grins hugely. 'Life goes on.'

Ah, Gareth's last try . . . The first I ever saw in an international match was at Twickenham, golly, two score years ago. New Zealand v. England, 30 January 1954. Still I throw a fond and rheumy glance left from Twickenham's press box to the Old Clock corner-flag. The first try I witnessed at the now rebuilt (into anonymity) but once beloved, cabbagey-green old amphitheatre was scored there – by Dalzell, of New Zealand, an oak tree of a bloke who crashed through a thicket of covering Englishmen to scatter them like twigs. It was the only try of the game but still, forty years on, my spirit yelps a cowering 'Timber!' at the memory of Dalzell's hurtling flop for the line. Our front-row school party, mittened and mufflered against the swirling snowflakes but hearts furnace-hot with the thrill of it, were right behind Bob Scott's torpedo-true conversion which bisected the H from an inch inside touch on the twenty-five. Scott was the man we'd come to see. The most famous full-back ever.

He was the first rugby player of truly global resplendence we had ever heard of. An all-time hall-of-famer, and, would you believe it, us under-sixteeners could have stuck out a hand and patted his backside as he lined up that kick. Or polished the tonsure that rimmed his almost coot-bald head.

Great Scott. He didn't let us down that day. Raucously, we were rooting for England, of course – and Regan and Rimmer darted, and Davies and Butterfield barrelled through the midfield, or fed their rumbling roll of thunder Woodward on the right wing – but as greatness had been thrust before us that afternoon in the shape of Scott, it was right and proper that he should display some. And how. Shining pate and smiling face, with opulent grandeur as last line of defence he felled each and every danger with stirring tackles as clean as Roy Rogers's lasso; and he caught everything thrown up at him into the swirling gales, and then would feint and dodge and hopscotch clear before setting up the counter-attack with a genial grin. A smile not of any remote swagger or strut. He was simply enjoying a jolly good game. Those men whom boys make their heroes have an awesome responsibility.

I have looked up the musty files. In *The Times* next Monday morning, the headline said simply: 'NEW ZEALAND A GREAT PACK – AND SCOTT.' In the following Friday's *Spectator*, the columnist and MP J. P. W. 'Curly' Mallalieu said the All Blacks had won 'because they had the one thing which neither England nor perhaps any other football side in history has ever had – a full-back like Scott. It seemed that danger vanished at the sight of him.'

A quarter of a century later, in New Zealand with the British Lions, I fell into conversation, at one of those interminable 'functions' thrown by Kiwi alickadoos, with a warmly gentle, soft-eyed, stooping man in his mid-sixties. He said he ran a couple of gents' outfitting shops. He was wearing a crumpled, faded All Black blazer which hung at his shoulders like a rope-slackened tent. I babbled on about this and that – you know, big time, serious bragging – till talk got round to Twickenham in 1954, and it transpired that he too had been at that match. So, suddenly, I twigged why he might have deserved to wear the All Black blazer.

'What were you?' I asked patronizingly. 'Assistant manager, say, or baggage man with that luminous New Zealand team?'

'No,' he said, 'I was playing that day.'

'You,' I said, surprised, 'what's your name then?'

'Scott,' he said. 'Bob Scott.'

Shhh-ugar and spice! I still feel just as cringing a turd as I write down the exchange all these years later.

Scott had played to the ancient full-back rules. It is a new game now – as the likes of Irvine and Hastings,

Karam and Gould and Roebuck have shown us. There are many who would say, and the wisest, calmest of judges too, that the man who took the full-back game into new realms once the touch-kicking laws had been tightened was the incomparable 'Japes': J. P. R. Williams, of Wales and all the world of rugby football. Time and again, his awesome, head-on and unflinching defence would rock the attack back savagely – and invariably you would see Williams then setting up the steam-hammer counter-charge, socks round his ankles, hair flying, the utter boldness and brass-neck of it stirring his comrades as well as the throng who watched, enthralled.

Williams's ability, almost obsession, to turn, in a trice, back-foot indestructibility into a creamy, full-pelt attack was the definitive stuff of sport. Once, on the way to a Welsh trial match at the Arms Park, JPR's Ford Capri crashed into a petrol tanker in a narrow lane near Llansannor. He was shaken, but hitched a lift into Cardiff and, of course, turned out that afternoon and went through his usual glorious repertoire. It inspired the some-time Welsh poet and troubadour Tom Bellion to pen a piece in praise, entitled 'JPR Collides With Tanker – The Tanker Spent a Comfortable Night In Hospital and Is As Well As Can Be Expected.'

But the grandest I ever saw? I agree I saw Scott, but apart from the aura, I was not old enough to fully appreciate him. But, for grandchildren's sakes, I lived through the whole era, the whole utterly resplendent career, of Serge Blanco, which ended with the last hosannahs and hurrahs in 1992. As a full-back, with counter-attacking propensities, and one who more than any dared to put his trust in gods who favour the foolhardy, Blanco turned an art form into a full-scale opera. The try which he inspired for his French confrères at Twickenham on his farewell bow to *les anglais* was probably, especially given the knife-edge circumstances, the most brilliant shining thing in the whole crazy canon of tries to the left of us, tries to the right.

Afterwards, down in the Twickenham dungeons, the

great man lit another cork-tipped cigarette and shrugged. How could he possibly 'talk us through it'? All he could offer was: '*C'est simplement le rugby. Il est instantané. Il est spontané. Il est spirituel. Il est instinctif.*'

He shrugged again, took another drag, and smiled slowly. '*Il est instinctif. Exactement le vrai rugby.*'

Which is our perfect cue to bring on the No. 10s.

2

An innate and presumptive conceit

Before Serge Blanco, the eighty-one international matches played by Michael Gibson had stood as Rugby Union's all-time record. In the fresh green finery of his youth, the Irishman Gibson had certainly been the best fly-half of his generation. By the time Barry John, three years younger, had made his debutant's curtsey in the hunting-pink of Wales, Gibson had moved to centre-threeequarter. As well as being stirring and chivalrous rivals on a number of Five Nations battlefields before John's premature abdication, the two of them in unison resplendently uplifted the arts and crafts of attacking rugby for the British Lions.

Off the field, any conceit or swank in either Gibson or John would not have half-filled a matchbox. But on it, both displayed an utter certainty that innate and presumptive conceit was a crucial stash in any regal fly-half's armoury.

One day, on the flight to New Zealand in 1971, Mike turned to Barry and remarked: 'Have you ever noticed that how your opposing fly-half acts in the couple of minutes before the kick-off informs you, without a glimmer of doubt, whether it's going to be a jolly good game or not?'

'Exactly,' enthused Barry as he leapt to the theme, 'and not only in top-class rugby. Even in a schools' match or a village pick-up, he doesn't have to have a number ten on his shirt for you to be able to tell which is the fly-half, just by watching both teams run onto the field.

'See how he holds the ball with relish, how he moves. Notice the swing of his hips. Is there a strut and confidence about him? Is he a-twitch with delight and anticipation? At what they call the "pre-match kickaround", does he try, say, twenty seconds' "keepie-uppie" with the ball – and with alternate feet? Then his party tricks – watch him flick it up onto the back of his neck, and balance it there before rolling it across his shoulder and down his forearm. Does he treat the ball like a close friend, a blood brother, almost a natural part of him? If he does, he is a God-given fly-half, and you can rub your hands and say to yourself, "Crikey, with this guy at fly-half there's every chance his team might do something different and exciting this afternoon."

'On the other hand, it's an expectation with a downside,' continued Barry, suddenly less bright-eyed. 'If the fly-half just wanders aimlessly out as part of the team, accepts a practice pass or two in desultory fashion and then just chucks it on to somebody else before folding his arms and standing there, leadenly, waiting for the ref to blow for kick-off – then you know, as sure as eggs, that it's ninety-nine per cent certain that him and his team are not going to be in the least bit different or exciting, and, in fact, everybody might as well go home there and then.'

For in any fifteen-man rugby team, the fly-half in the No. 10 jersey – and feel free to call him the 'stand-off', 'out-half' or 'first five-eighth' if you want – is the pivot and playmaker, the conductor, producer and director. He is both strategist and swankpot, fulcrum and fancypants. The fly-half calls the shots, and carries the can (and mixes the metaphors!). He can be no distant hilltop general, hiding behind a map; the fly-half's patch is in perilous no-man's-land, encircled by snipers. He is both the intellectual and the physical link between the forwards and backs, the footsloggers in the trenches and the knights in their flamboyant finery. Gunsmoke sears the eyes of even a half-decent fly-half. He operates in the very cannon's mouth. It goes without saying that a tip-top fly-half must be courageous and *sans peur*.

In rugby's history the fly-half is, however, the newest order of chivalry. But almost as soon as the order was founded, the structure and basic strategies which harness and bless the game today were – 'amazing, just like that', as Tommy Cooper used to say – in permanent and immovable place. Once the position was 'invented' (by the Welsh) and rumbustiously taken to by the Irish and South Africans before being organized, honed and polished by the English, then modern, worldwide Rugby Union could be said to be strictly codified and under way. The Scots, happy hackers content with the boisterous footrushing game they had learned at their schools, resisted the fly-half 'revolution' for a time; so, more defiantly, did the New Zealanders, who came up with their own 'double fly-half' system which they named 'first five-eighth and second five-eighth'. A Kiwi today will still gulp before uttering the word 'fly-half'.

A general basis for the game's rough pattern and outline began to take shape once it was agreed, by the six-year-old Rugby Football Union in 1877, that any international team should play fifteen men instead of twenty. By the mid-1880s, each of the four fledgling 'Home' Unions was well enough established, and there seemed a tacit agreement that the formation on the field consisted of eight front forwards and three 'whole-backs' (or full-backs) with, in between them as link-men, and logically, one quarter-back (to all intents, the scrum-half), and three 'threequarters'. In the late 1880s the innovative Cardiff club – inspired by their captain Frank Hancock, a Somerset man working at Cardiff's coaling dockyards – began to play with only two 'whole-backs' and a revolutionary four 'threequarters', and soon experimented with just one 'whole-back' and an extra 'half-back'. This latter pair would share duties behind the pack of forwards, as the mood and the suddenly varying context of the game demanded, sometimes just playing 'left and right' depending on the side of the field where play was taking place (as some flanking wing-forwards still do today). The grand three rival clubs, Swansea, Newport and Llanelli, soon copied and so, inevitably, did the national side, which at once found itself embarked on the first of its hymned and irresistible 'golden ages'.

Two unlikely, but deservedly sanctified, Swansea brothers, David and Evan James, both impoverished copper workers, together took it in turns to pioneer the revolution – alternating 'scrum-half' or 'fly-half' (although the names were not yet coined, of course), first for Swansea, then for Wales. After them, you might say, for the brand-new position 'the dai had been cast' – and before the end of the century George Llewellyn Lloyd, a Newport solicitor, was to pick up the Jameses' bright red mantle and become, most agree, the first 'pure' fly-half. In turn he was to hand it on to such compatriots – and still luminaries of the lore of early fly-half history – as Richard Jones, Percy Bush and Willie John Trew . . . By the time Bush and Trew had gone, about 1910–11, the word 'fly-half' was unarguable and inviolate in all rugby's dictionary (except, of course, New Zealand's and their ruddy five-eighths) – and, to be sure, had also found its most articulate champion at Twickenham itself, in the shape of Adrian Stoop.

Writing this chapter in 1993, one realizes that an exact century ago was a momentous time for rugby – no matter that the James brothers had already played their first match as these new-fangled joint 'quarter-backs' for Wales in the defeat of Ireland at Llanelli's Stradey Park two winters before. In 1891 the International Rugby Board was founded. A year later, the 'home' international championship was played for the first time under the points scoring system which still applies today (although some points values have been marginally altered since). In 1893 the referee was entrusted with sole responsibility for running the game and its discipline – and the crucial 'advantage' law was passed. The social turmoil over a working player's 'broken-time' payments was resolved – well, more or less – when a motion proposing remuneration was roundly defeated at a meeting in London of the Rugby Union, which resolved to remain pristinely amateur; those who disagreed could lump it or 'go north' to the soon-to-be founded professional Northern Union (which did not, in fact, call itself the Rugby League till 1922). Among the first to 'go north', as we shall see, were the James brothers from Swansea. But not before they had sown a tiny seed which in no time was to be nurtured and cultured into vibrant life. The fly-half would make rugby a whole new ball game.

So, as the old Queen approached no-side, and the bells prepared to peal for a brand-new century, within three decades of the first-ever rugby international match a most bonnily bouncing, sorted-out and stable pastime had been launched which, well before its next century was through, would girdle every continent on earth – and its World Cup competition would mean just that.

As soon as fly-halves had burst upon the game, the Scots, for very different tactical reasons from the New Zealanders (who, you could say, wanted to play two instead of one) and with characteristic wariness, were totally unimpressed. As ever, they had been happy up there behind old Hadrian's ramparts with their own way of doing things. Don't forget, Scotland in those prehistoric days almost claimed rugby as its own. In that first-ever international, at Edinburgh's Raeburn Place on 27 March 1871, Scotland had beaten England by a goal and a try to a try, and were, said the contemporary reports, 'far more the efficient in combination and sustaining in stamina'. That game was played between fourteen forwards each side, three 'whole-backs' and three 'threequarters'.

The nice paradox of this skimpy history so far is that, without knowing it, Scotland probably fielded the first 'natural' fly-half of the whole canon – in everything but name. And fully a decade before Hancock's Cardiff and the James boys' Swansea claimed they had 'invented' and then proselytized the fly-half as a 'missionary position' on the field. Through the 1880s, one Andrew Don Wauchope played in that first 'receiver's'

38

threequarter position which lined up loose of the marauding, tally-ho hackers who made up the forwards. Wauchope, for that reason, was probably the first famous rugby star. Had he but known it, he could have been the unquestioned pioneer of fly-half play. But he abhorred the very thought, and continued to do so long after he had hung up his tasselled cap, when whispers came up from Wales of new strategies and the free-running possibilities a fly-half could offer.

Wauchope was educated at Fettes, then as now a proud nursery college of the game. For young Wauchope rugby ever was, ever should – and ever would – be based on trenchant, collective, forward rushes in strength. When word seeped up across the Border, he pooh-poohed such lamentable milksop modernity as tantamount to heresy. Scots, he sneeringly insisted, should resist all such lily-livered infamy – 'forwards who are asked to continually play to their backs will always and unremittingly be beaten', he seethed, and followed up with a snorting article in the *Scottish Athletic Journal*: 'This "new" game I strongly oppose. Beat them well forward and you have the game won. Swing the scrummage occasionally, then it is that backs get a chance; but then it is that the opposing backs are run over by our forwards. If Scottish forwards will play their own good game, I shall never have any doubts of victory.'

That this championing of an out-and-out forward game should be expressed by such a player as Wauchope can only, at this distance anyway, be put down to the old-dog-and-new-tricks syndrome. Because Wauchope seemed to be the very model of a 'modern' fly-half (whatever that might be, I agree, for they have, and do, come in all shapes and sizes, speeds and gears and gumptions). But take note of the Scottish Rugby Union's first-ever historian, R. J. Phillips, logging Wauchope's legend for posterity only the very winter after the summer of 1880 in which young W. G. Grace made his first appearance for the England cricket team. A long time ago.

The ancient historian Phillips was in no doubt that, at

rugby football in the 1880s, 'no man has yet arisen to bear comparison with A. R. Don Wauchope'. Now here must have been a 'fly-half' (and a half) if ever there was one, for Phillips went on to record that Wauchope was 'a completely equipped all-round player. Heavily built around the haunches, he ran with a comparatively short stride, and had the power to abruptly change his course within a very small space of ground. One international player and a great tackler of his time did not believe that any player could tackle Don Wauchope.'

If that last claim remains, a century and more later, though tabloid-understandable, more than a touch far-fetched, well, re-read the historian's earlier testimony; who could those of my generation picture with such short-striding haunches and change of direction? Well, just off-hand and for a start, a quartet which spans my ken – so how about Cliff Morgan or Dai Watkins or Jonathan Davies or Stuart Barnes?

In that strategic, tactical and politically traumatic last decade of the nineteenth century, when Rugby Union discovered the fly-half and so came of age in the form we still enjoy a hundred years later (in many ways the game's true centenary could be celebrated at the 1995 World Cup), another series of historical landmarks was being erected across the Atlantic which were relevant to sporting history.

Not only had the professional Northern Union dramatically flown the nest in 1895; so too, in the same decade of turbulence, did rugby's blood brothers in the United States 'do a runner'. Through the 1870s, it had seemed certain that the North American intercollegiate football tournament would codify its local frills and home-grown rules and be happy to play under the aegis of the new Rugby Football Union of England. Montreal's McGill University were out-and-out devotees of the English game, and in 1874 played three games against Harvard, after which the latter themselves became so enamoured that they challenged Yale to a match under the same rules. Thus the first of the great college football rivalries was established with the game on 13 November 1875. The following year, representatives from the university football clubs of Yale, Harvard, Princeton and Columbia met to form the Intercollegiate Football Association, 'and adopted the English Rugby Union code except for one slight change in the scoring rules': a 'field goal' (today a drop goal) would not be more valuable than a 'try', i.e. a touchdown.

Through the 1880s, discontent grew in the US with the ruling body in England – just as it was doing nearer home, in Wales and Scotland, as we have seen. Under the zealous inspiration of one man, London's rules were first whittled, then flouted, then unceremoniously scrapped. The first paid, full-time Rugby Union coach to make his presence felt in the history of the world was undoubtedly Walter Chauncey Camp (1859–1925). He played for Yale till 1881, became the team's coach for ten years, and was then at Stanford University till 1895. He is still accepted as the father of American Football, as through the 1880s he discarded most vestiges of Englishness from his brand-new game. By 1890 Camp had persuaded the intercollegiate committees to forswear the English scrummage and reduce the number of players from fifteen to eleven; he had totally revolutionized points-scoring values, welcomed the forward pass, and established the field alignment that became standard – a full-back, two half-backs, seven linemen and (crucial to our thesis here) one *quarter-back*. In other words, the fly-half was invented in America long before the British realized his possibilities. And when they finally did, of course, the very game was revolutionized. No-one should doubt Camp's part in that revolution; it is inconceivable that, once he had re-formed his alignments on the field, word did not come back east across the ocean that rugby would be a far better game given a playmaking pivot able to orchestrate and then conduct the harmonies and tunes between the piano-shifter forwards in front of him and the piano-playing threequarters outside.

Thus, a few years before the turn of the century,

American Football had swum off on its own sweet way, leaving Rugby School far back in the wintery mists of rugby prehistory – but bequeathing to that old foundation and its heirs, as first cousin to Walter Camp's quarter-back, the fly-half as both creative boffin and unflinching brave at the very eye of the storm. Nor, as we begin to stoke up a head of steam to get this enjoyably zig-zag round-the-world whizz under way, must we ever forget the bravery and courage which go without saying in appraising and lauding this forthcoming litany of legendary figures who have worn, and are wearing, the jersey numbered '10'. If one or two – certainly no more than three or four from the whole canon – may have been logged as lacking somewhat in bravery and stomach, then that will be mentioned. For the rest, take the courage and utter 'bottle' for granted. Even in those who seem the frailest and most modestly retiring of men, from the tiny feast-founding James brothers of Swansea to, say, Ollie Campbell and Rob Andrew in modern times, there has been a dauntless valour in their defensive tackling and, in attack, a resolute nervelessness about looking danger in the face and not for a moment flinching. Such qualities, too, did Cousin Quarter-back across the Atlantic inspire in Paul Gallico, one of all sports writing's purple eminences, nearly sixty years ago:

'Nearly every boy can run, jump, swim, play a passable game of tennis, or hit a golf ball, but not every boy can play quarter-back at football. That calls for an extra-ordinary amount of physical courage and combativeness. If you do not think so, picture yourself hurling yourself into the path of a 200-pounder who is charging at you full speed, picking his knees up to his chin as he runs – and sometimes unwittingly leading with his skull that itself can be a dangerous and powerful offensive weapon that can well smash a man's nose level with his face, split his eye, or break his jaw' (as we shall observe later in this chronicle).

'The game demands, too, a great deal of skill. Well, the catching and holding of a pass on a cold, wet day will always make for a good yarn – but you might get a better one out of it if you happen to know from experience about the elusive qualities of a hard, mud-slimed, oval football rifled at you through the air, as well as something about the exquisite timing, speed and courage it takes to catch it on a dead run, with two or three 190-pound men reaching for it at the same time, or waiting to crash you as soon as your fingers touch it. Unless you have had some experience at this, you won't hang on to one out of ten, besides knocking your fingers out of joint. But if you have any imagination, thereafter you will know that it calls for more than negligible nerve to judge and hold that ball and even plan to run with it or the exact second to pass it – for those two husky ends are bearing down at full speed preparing for that head-on tackle.'

You sometimes wonder why any athlete chooses to be a fly-half. Till you realize that only very special athletes do.

3

The rubber-boned illusionists

The James brothers had laid down the necessity for valour from the beginning. Their captain in the first match the brothers played for Wales together – at Stradey Park against Ireland in 1891 – was A. J. 'Monkey' Gould, the centre-threequarter and undoubtedly the rugby world's first superduper star. On his retirement, Gould summarized his career in a memoir which spared no blushes of officials (especially) or fellow players if he reckoned criticism was in order. But his recollection of the James brothers began with admiration for their courage:

'They were not merely attackers. They were deadly tacklers and fine defensive players. Never have I seen two men more utterly fearless of danger on the football field, and the way they have stopped rushes of enormous forwards has been simply marvellous. As for their pluck, one only has to remember that Evan James sustained serious injury to his shoulder soon after the English game began [in 1899 at Swansea; Wales won 26–3] and yet he played to the end. His brother is just as plucky.'

The first, apparently verbatim pre-match exhortation before an international rugby team took the field was that of the grand Irish captain, Victor le Fanu, agent to Lord Meath's estates and the first Irish cap to play in the University Match (for Cambridge). At Lansdowne Road before the match against Wales in 1892, le Fanu gathered his team around him to demand: 'Every man of you, go for the James boys – and never mind whether the little varmints have got the ball or not, *because by the time you reach them one or other of 'em's sure to have it!'* The tactics probably worked: Ireland prevailed that day by 9–0.

Understandably, the brothers' attacking play left their international captain less swooningly awestruck than those behind the touchline, but his considered appraisal is probably the more valuable. Gould even confessed that much of the Jameses' artifice came to naught 'through the inability of us threequarters to take advantage' of the openings presented to them. This last was not wholly confessional, for do not forget that Gould played far more often against the brothers, for Newport, than with them, for Wales.

'From some reports', wrote Gould, 'one might be led to think the Jameses were not a bit like ordinary players, but that they played some marvellous, bewildering sort of game, with conjuring or legerdemain introduced into football. They are not conjurors but they are an exceptionally clever pair of halves who have brought back play to a state of perfection. They never wrangle, they hardly speak on the field, and no matter how much they are knocked about they go on playing as if they were proof against injury.'

These two astonishing little squirrels behind the pack would alternate on whim which of them played scrum-half or fly-half – as we know the positions today. David, born in 1867, was the older by two years. He was also bigger than Evan, 5 ft 7 in. and ten and a half stones, against 5 ft 6 in. and ten stones.

As a boy, their father had crossed on the ferry from Wales to Ilfracombe and walked to Truro to find work in the Cornish tin mines. There he married a beautiful Jewess, and he brought her back to West Wales's capital when she was pregnant with David. If Cardiff and Newport were the world's most important ports for coal as the nineteenth century approached its end, then Swansea's docks had long been the international clearing yards for more than the black gold which fired and drove the Industrial Revolution – copper, zinc, tin and nickel as well as coal. The Jameses set up home downtown on the banks of the Tawe – significantly, not far from the Swansea Football Club's rugby sanctum at St Helen's – and from the age of thirteen the boys were signed as ladlers at Swansea's great White Rock copper works.

They were apprenticed to their rugby with the local Harlequins of St Thomas, but it was only a matter of time before they were gathered in by the great town side that played at St Helen's – and their first games for the 1st XV were in the 1888–9 season. When the neighbours and rivals Llanelli were overwhelmed by five goals and two tries to nil, one of their first notices in the *Llanelli Mercury* grudgingly faint-praised that 'their tricks with the ball and with their bodies remind one more of circus performers than of football contests'.

The circus allusion was an illuminating one. This was the time, if ever there was, and with knobs on, of the travelling illusion show – the big top, the menageries, the African lions, the Bengal tigers, the Ceylonese elephants, the Indian snake-charmers, the fire-eaters, the two-headed ladies, the Buffalo Bills, the Oriental wrestlers, the very wonders of the world, far away from the deprivations of industrial squalor and servitude and breadline weekly wages.

But the circus did not hit town every week. Sport had just begun to, however. And the illuminations of spectator sport cost fewer pennies to enter than the big top. Everywhere else, in the sooty, perspiring filth of industrial cities towards the end of the nineteenth century, association football gave fantastical and merciful release for an hour or two each Saturday afternoon. Sport became the people's theatre in London and Manchester and Sheffield and Glasgow and all the concentrations of the desperate east and west – but in south Wales, not soccer but Rugby Union football took a hold on the common people which will never, one fancies, be prised away. Unconsciously, the diminutive, daring, 'rubber-boned illusionists', the James brothers, were the two for the time – for the people and for the game itself, because we are not going to let go the certainty that without the fly-half Rugby Union would not possibly be the fully rounded, globally garlanded game it is. Let's face it, rugby could well have gone the way of real tennis, roller hockey, rugby fives, rounders or rackets, but for the brave young bloods of the 1880s and 90s. Like, particularly, the two James sons of a Jewish mother (she called her two boys 'my beloved Greek gods') and a solid, song-loving Celtic father.

Apart from instinctively presenting glistening new ways of linking scrum and threequarters, the two boys were also obviously a-twitch and aware of this new theatre and its dramatic qualities. That's entertainment! If, for his party piece of shinning up goalposts, their captain Gould was nicknamed 'Monkey', the Jameses, in tribute and confraternity, were known by Swansea as 'Our Curly-Haired Marmosets'. The two of them bounded out to play a match with a series of somersaults; before the kick-off they would literally walk on their hands from each corner-flag to goalposts and see which made it first (while bets were being taken by the throng). But they were also firsts at rugby as the wide world now knows and loves it.

Noted the joint historians of that sublimely evocative and enlightening Welsh history, *Fields of Praise*:

'[The Jameses] had not only built upon the advances of earlier half-backs, they had initiated tactical ploys which were effective *and* crowd pleasing. They were the Merlins of Welsh rugby and their lineage has proved as long as that of the graceful "King" Arthurs begotten by Gould . . . Rugby in Wales became a popular game not merely because of some success or local patriotism, but because it displayed an excellence that was not confined in spirit, that was questing for a rounded presentation of physical and mental agility and, in this, the James brothers were, literally, a marvel.'

Fully eighty-eight years before the classic *Fields of Praise*, rugby had seen publication of its first defining treatise, *Football – the Rugby Union Game*, by an English clergyman headmaster, the Rev. Frank Marshall of Almondbury, Yorkshire. It was published in 1893. Marshall had no doubt how, between them, the two little brothers could claim to have pioneered half-back play and, with it, created the still unnamed position of fly-half:

'They played in conjunction at half-back for the first time in an international match and are undoubtedly the finest pair of halves in Wales that play regularly together. Considering their size, they are recklessly daring in defensive tactics, tackling with great resolution and effect. David generally works the scrum, picking up smartly with low and rapid transfers to Evan, who handles brilliantly. Both dodge and feint cleverly, David, particularly, being very clever near the line. They are remarkably difficult to stop when clear of the forwards. They are skilful dribblers but rarely resort to kicking.'

By the time Marshall's book was published, however, the birds had flown. The schism in rugby was still two years away from being official, and although the 'Northern Union' had not yet cut the umbilical cord with amateurism, there was money and perks in plenty being offered for the new southern 'stars' of the game to look north. None of these were more luminous than the twinkling James brothers, as readers of Swansea's *Cambrian* were to find out on the evening of 27 January 1893, under the headline 'Where, oh where, are our famous half-backs?':

'To-night a committee will sit in solemn conclave to receive evidence relative to the flight of the brothers James from Swansea to Manchester when it is expected some startling statements will be made. The case of the erstwhile Swansea halves is exciting great interest throughout the whole football world, for upon its result will depend the future of professionalism. For the brothers to deny they were induced to leave the home of their birth by pecuniary considerations is absurd on the face of it. No men would leave a town where they could get fairly regular work and pay and fly to a far distant town in the "hope" of finding employment. Lancashire and Yorkshire people may believe such a "cock and bull" story, but we in South Wales and those who conduct the Rugby affairs of England and Wales are not to be misled by such a story.'

My readers would probably like to know the circumstances under which the 'curly-headed marmosets' left Swansea.

A few days prior to their sudden flight, a Swansea man was in the High Street, when he was accosted by a well-dressed man who appeared to be a stranger to the town.

'Could you tell me where I could see the brothers James, the famous half-backs?' he said.

The Swansea man gazed somewhat at his questioner and, with a merry and wicked twinkle in his eyes, replied: 'Yes, I know where they are, but what do you want them for?'

'Oh, I am a cousin of theirs and have not seen them for some years. I belong to Gloucester and have just run down for a trip.'

The twinkle in the Swansea man's eye grew merrier and more wicked. 'Get along with you,' he said. 'Do you think I don't know a Gloucester man from a Lancashire man? I know what you want. You want them to play for some club.'

The stranger seemed taken by surprise. 'Well, eh, as you have guessed my object I think I may as well tell you that a club in Manchester is hard up for a pair of half-backs. We want a good pair. Do you think we could get the brothers James? Are they hard to satisfy?'

They were not too hard to satisfy. They were each offered £2 per week and win-bonus money. Their 'official' jobs would be as warehousemen. They played for Broughton Rangers and at once helped the club win the Lancashire Cup. On behalf of the Rugby Union, the brothers' 'professional' case was examined by one of its most fervently amateur 'witchfinder-generals' in the north, the Rev. Frank Marshall, rave reviewer of the Jameses in his still-to-be published book. He found them both as guilty as sin.

Three years later, homesick for South Wales and with the Northern Union now a fact, the brothers appealed to the Welsh RU for reinstatement. That body asked London for a ruling. The Rugby Union grudgingly gave permission. When the news came through, there was a torchlight procession from the Swansea railway station to St Helen's. In 1899 the Jameses were even selected to play for Wales again, on their home ground and against England. A record crowd of 26,000 thronged St Helen's – over twice as many as had attended the previous international at the arena. Swansea's 'boys' – although David was now thirty-two and Evan thirty – went quite gloriously potty, making fools of the English ('who had started in a rush and confident frenzy which initially dashed the Welsh pack off its feet') and, as the patterns developed, inspiring run after run.

Wales won, incredibly, by 26–3. That was twice as many points as England had ever conceded in the 64 internationals they had so far played in history (Wales had scored 12 against them in the 12–11 victory in 1893, and two years earlier Ireland had scored 13 in their 13–9 win). But this score was sensational – and no fluke, for it set Wales off on a sumptuous passage in which they would lose only five of their next forty-six matches in the following dozen years, firmly cementing the principality's national game.

England, who were not to beat Wales in their next eleven meetings, were shamed. Their captain, Arthur Rotherham, was seen to lose his temper, 'with no thought of chivalry or his class', with the James boys, whom he was meant to be marking. Rotherham (Uppingham and Trinity College, Cambridge) was a senior psychiatrist at St Thomas's Hospital, London (he was to end his medical career as the Government's 'Visitor in Lunacy', 1931–44), so he might have best appreciated the report on the sporting pages of *The Times* the Monday after the rout at St Helen's: 'Rotherham wasted himself in empty retort throughout the occasion, with no thought for his forwards being reduced to a rustic collection of delinquents.'

At the final whistle it was observed that Rotherham refused to shake hands with the Jameses. He never played for England again – nor would the poor fellow have expected to, after reading not only the English newspapers in the following week but also the reports in the following *year*, like this in *The Athletic News Football Annual*: 'England's pack was beaten and out-manoeuvred, and the brothers James, with their marvellous legerdemain and their constant change of relative positions, completely fogged and nonplussed Rotherham and Livesay.'

Rotherham was no mug. Before the match, in trepidation, the *South Wales Argus* had profiled him as 'one of England's finest halfs ever seen, sharp as a needle, solid brawn and muscle; when running his free arm works like a piston and, in handing-off, he has the kick of a Brazilian mule.' After Rotherham's performance at St Helen's on that famous first Saturday of January 1899, however, the *Argus* noted his 'unseemly waste of energy in empty protest when he discovered the brothers James quite too good for him.' On the same day London's *Morning Leader* laid the blame for England's humiliation not just on Rotherham himself, but on all his fellow university men and the RU's oligarchic coterie:

'For many years the Rugby Union has been a close corporation, composed of men with the mistaken idea that only public schoolboys and University men could play the game. The middle class and working man footballer was barely tolerated. And yet it is the latter class rather than the University player that furnishes the majority of the best footballers today ... I can imagine a meeting of the Rugby Union five years hence. The selecting Committee meet to choose the Rugby XV to meet Wales. "Let me see", says Rowland Hill, secretary of the RFU ... "We will have four men from Oxford, four men from Cambridge, four from Blackheath and three from Richmond." Carried nem. con. Enter a telegraph boy who hands R.H. a message. "Gracious alive!" he exclaims. "Wales declines to meet us, and prefers to play the rest of England!"'

Ninety years on, the historian John Griffiths was still wincing when he wrote his definitive *Book of English International Rugby* for the delectation of Twickenham's mandarins as another century ran to its conclusion. No other match report of the 380 in the book is more scathing:

'The work of the James brothers enabled the brilliant Welsh three-quarters to entertain the 25,000 spectators with their full repertoire of handling and running skills. In a seven-minutes purple patch during the second half, the Welsh backs clocked 15 points and the poor Englishmen scarcely knew what had hit them. The forwards were overwhelmed in the tight and loose, and the backs were unable to find any rhythm or combination in their play.'

David and Evan, and all of Wales, looked forward to travelling to the next match against Scotland, at Inverleith two months later, in March. A week before the game, they both cried off, pleading injury. That Saturday, instead of bemusing the Scots they were playing in front of a few hundred – back at Broughton Rangers for £200 down for each of them and their old £2-a-week jobs as 'warehouse-men'. Within three years Evan, aged thirty-three, had died of tuberculosis. David returned to Wales – and to his first job, toiling in the sweatshop of Swansea's White Rock copper works. He died on the job, wizened, bent, and impoverished, aged sixty-one. And, doubtless, quite oblivious that he, in tandem with his beloved younger brother, had 'invented' the pivotal and absolutely crucial role of fly-half in a pastime which had already captivated the whole of the British Empire and far beyond. (Talk about *Chariots of Fire*. Colin Welland should write a film on the brothers James of Swansea and the Universe.)

The baton had been firmly grabbed by Wales as soon as the Jameses had, for the second time, 'gone north'. Llewellyn Lloyd, of Newport – 'the calming, talented link in which the distinguishing quality of his greatness was the perfection of his judgement' (*South Wales Echo*) – at once developed the idea of a 'standing-off' half-back for

52

the national side. Then, having founded the feast, as it were, Swansea demanded the second and third helpings for St Helen's – for in quick succession came what could only be described (even by our specialized standards of today) as fly-halves pure and simple. Dick Jones was one half of the 'Dancing Dicks' – the outside one with the apparently incomparable Dickie Owen, a genuinely specialist 'scrum-working' half-back. Then came the boilermaker, later the town's favourite publican, Willie Trew – two inches taller than the 'marmoset' Evan James, but under ten stone. Trew, enthused the *South Wales Graphic* graphically, was like 'a wraith whose rapid swerve could double opponents up, and it is near the touch-line he is very resourceful, and if in difficulties can often put in most judicious kicks and extricate himself with ease. He invariably receives the ball in an upright position and rarely muffs a pass. It is not very often that Trew is baffled – and now ... he has a complete control over his body at whatever speed he gets up ... indeed, he has at times been seen to jump bodily over one of his opponents and score.'

Just as, over eighty years on, Jonathan Davies might have thought of doing.

Then there was the onliest Percy Bush, a Cardiff school-master who was to become British vice-consul at Nantes on France's Atlantic coast. Bush was capped only eight times for Wales between 1905 and 1910, but unquestionably he garlanded with coloured bunting the ship which James – then Lloyd and Jones – had helped to launch. He seems to have been the finished article with shiny brass knobs on: tactical control; cocksure, close-quarter running; pluperfect presentation of the pass; unflinching in the tackle, and geometric and teasing when kicking in attack. In one match when he was working in France, playing for Nantes against Le Havre, he scored 54 points on his own – ten of them tries. His friend, the grand Welsh centre Rhys Gabe, once said, 'I can sidestep one way or the other; Percy can do it both ways all the time.' Photographs make Bush look a dead ringer for Robert

Jones, fine little Welsh scrum-half of the 1980s and 90s.

It was said that Bush made comparatively few appearances for Wales because he could not hit it off with the great scrum-half Owen. Both liked to be senior partner. Before he was capped, Bush was chosen for the 1904 British tour Down Under. In the one Test in New Zealand, the *Wellington Times*, unknowingly setting the tone and pattern for many future encounters, wrote: 'It was a struggle between the clever and fast forwards of New Zealand and tricky, resourceful, hard-striving British backs; and one man stood in strong relief from all the others – the little Welshman P. Bush. Whenever the ball reached him in the second spell there would be seen a rush of New Zealand forwards to fall upon him lest he might . . . turn his side's probable defeat into victory.'

Back home, the supply of grizzled greybeards has only recently dried up in Cardiff who could spend hours over a drink telling you every detail of 'Bush's Match' – against Ireland at the Arms Park in 1907, won by Wales by a then record margin of 29–0. Luckily the files of the *South Wales Argus* are still 'alive' with the memory:

'From a scrum David sent the ball back to Bush, and he dropped a goal. When Wales were driven to their 25, Bush, with one of his most brilliant efforts, threaded his way through the defence, and that led to a try by J. L. Williams after a run from half-way. Winfield converted, and Wales led by twenty-one points. Once more Ireland, chiefly through Maclear, reached the Welsh line; and once more Bush relieved with a dashing run. Williams scored his third try after a great run by Gabe; and finally, with the Irish three-quarters lining up level with the scrummage, Bush dodged one man with his best swerve, and had only the full-back to face. He left Hinton standing, and scored behind the posts for Winfield to convert again. Yet again Bush went through with a brilliant run. Maclear flung himself at the place where the Cardiff man's legs had been, but by that time his body was somewhere else. Bush went on and looked like scoring himself, but on facing Hinton he passed to A. F. Harding, who threw the ball out of the reach of D. P. Jones. Perhaps this record does not seem to justify the claim that this was "Bush's Match", but, in truth, no statement of the facts of the game can indicate how great and persistent was his influence upon the play of the whole team. Throughout the game he was the pivot of attack – audacious, confident, supreme in skill. He showed real subtlety in dealing with the Irish defensive tactics: when they lined up level with the scrum he was not intimidated and put off his game – he made what they took for defensive strength into a weakness, and scored his one try through an individual effort when he was expected to pass. It was "Bush's Match" indeed!'

Thus was born the 'fly-half' – even in name, perhaps, before old Queen Victoria had died. If Mr Richard Llewellyn got his research right, that is – for in his glorious novel *How Green was my Valley*, he writes of Davy's red jersey of Wales in the glass case on the wall next to the picture of the Queen and, of course, the fly-half at the match:

'In goes the ball, and the tight, straining muscles are working, eight against eight, to hold one another and then to push each other the length of the field, but the ball comes free behind the pack, and their fly-half has it so fast that nobody knows till he is on his way toward our touch line with his three-quarters strung behind him and nothing but our full-back in his way.

'Shout, crowd, shout, with one voice that is long-drawn, deep, loud, and full of colour, rising now as the fly runs pell-mell and Cyfartha Lewis dances to meet him, and up on a rising note, for inches are between them, louder with the voice in an unwritten hymn to energy and bravery and strength among men.

'But Cyfartha is like a fisherman's net. The fly has been too clever. He should have passed to his wing long ago, but he is greedy and wants the try himself, and on he goes, tries to sell a dummy, and how the crowd is laughing, now, for to sell a dummy to Cyfartha is to sell poison to a Borgia. The fly is down, and Cyfartha kicks the ball half-way down the field to our forwards, and has time to offer his hand to poor Mr Fly, who is bringing himself to think what happened after the mountain fell on him.'

Rugby itself, of course, had already moved from those black-grimed, once green valleys. At a tremendous lick. Rugby's own travelling circus of tumblers and illusionists had begun to open up the world – and almost immediately with a two-way reciprocity. In 1888 the cricketing entrepreneurs Alfred Shaw and Arthur Shrewsbury, having shown a profit touring with their summer sport, took twenty-one rugby players to Australia and New Zealand. No international matches were played, and although an amateur England cricketer, Stoddart, who played rugby for Blackheath took over as captain when Seddon was drowned while boating on the Hunter river near Maitland, the Rugby Union looked with distaste on the adventure (the bulk of the players were working men from clubs such as Batley, Bramley, Salford and Swinton, only seven years away from joining the professional Northern Union), and on their return the players all had to sign RU affidavits swearing their amateur status had not been infringed on the trip.

To the team's surprise, its welcome on the New Zealand part of the tour had been overwhelming. Indeed, wrote T. P. McLean, literary keeper of subsequent All Black legend, 'that first British tour was epochal, for the visitors revealed to Colonial players the possibilities and opportunities of attacking through the backs – hitherto New Zealanders had believed this to be prohibited by the laws of the game because it meant ball-carriers were being screened by team-mates (the forwards), who must be operating from offside positions.'

Elementary enough on the face of it – but the eye-opener was to revolutionize rugby in New Zealand within ten years and, of course, hasten immeasurably the world game's tactical appreciation. If the birth and evolution of the fly-half took place somewhere else, in no time New Zealand had invented its 'five-eighths' formation, in which, McLean wrote, 'the two backs next to the [scrum-]half were called "first" and "second", on the understanding that either might attack on whatever side of the scrum he chose.' The tactic was born in Dunedin, and was delivered by James Duncan, a five-eighth with a bald head (which he concealed with a cap), a drooping moustache and, said McLean, 'a massive opinion of his own talents – Duncan was all but anointed for his powers as a tactical Napoleon. At once, from further south, came a boot-clicker, Billy Stead, whose Maori blood was indiscernible in his faintly tanned, freckled face. Now here came a first five-eighth *sans peur et sans reproche*, esteemed by his colleagues as a back in a million.'

Duncan, a saddler originally from Kaikorai, Otago, captained New Zealand's first official tour, to Australia in 1903; and Stead, a Southland bootmaker and later a vibrant newspaper columnist, was vice-captain and immortal five-eighth on the, in turn, 'epochal' 1905 New Zealand tour to Britain, when the 'All Blacks' were born.

Thus the southern hemisphere began to take ravenously to the game, and especially to the tactical developments it was so obviously ripe for – not least in the strict demarcation between forward responsibilities and those of the threequarters. The arbiter, still without a name as yet, was the 'fly-half', the man 'standing off' from the pack and its 'scrum-half'.

In 1891, the same year the James brothers had first played together for Wales, taking it in turns, almost, to play 'fly-half' or 'scrum-half', a British side of mostly Cambridge University men (and very different from the 'northern' side Stoddart had led to New Zealand three years earlier) toured South Africa, led by W. E. Maclagan, of London Scottish. It was no more than an exhibition tour – the team played nineteen games, won all of them, and in scoring 224 points had only a single point scored against them. The British returned home, Maclagan saying that the South Africans would be 'fast at learning' and that the tourists had been particularly impressed by two players on the home side: 'both cricketing men, Herbie Castens, a forward who had attended Oxford University, and Alfred Richards, a half-back from Western Province, who stands off some paces from the forward tussle from where he orders the speed and fluctuations of the play.' Castens and Richards were both to play cricket for South Africa – but of most significance is that, unbidden by any outside influence and solely out of his own obvious sporting nous, Alfred Richards had become South Africa's first fly-half.

Of equal moment for the game as a whole was the fact that such a missionary endeavour as Maclagan's. tour must have made hundreds of converts to rugby at every turn. Do not forget that Association Football was already well embarked on its wild-fire spread around the rest of the world. So, for rugby, the timing of the 1891 tour could not have been more propitious, for South Africa was in a state of enormous upheaval, with thousands of fortune-seekers pouring in by the week: gold had been discovered in Johannesburg hot on the heels of the vast diamond finds at Kimberley. In the general boom and excitement of this adventurers' playground, rugby proved just the ticket, and by the time another British party arrived in 1896, the game and its culture had grown healthily deep roots. To be sure, even the cruel and passionate Boer War between 1899 and 1902 could not uproot South Africa's rugby, as witness this letter, translated from High Dutch, and addressed to a Major Edwards of the British Army, stationed at O'Kiep:

'Dear Sir – I wish to inform you that I have agreed to a rugby match taking place between you and us. I, for my side, will agree to a cease-fire tomorrow afternoon from 12 o'clock until sunset, the time and venue of the match to be arranged by you in consultation with Messrs Roberts and Van Rooyen whom I am sending to you.

'I have the honour etc.

pp. S. G. Maritz (Field General, Transvaal Scouting Corps).

Concordia, 28 April 1902.'

To be sure, within months of the guns being stilled across the veldt, a British rugby side was again on its way.

Two Tests were drawn and in the third and last, at Cape Town, South Africa recorded their first international victory. They had also found an obvious heir to the pioneer 'fly-half' Alfred Richards – for now, from Griqualand West, came Fred Dobbin.

His captain, Billy Millar, was to describe him thus – and most significantly: 'Dobbin is essentially a "stand-off" half-back and not a "scrum" half-back, and he is cleverness personified, always drawing a section of the defence before passing, and his feinting repeatedly deceived opponents. South Africa owes more to Dobbin than to any other single player.'

But shades of green-jerseyed things to come. The esteemed *Cape Argus* sporting journalist, A. C. 'Ace' Parker, noted that, 'while Dobbin is one of the wiliest players of his day, with a particularly deceptive "dummy", his centre-threequarter from Stellenbosch, Japie Krige, felt that after the first drawn Test of 1903 in Johannesburg he had not had any chance to show his quality, so declined an invitation to play in the second match at Kimberley, privately telling friends that it was because he would "never see the ball" with Dobbin playing inside him.'

A centre-threequarter's prophecy, not – as we shall see – to be heeded by Dobbin's fly-half heirs with the prancing Springbok at their breast, Benny Osler and Naas Botha!

Incidentally, the famous green livery preceded the springbok motif. Before that third Test at Newlands in 1903, South African teams had played in white shirts (which, had they continued to do so, would have proved to be pointed symbolism sixty or so years later when the international moves to ban them for their government's racism began to gather strength). Then the local club, Old Diocesan, folded up and bequeathed its basket of myrtle-green jerseys to the fledgling international team. Three years later, when the first South African side toured England in 1906–7, gold trim had been added to the collar and cuffs, and on the left breast 'a small African antelope, a springbok, was sewn in mouse-coloured silk', according to the reporter from the London *Daily Mail*, who had met the Union Castle ship *Gascon* on its arrival at Southampton on 20 September. In next morning's newspaper, predictably, the headline writer called the new tourists 'Springboks'. The captain, Paul Roos, wrote at once to the *Mail*'s editor, pointing out that 'Springbokke' was the Afrikaans plural. Bad luck, Springboks fitted the headline space and Springboks they stayed.

In the same way, the year before, the New Zealanders, with Billy Stead, first 'great' of the first five-eighths, had also been christened for all time on their debutants' bow of a first full-strength tour. The New Zealanders of 1905 were given no chance by the Brits, of course, and arrived almost anonymously at Plymouth after a scary journey when their steamship nearly foundered off Cape Horn – indeed was saved only by the team in rota helping to stoke the boilers for three successive days till they could make an Argentinian port for repairs.

Thus, arriving late in Plymouth, they discovered they were due to play their first fixture, against Devon, the very next day. Devon offered smugly to postpone the game for a few days, but no, said the New Zealanders, still without their land-legs, we'll give it a whirl. The result was 55–4. The Fleet Street news agencies received the flash that afternoon, did not believe it – and changed the score to Devon 55, New Zealand 4. This was relayed to the London newspapers. Half an hour later a report came up the line confirming that the tourists had indeed won. So all the agencies presumed a cock-up only in the size of the score – and released the correction for second editions that the result had been 5–4 to the Kiwis, so outrageously impossible was a half-century notch. When, in time, the full report of the match and the list of try scorers winged up, the agencies had to apologize again and send out a brand-new story for the third editions. New Zealand rugby was off and running and terrorizing the Brits.

The New Zealanders continued a trail of runaway victories around the land. They played in black shirts, but their nickname remained 'the Crafty Kiwis', so we are told. In their sixth match, at Hartlepool – then a strong-hold of the union game – the tourists romped in by an astonishing 63–0, prior to which a leading writer of the day, a Mr Vivian of the *Morning Post* in London, wrote a prelim explaining that the upstarts' colonial game was based on the simple premise of every man, in whatever position, being immensely fit, fast and athletic, with a good pair of hands and a ferocious pruning-shears tackle – unlike the British tradition of rather lumbering, butter-fingered forwards and darting, dodging, dainty backs. (Exactly the two definitions that still prevail today.)

Anyway, Mr Vivian wrote this perceptive piece, and his Fleet Street sub-ed put up the headline THEY ARE ALL BACKS – and included a few similarly inscribed billboard board-ings to be nailed onto trees around the Hartlepool ground the next afternoon.

Up they came on the overnight newspaper train. The billings puzzled the Hartlepool newsagent. He was a cricket man and didn't twig the reference. But he did know that the touring team played in black shirts and shorts. So he changed the billboards to THEY ARE ALL BLACKS.

The name stuck. With a vengeance. So, of course, did another name for that obviously mesmerizing, marauding side of 1905 – 'The Originals'.

On the following year's tour by the South Africans, in which Dobbin shone ('combining well with his inside half-backs, either H. W. "Paddy" Carolyn, an extremely brainy player, or D. C. "Mary" Jackson, extremely sound', said the *Daily Mail*), the visitors won two of the four inter-nationals, against Ireland and Wales, drew with England at Crystal Palace, and lost to Scotland.

Against Wales and England, the brand-new Springboks came up against, respectively, Percy Bush and Adrian Stoop. Dobbin could witness their play at close quarters – and see a *real* fly-half, a genuine out-and-outer. Bush and Stoop were perhaps first of the line of fly-halves we would unfailingly recognize today. Bush might have played like Phil Bennett was to, over half a century later; ditto Stoop and, say, Richard Sharp.

4

'Not good enough, no opposition'

Mind you, when both Wales and England played those All Black 'Originals' in 1905, the selectors were still hedging their bets about the way to counter the New Zealanders' five-eighths system. Dai Gent, a Welshman born in Llandovery, educated at Cheltenham and a player for Gloucester (whence he chose to be capped by England), was the half who worked the scrum at Crystal Palace in England's 15–0 defeat by the All Blacks. In the RFU's official centenary history Gent is described as 'a pioneer of specialist half-back play', and to him a scrum-half was a scrum-half and a fly, a fly: 'no alternating for its own sake, or depending who was first up, or playing "left" and "right".' Gent was a schoolmaster who wrote elegantly on the game for the *Sunday Times*. After the dust had settled on that famous and brazen All Blacks tour, he wrote in his newspaper: 'Their arrangement of a scrum-half, two five-eighths, three threequarters, and a full-back has never appealed to us for any length of time. I saw the other day that when the Wales–New Zealand game of 1905 was being recalled, that victory of Wales was described as a "triumph of orthodoxy". Actually Wales played eight backs that day: an inside-half, two outside-halves, four threequarters, and a full-back, as England did the same season against New Zealand.'

(When Gent himself was 'inside-half', the centre, Raphael, was co-opted to play what you might call 'spare-outside-bod-at-Gent's-elbow' – what, in Wodehouse parlance, would be a 'gent's gent'.)

'But we have never liked the formation, and when we have adopted it, it has been solely out of fear of our opponents, or for sheer experiment. What the New Zealanders maintain is that the distance the normal outside-half stands away from the scrum slows up the passing movement at its inception, and consequently delays the moment when the threequarters are really under way. The nippiest of all these backs must be the first five-eighth. He must be away in a flash, and by his speed and direction he starts the whole machinery going.'

Not long after the turn of the century, newspapers had woken up to rugby. Many already retained their own specialist correspondent, as the *Sunday Times* did with Gent. Much of the straight match reporting was turgid, lengthy and colourless, but there were some gleaming exceptions, such as 'Old Stager' (W. J. Hoare) on the *South Wales Daily News*, 'Dromio' (W. J. Townsend Collins) on the *South Wales Argus*, and the splendidly singular cricket-'n-rugger man E. H. D. Sewell, who cast a beadily observant eye on both games for the London *Evening Standard* (combined often as sports editor) for almost half a century, right up to his death aged seventy-five in 1947. Sewell played 'muscular and aggressive' rugby for Bedford and Harlequins in the 1890s and cricket for Essex in the seasons 1900 and 1902. *Wisden* of 1953 lists him, mysteriously, as having played one game for India, but I can find no further details, hard as I have tried. Anyway, he knew his stuff. He was once no-balled at Lord's for delivering with both feet off the ground, and remarked to the umpire, 'Sir, that is the first time in my life I have been mistaken for an acrobat.' In print he could turn his hand, with a scatter of glitter-dust, discursively and at length on the first thing that came into his head – be it cold baths after the match, the pointlessness of scrum-caps, referees, oval balls, wives, or, at cricket, a pleading demand that batsmen aim for, and smash, more pavilion windows. One of his books was titled *Rugger* –

the Man's Game. C. B. Fry, whom he employed as a columnist on the *Standard* in the 1930s, said Sewell 'may safely be backed to produce his facts and argue his case against anybody, though there is a large barrister named G. D. Roberts, KC, whom I would much like to pit against him in open court. Just to see.'

With Sewell's diamond-sharp, day-to-day, deadline-urgent brilliance mouldering away, unread, except by boring burrowers, in dingy cuttings libraries or, perhaps, granted a few carelessly chosen paragraphs in modern rugby and cricket anthologies, it has been a joy to discover him (in only a few cases, to rediscover him) while delving for this offering on rugby's playmaking No. 10s. Sewell, I am glad to report, was advocating the 'pure' one-man-one-job fly-half even before Bush came up against Stead and his second five-eighth at Cardiff in 1905 – and the no kicking into touch on-the-full outside the twenty-five rule was a campaign of Sewell's long before Stoop thought of it – and sixty years before the RU woke up and decided on the law change. But it was not so much what Sewell wrote, it was the way that he wrote it. When that regular crass cry goes up again that rugby, unlike cricket, has no remotely readable literature, just say 'EHD'.

This, for instance, is how the already veteran Sewell signed off for the *Standard* after the final international of 1939, with Hitler's guns already thundering around Europe and British papers subject to stringent newsprint rationing. At Murrayfield England had drearily eked out a victory by three penalty goals to two fine Scottish tries. But, first things first, Sewell felt the need to curse the German army for yet again, only twenty-one years later, interrupting the rugger programme, so that it looked unlikely that he would increase his tally of not mere attendance at, but reporting of, 187 international matches in six countries. What an Intro: any of us Twick-hacks today, in the final ten minutes of the century, should stand to applaud a predecessor, 187 'reporting' international matches squiggled into his notebooks over forty years, beginning like this – and, don't let them forget, as the

Standard's sports editor as well, EHD surely signed his own expenses:

'Murrayfield, Saturday: – Scotland 9, England 6. In the existing paper and space shortage, due largely to the daily publication of astrological prophecies, none of which tally, and of feminine fashions few of which would suit anything but a Belisha Beacon after a Boat-race night, I am far too patriotic to join the wasters. But, in the witnessing of what, were it not for Huns, would now be a list of over 200 such matches I have experiences and reminiscences of my meetings with some grand chaps.

'However, if anybody among my readers wants to cross sword with me as to whether it is good Rugby common sense that a referee's awards (whether these are right or wrong is definitely not the point here) should make it possible for a side which cannot score a try to be returned the winner against an opponent who has scored two, one of them a beauty, then let him supply me with stationery, and pay my fee for time and labour and incidentals – don't forget them! – and I'll be only too pleased to enlighten him.

'In this farce the English three-quarters got the ball, well served by an attacking pair of half-backs, J. Ellis (Wakefield), scrum, and T. A. Kemp (St Mary's Hospital), from more than fifty scrums, plus many line-outs. They then performed the unheard-of feat, the quality of their munitions duly considered, of never so much as looking like making a try on their own. More incompetent centre play in the circumstances has never been seen in a match of importance . . .'

To cover 187 international matches in six countries in over thirty-five years – allowing for those four years snatched by the Huns! – was some going for those days. No quick black cab to Heathrow's shuttle and, hey presto, you've arrived for a Five Nations match before the coffee's cooled. Same for the players, of course. It was the Friday-night sleeper to or from Edinburgh for the Calcutta Cup, ditto the night ferry to Dublin. The players complain about an abundance of travelling now. They should be so lucky.

In February 1905 Ireland played England for the first time in Cork. Twelve thousand watched the match, paying £900 for the privilege, which at the time were record gate takings for all rugby. Ireland won by 17–3. Sewell travelled with the England team:

'Such was the parsimony of the staff management in those days that the English team travelled from Dublin to Cork packed in third smokers! Anybody familiar with train journeys in Ireland will be able to tell the reader something of what that preparation for a "forty each way" must have been like. With only one exception, that was the most irksome match, so far as travelling was concerned, I ever had. We left Euston on the Friday night for North Wall via Holyhead and caught some kind of a train to Cork. We seemed to stop at every station and between several. Eventually I got to the ground, sat in the open, the weather, glory be, happening all right, caught the first train back, missed the night boat, had to put up at the Shelbourne, was called at 5 a.m., caught the first boat from Kingstown, travelled all Sunday and fetched up at Shoe Lane around 10 p.m. to find a wad of "copy" about two foot thick on my table! Not one word of Saturday's sport had been handled – my so-called assistant had taken his "Sunday off" properly, forgetting I had gone to Cork. As he was a Soccer enthusiast he may have hoped I'd gone to blazes. I was ready for bye-bye when I fell into bed at nigh 3 a.m. on the Monday at Anderton's in Fleet Street. So ended for me Basil Maclear's first game for Ireland.'

Sewell was not going to miss that. Basil Maclear was about to become the shining emerald gleam in Irish rugby for the first years of the century. He was a natural at wing or centre, but he qualifies here because (with the visit of the All Blacks and the great debate about five-eighths) Ireland played him three times in the 1905–6 season at 'fly', just outside the scrum-working 'half'. Maclear was, to all intents, English. But he had an Irish father. Basil was in the British Army, a captain in the Royal Dublin Fusiliers, and had been stationed briefly at Fermoy in County Cork, so Irish rugby knew all about him and looked ready to pick him at the first opportunity. In England Maclear played for Blackheath. He had been educated at Bedford School. So, it happens, had E. H. D. Sewell; thus the journalist knew all about the young man's massive talent, which recommendation he passed on to the all-powerful mandarin and Rugby Union Secretary, G. Rowland Hill, who was also eminence of the England selection committee. 'All right, I'll have a look at him,' Hill told Sewell. 'Arrange a match.' Such was the way of the freemasonry in those days. Hill said he would disguise himself as a touch judge to see better this alleged Bedford School prodigy, and Sewell whistled up his Old Boys' XV, plus Maclear: 'Thus on January 17, 1905 there was arranged a mid-week frolic at the Richmond Athletic Ground, between Old Paulines and Old Bedfordians, and I was to have been one of Basil's partners if some other optimist did not turn up. I was not sorry he did, since sports editing almost by yourself, watching games and scribbling all day, and "seeing the page to bed" up to any old hour at night is not an ideal training for even second-class Rugger. Anyway, I looked on while Rowland Hill judged touch and Basil Maclear converted eleven tries out of twelve, scored in something of a walk-over by the O.B.s over their always very good friends the O.P.s. I forgot how many tries Maclear scored, not many, as he was centre that day, nor does it matter, but I remember that Rowland Hill's summing up was: "Not good enough, no opposition."'

And that was that – and Ireland picked Maclear to play against England just over three weeks later in Cork. Poor old Rowland Hill: in Maclear's three matches against England of the eleven he played for Ireland, he was on the winning side each time, and to the tune of 13 tries to 3! He was a handsome, fair-haired fellow who could run like the wind blowing a gale, and was, apparently, without 'an atom of side or swank in his make-up'. He unfailingly played in white kid gloves – 'and a smile on his face from beginning to end' – and could tackle like a cowboy at a pair of horns. His hand-off was famed. In at least five of his eleven games for Ireland, an *Irish Times* tag on the headline read MACLEAR'S MATCH.

There were two particular stormers in his season as a 'fly' in 1905–6. Wales, at the zenith of their first 'golden age', were going for the Triple Crown at Belfast in March 1906. Ireland were down to thirteen men for most of the match – but won, heroically, by 11–6. 'Dromio' was there for the *South Wales Argus*: 'Every time a Welshman got the ball, an Irishman downed him, and Basil Maclear downed 'em three at a time. If this appears to be an exaggeration it is a pardonable one. That is the way Maclear downs 'em. Ireland, against all possible likelihood, won and this was one of the matches where fate overcame the facts.'

After his 'blinder' in 1905 against New Zealand (which Ireland lost so narrowly by 15–12), the following season saw 'Maclear's Try' against the newly christened Springboks. 'Dromio' was again at the press table:

'At the beginning of the second half the score was 12–3 in the Springboks' favour. Parke, the lawn tennis player, kicked a penalty goal to make it 12–6; then, in the middle of a sustained South African attack on the Irish line, Maclear intercepted a pass and set out on his long trek towards the enemy line, beginning with a flying leap as he took the ball, and then going straight on. He had very nearly a hundred yards to go but, with a combination of force and swiftness, he passed man after man until he reached the half-way line. As the whole South African side had been up in the attack, there was nobody between him and a try but the full-back, Steven Joubert, and, of course, the second half of the field. The back made to tackle his man and was half bowled over. Maclear went on and the back came after him; there was a second tackle, courageous but only half-successful. For the next few yards Maclear staggered along, carrying the full-back draped around him like a cloak. Then, with a hand-off that was a gesture of royal dismissal, he broke away and scored.'

Sitting next to 'Dromio' (I daresay) was Sewell of the *Evening Standard*:

'Joubert is a small but very plucky back and it needed three hand-offs before Maclear, going a cracker all the time, finally disposed of this terrier, and was able to finish his gallop with a try about midway 'twixt post and corner. Nowhere else at a Rugger ground have I heard such a din as then arose. The mere sight of such a splendid figure of a man as was Maclear going all out on business on a Rugger field is not seen every day. Inasmuch as, added to that, was the fact that he was on an Irish ground in an Irish jersey, and the try might prove to be the turning-point in what was in any event sure to be a very close thing, well, there was ample excuse for the Whirroos and Be Jabers to become unusually vocal! I, at all events, have nowhere else at any game witnessed or heard such a scene.'

The try was not converted. South Africa won by 15–12.

Maclear's penultimate match for Ireland before his regiment was posted abroad was later that season, against Scotland at Inverleith. In his *Rugby Recollections*, Newport's bard of ballgames, Townsend Collins, wrote:

'Maclear's most relished annual tussle was when he fought and gloried in his battle with D. R. ("Darkie") Bedell-Sivright, Scotland's captain. What a pair of beloved enemies! Each was a powerful, full-blooded male; each was a deadly tackler, and for a time Darkie had the best of it. Then suddenly they met in head collision. With all the strength of Maclear's steam-hammer hand-off, the irresistible force met the not quite immovable body, Darkie lay still. "Ho, Darr-kie!" roared a voice from the ring. "Ye've been asking for that and noo ye've got it!"'

Bedell-Sivright had captained the 1904 British touring side down under – during which time he won the New Zealand heavyweight boxing championship. He became a surgeon in the British Navy and was killed at Gallipoli on 5 September 1915 – living just four months longer than Basil Maclear, who fell leading his company of Dublin Fusiliers 'over the top' at Ypres on 26 May. He was thirty-four.

Shades of Barry John's conversation with Mike Gibson

in 1971 – as Dai Gent wrote of Maclear: 'As a boy I used to go and see him – just to watch him walk out onto the field.'

Maclear's famous white kid gloves were not particularly novel. His most celebrated predecessor on the Irish side was Louis Magee, a veterinary surgeon who played in his own, patented 'string' gloves. Magee must have been a heck of a player – 'undoubtedly our genius at half', said the *Irish Leader*. Magee was a Bective Ranger (as had been Ireland's pioneering half-back of the early 1890s, Ben Tuke). He had, by all accounts, enchanted South Africa with his skills on the tour of 1896. For Ireland he usually worked the scrummage 'left' or 'right' with C. G. Allen, of Derry. Magee played, in all, twenty-seven matches with the shamrock on his jumper between 1895 and 1904. After Maclear's 'experiment' at 'stand-off' (which must have been deemed a success) in 1905–6, 'Dicky' Lloyd, an Ulster army officer, was soon to begin a long span as an orthodox 'fly' who developed hugely the kicking possibilities of the position. 'He was the completely equipped player, but excelled as a kick,' wrote Townsend Collins. 'Opposing captains might tell off their wing forwards to suppress him, but he would circumvent them. Other men have kicked as quickly: no player of modern times has been so accurate.'

The Scots, meanwhile, continued to be half-hearted about the possibilities of making one man the permanent pivot, a half who always 'stood-off' the scrum to be fed by an inside-half. A. R. Don Wauchope's early antagonisms were holding fast north of the Cheviots. By the way, Sewell's elder brother, RAD, had been educated at Fettes with Wauchope, and the journalist recalled being told: 'Don Wauchope was something truly out of the ordinary at half-back . . . and I've seldom met a rugger Scot who had not something to say about this wizard who always played in ordinary street shoes.' Scotland persisted with the half-backs sharing duties long after Wauchope's final international in 1888. John Gillespie was firmly a 'Wauchopian' – 'the more dangerous because he understood and practised the combined game.' The *Scotsman* added that he was 'also a most effective dribbler', which underlines the fact that there was no remote suggestion of his being any ancestor of the modern fly-half.

Perhaps Ernest Simson was at least nearer the finished article. He was a doctor who played in the first years of the century. Townsend Collins saw him in all five of his matches against Wales (each of which Scotland lost) and, after the last, became quite carried away about Simson. Perhaps because Wales had, to all intents, invented the pure fly-half, Collins, in his dotage, was feeling inclined to welcome at last a glimmer of the genuine article from the boys in blue:

'Never was there a pluckier player; no half ever played the uphill game with greater resource. He was not stylish, but he was effective. In attack he got away from the scrummage with flashing swiftness; in defence he performed prodigies – quick on his man, a tenacious tackler. His play was great, the spirit of the man was greater. To me he seemed heroic: after forty-five years he remains for me the greatest of Scottish halves. There are some things in everyday experience we cannot explain – perhaps because they have their origins outside everyday experience. I cannot explain why E. D. Simson made on my mind an impression no other player has made. He seemed – and still seems – a man apart. It was not his play alone, great as it was: it was an inner quality which made him, of all the thousands I have seen playing Rugby football, the one man who seemed "devoted", "dedicated". I knew nothing about him – who he was, what he was, what home he came from, what career was his aim: I only know that his play spoke to me of unique devotion, the inspired fulfilment of a sacred duty: to what? – Scotland? the game? or to some ideal of perfection? As I look back, he seems to me "The Devout Lover" of the greatest of games, eager to "do her behests in pleasure or in pain".'

Simson left Scotland and rugby at twenty-six, immediately after his final international match against England;

'he dashed over in splendid style for the winning try in the second period', said the *Scotsman*. He went to help garrison the Empire and joined the Indian Medical Service. Within two years he had died of cholera. Simson's two cousins, JT and RF, were also capped by Scotland, respectively wing- and centre-threequarter. Oh, the bloodiness of war and the quirkiness of luck – RF was the very first of the many rugby internationals to be killed in the Great War (at Aisne on 14 September 1914, before a trench had been dug); JT went right through the mud-slimed holocaust as a medical officer at the front and lived till 1976, when he died in bed as the oldest of all British rugby internationals. The rub of the green, the bounce of the ball . . .

Two knights-to-be then pulled on the blue jersey labelled '10' – not true in Scotland's case, in fact, because the autocratically conservative secretary of the Scottish RU, J. Aikman Smith, flatly refused when 'Twickenham' ordered numbered shirts to match the team listings in newly introduced match programmes. 'Do you also want me to pierce their ears with identity-tags?' he snorted. 'We are organizing a rugby match here, not a cattle sale.' It was not till 1926 that Scotland numbered their shirts.

Louis Greig (later knighted) and Simson had played together as alternating halves, left and right; they were instigators in Scotland's exhilarating, if losing, challenge to the All Blacks in 1905. Scotland had fielded eight backs to counter the colonials' dastardly five-eighths ploy, and it worked outstandingly till, with the Scots down to fourteen men in the final ten minutes, New Zealand scored their two winning tries for victory by 12–7.

Now, with Simson off to the ravages of India, Greig took the main role. He was just embarking on a brilliant, and decorated, naval career after Glasgow University, and was one of the first United Services players to win international recognition. For the rest of the half-century there were to be all too many servicemen also qualified to wear the funny little tasselled cap of blue, red, green and white – and round the Empire too, of myrtle-green, yellow ochre, and black. (Not yet to mention, which we are saving up, the more washed-out, paler blue of France.)

Unlike the estimable Greig, George Cunningham was to win his 'K' for work on terra firma, in the Indian Civil Service. He fought the Great War in the Punjab Light Horse. Cunningham, too, partnered Greig as 'alternative half' before he presumed to be senior in the partnership. Like Sewell's brother, Cunningham was an Old Fettesian, so the writer had to be a fan: 'a very clever stand-off or centre; expert at the cut-through, and a good handler and passer.' (That, now I notice, is the first time a Scottish half-back, according to these flimsy researches anyway, has been mentioned as a 'stand-off': this was 1910-ish, the century was already into double figures, and the Scots were catching up.) Significantly, Cunningham had gone up to Oxford in 1906, but had not won a Blue as a Magdalen fresher because of the 'brilliance and originality' at half-back of two Rhodes scholars from St Andrew's, Grahamstown, W. K. Flemmer and R. H. Williamson, who did not take it in turns to put the ball into the scrum, or play 'left' and 'right', and thus became the first authentic fly-half and scrum-half to play in a University Match. The following year, Williamson partnered Cunningham and there was another handsome victory for Oxford.

It was all coming together, and suddenly Scotland and faraway South Africa were following the first revolutionary torches lit in Wales and were imposing on Rugby Union, for its enlightening and necessary benefit, a crucial tactic and formation at half-back. The last rivet in the hull. Nor, as we shall see, were England far behind. Not far at all – for, intriguingly, two years before the South Africans' Varsity Match, the Oxford captain had been one: A. D. Stoop, a half-back who had come up from Rugby School (wouldn't you know) with an intense fascination for the sciences of a still rudimentary game and who had, through the term, chivvied his team into experimental plots with no end of original formations. He possibly encouraged the two South Africans to stay settled at inside- and outside-half in the 1906 match.

Certainly, it is highly probable that Stoop inspired his inside partner in two Varsity Matches, a wiry, enthusiastic Scot, Patrick Munro. For by the time, half a dozen years later, Munro had established himself in the Sudan Civil Service and was able to choose when to return to Blighty on long leave, he would come back to play for London Scottish. At Christmas 1910, he was seen to have picked up the threads so instinctively with the London Exiles' XV that (Cunningham having been dispatched to help run the Raj) Scotland picked him as their second authentic, pure and simple, fly-half after Cunningham. By which time, of course, Stoop had long and glisteningly been putting his same ideas into practice for England. Munro played the first three internationals of the 1911 season, against France, Wales, and Ireland, but – doubtless infuriating for the two old friends – by the time of the England match in March the Scot was back at his desk in the Sudanese bush. So he and Stoop, who had played 'alternate' halves together for so long as students (but forever practising and discussing the 'alternative to alternating') never marked each other as pure fly-halves in an international match. In 1939, long back in Britain, Munro was elected President of the Scottish RU. Three years later, he was killed on air-raid duty in London, aged fifty-nine. 'He was the best all-round stand-off half I ever saw in a Scots XV, and one of the first four or five of all,' wrote Sewell in Munro's obituary, 'an accurate punt and uncanny powers of intelligent anticipation in both attack and defence.'

Meanwhile, this chronicle must not hop ahead so hastily. There was a First World War to get through yet, alas – as the youthful Munro would have been all too aware in his Sudanese outpost. But the guns were still a million miles away in 1910, the year after Cunningham's final University Match for Oxford, which was won by the Dark Blues. For the 1911 match, Cambridge chose a twenty-one-year-old Scottish fly-half of the new orthodoxy, John Bruce-Lockhart. He was known as 'Rufus' (whether for other reasons than being either red-haired or unready, I don't know) and had been educated at

Sedbergh. In 1913 Scotland blooded him at fly-half against Wales at Inverleith. After war service with the Seaforth Highlanders, Rufus was to play one more game for Scotland, in 1920. Two sons, Rab and Logie, were both to grow up and play fly-half for Scotland – Rab just before the second war, Logie just after it. Both were schoolmasters, like their father. The other day – in 1993 – I came across this parchmenty old cutting, undated, written by Logie and torn from some back number of the *Field* magazine. It was headlined 'How To Win At Rugby' and as it set down the basics I was warmed that the junior of a rugby dynasty of international fly-halves, begun in a match at Inverleith all of eighty years before, so precisely captured the point of it all. I wonder how much of this credo was unconsciously passed on by old Rufus as he sat his son on his knee and told tales of what rugger could become – if your fly-half knew his onions? This was the Bruce-Lockhart definition:

'To handle beautifully and pass swiftly, whether you are a forward or a back; to kick or thrust your way beyond the advantage line and behind your opponents; to use accurate kicking to keep play in your opponents' half; to ruck swiftly, remaining on your feet; to get support to the ball carrier, always in greater numbers than the opposition; to retain possession, never losing the ball in a tackle; to keep thrusting until the opposition defence is exhausted, outnumbered and disorganized. Not to line back too steeply in the backs; to cultivate the swift long pass to an outside centre lying fairly flat in order to outflank "drift defence". To attack on one side or other of that centre, using short or long passes, loops, scissors or dummy scissors, introducing the full back and the blindside wing . . .'

Adrian Stoop would no doubt have called 'Aye!' to that testament of possible grandeur even before old Rufus Bruce-Lockhart. If Stoop was first to articulate clearly and then dominate the fly-half advances up to the First World War, England had fielded before him a litany of half-backs still alternate scrum-workers or forward adjuncts. Those who, from my reading, could possibly have advanced even by a smidgeon the coming of the 'pure' fly-half – though with nothing like the blazing trails laid by the James brothers and the other Welsh pioneers – deserve mention. Not least because their backgrounds, lumped together, illustrate the 'type' that made up the game as the old century melted into the new. The trio who were each given most of a run as senior of the England half-backs while the Empire still bathed in the safe aura of the venerable Victoria were Cyril Wells (Dulwich, Cambridge and Harlequins), who taught at Eton and once scored 244 for Middlesex against Nottinghamshire at Lord's; R. H. Cattell, an Oxford theological student who, on his ordination in 1897, switched promptly to association football 'for pastoral reasons' and turned out for years for Welwyn & Tring AFC; 'Dromio', the Welsh scribe, had said of his rugby that 'like about 30 per cent of all England players it was far better in international matches than in club games where they appear to have no special gift apart from weight, height, and strength.' Then there was Harry Myers – 'very lively and clever, a student of the game' – who kept a hotel in Keighley, Yorkshire, and switched in 1900 to Rugby League, in which game a tackle broke his back and killed him outright on the Saturday before Christmas in 1906. Robert Livesay was an England half, via Wellington and Sandhurst, who went through the Boer War and the 1914–18 global one – to emerge as a Brigadier-General and a member of the Légion d'Honneur, having been mentioned in dispatches six times. His successor in the white shirt was less lucky; R. O. Schwarz survived the trenches but died of influenza, still in France, on 18 November 1918, one week after the Armistice had been signed. Still Schwarz had, overall, been a more successful sportsman than the Brig.-Gen.; he was also a celebrated bowler of googlies at cricket and on the South African tour of England in 1907 had taken 143 wickets at just 11 apiece.

E. W. Taylor ('Little Billy'), from Northumberland, and Bernard Oughtred, from West Hartlepool, were two pioneer 'flies'. Taylor kept a shoe shop, was described by the *Northern Echo* as 'the prince of all halves', then sold everything and became a golf pro. Oughtred was a naval architect who was witness at first hand to the mighty Battle of Jutland; he was fortunate to do so, for when the 1903 England team, of which he was captain, had gone to Dublin to play Ireland, he was one of three in the party to catch typhoid. Oughtred recovered, but Reginald Forrest, the winger, and Robert Whalley, a former president of the RFU, did not: no side. Walter Butcher, an engineer, took over Oughtred's No. 10 shirt for a few matches, till he sailed to help build more routes for the Indian State Railway Company.

To counter the daunting brilliance of the 1905 All Blacks and their mystifying five-eighths tactics, England's hitherto presumptive but totally lackadaisical approach to new theories at half-back forced them to sandbag the areas immediately outside the scrummage, and they asked their outstanding centre-threequarter, a bright barrister John Raphael, to move one place inside to mark Billy Stead, the New Zealand wizard, with Dai Gent as Raphael's 'scrum-half' lieutenant. To no avail, of course, and in front of 45,000 at Crystal Palace England conceded five tries to nil.

The following week, Raphael wrote in the *Athletic News*: 'The difference between English and New Zealand rugby is the difference between a team which apparently has nothing more to learn and a team which by slavish adherence to cobwebbed tradition has much to unlearn. People keep saying, "Wait till they meet a nation!", forgetting that all New Zealand is not much more than a county. The success of the New Zealanders is the best thing for English rugby, since it will compel divorce from tradition and encourage the free indulgence of intelligent thought.'

Another English critic wrote: 'Nothing quite so brilliant as the intuitive combination of New Zealand back-play has ever been seen.' And the correspondent of the *Daily Mirror* could scarcely be restrained:

'They move like blood-horses, while the gait of the Englishmen is more suggestive of a Shire stallion . . . They play as if their hopes of eternal welfare depended upon success, every nerve and sinew braced all up to snapping point. They are as persistent as a lot of wasps, as clever and alert as a crowd of monkeys . . . They work together like the parts of a well-constructed watch . . . The New Zealanders are here, equipped for victory, and they have gained their equipment by recognizing that nothing but hard work and thorough drill can win success.'

Poor England's shire horses. But riding to their rescue was a young man, a genuine out-and-outer – a real fly-half.

5

Stoop begins to conquer

England's thrashing by New Zealand had been administered on 2 December 1905. For their previous match that year, against Scotland at Richmond in March, they had chosen Adrian Dura Stoop to share duties at half-back with the railway engineer Butcher. It was the year after the third and last of Stoop's Blues for Oxford, and he was one week away from his twenty-second birthday. Scotland won convincingly. 'Stoop showed promise early in the match', notes Griffiths' splendid history, but generally 'only Raphael's play earned any praise among the England backs'. Whether Stoop was seriously considered for the new formation to counter the wiles and guiles of the All Blacks eight months later is not known. Certainly he was not picked, and was probably fortunate not to be. In the last two matches of 1906, however, he was back for victories against Scotland (9–3) and in England's first ever match against the fledgling French (35–8). In both games Stoop shared the half-back role, alternating inside and out with James Peters – an English rugby pioneer with a difference.

As the twentieth century runs its course, the presumption is that the darting Nigerian Chris Oti was the first coloured man, in 1988, to play Rugby Union for England, soon to be followed by Andrew Harriman, Jeremy Guscott and Victor Ubogu. But James Peters – the Rugby Football Union's official history was still calling him just 'Darkie' Peters, as was their wont, in 1970 – beat Chris to the white shirt by over eighty years.

Peters was born in Salford in 1880 of West Indian parents, and his father moved to find work in the Bristol docks. The boy was educated at Knowle School. He learned his rugby at both inside- and outside-half. From the junior Bristol club Dings, he was soon poached by the city's illustrious senior side. In sepia team photographs, cross-legged-squat in the front row as all half-backs used to be, he suggests the quicksilver reactions and coffee complexion of Sugar Ray Leonard, the welterweight boxer.

When Peters's first appearance for the Bristol XV was announced, a letter in the local *Post and Mail* warned that the selection of 'this pallid blackamoor' might open the 'floodgates', and 'all and sundry might swamp a noble English game'. Following that first match, the same newspaper's sporting reporter wrote:

'Peters's ambition appeared to be to break away as he might do playing junior football and the result was that time after time he was collared with the ball. His excessive lack of judgment had a severely detrimental effect on his inside partner, Billy Needs, and the result was that all Bristolians present had the mortification of seeing the worst half-back play that has been witnessed since the city club became "first-class".'

Peters took a job at Devonport dockyard and stuck to his rugby with Plymouth. Soon he was the talk of Devon. I wonder if that Bristol reporter was one of those who lent voice to the chorus that Peters should play for England? He was blooded in the 9–3 win against Scotland.

'A delightful, running show was provided by Peters', wrote the *Manchester Guardian*. 'Peters's performance was most pleasing', purred the *Sunday Times*. He kept his place for the next five internationals. He inspired Devon to win the County Championship. Then he lost three fingers in a dockyard accident. When the wounds healed, he continued, remarkably, to turn out for Devon. He played till he was thirty-two, now in charge of a whole division in the naval dockyard at Devonport. When he gave up Rugby Union, Peters suggested enthusiastically that the workers should form a Rugby League side, to be paid for time off as a 'southern league' branch playing matches against their working-class confrères in the north. Twickenham banned him for life. He smiled softly and, appropriately, two-fingered a salute to the RFU, joining Barrow in the Rugby League. James Peters died in March 1954: a pioneer in more ways than as a fly-half.

Peters had even superseded Stoop as senior half-back partner at the end of their combination. In 1908 he partnered for England the brilliant South African 'inside' Rupert Williamson, who had so thrilled Oxford a couple of years before. What with a broken collarbone and his Bar exams at Inner Temple, Stoop faded from the selectors' list of Probs. It was not till another bad defeat by Scotland in March at Richmond that, for the following season of 1910, they turned again to Stoop – and made him captain for the first ever international match to be played at the newly built arena, surrounded by orchards, allotments and nursery gardens, ten miles from the city, just south of the Thames and hard on the River Crane. It was a tremendous occasion, a fiesta. The King was in the Royal Box, and the span-spick stadium, not yet splintery and venerable as it was to become, was rafter-packed with celebrants. 'Throughout the morning', reported the *Illustrated London News*, 'the throng continued to pour into the picturesque country village of Twickenham . . .'

While he had been, so to say, 'sitting on the bench' for two years, Stoop had cemented his ideas about half-back play; and now he had, also back again, the irrepressible Gent, a 'real' scrum-half if ever there was one, working at the back row's heels.

The teams were introduced to the King. Then Stoop won the toss. Wales to kick off. Of a sudden, the vast, buzzing multitude are pin-drop silent for a split second as the Scottish referee, John Dewar Dallas, raises his left hand before, with his right, blowing his whistle . . . Ben Gronow, of Bridgend, kicks off towards the right touchline, deep into England's twenty-five ... Stoop catches it calmly ... he feints to the right as the Welsh thunder down on him ... but he is not kicking for touch ... he's wrong-footed them ... he's going left, lancing fast across the midfield ... he's up almost to his ten-yard line as Wales attempt to regroup ... they are across at him now ... he puts up a short kick ... a beauty ... Jones goes down on it desperately, but the English are at him like tigers ... a fierce maul ... the ball's out for England ... Gent like an arrow to Stoop ... Stoop dummies his man and hands on to Solomon at pace ... the Cornishman's ripped through his man and passes to Birkett ... only Jack Bancroft to beat ... Birkett draws the full-back ... and flips it to Chapman, his winger ... Chapman must score ... *Chapman scores.*

No radio then, of course. But that is how it might have sounded. For it really did happen. Twickenham's first ever try – within a minute of the kick-off and inspired by Adrian Stoop in his first match as captain. Many years later, Stoop was to recall it – with typical modesty and a spiky dismissal of one of his forwards, Dyne Smith, a stockbroker and forward 'donkey':

'I caught the ball from the Welsh kick-off, feinted to the right to pin the Welsh forwards, and then swung left and through them. I put up a short kick when I found myself involved with the Welsh backs; then there was a scramble and the ball went out to Chapman, who scored. D. F. Smith claimed the other day that he was mixed up in it all; but as he is still under the impression that he fielded the kick-off before passing to me his evidence is worth nothing.'

Cornishmen still tell a bitter-sweet story about England's centre that day, their compatriot Bert Solomon, who they still laud in the Duchy as the grandest of all their grandeur. He played a blinder, but it was the only game he was to play for England. He had come up on the milk train from Redruth to Paddington, then battled his way with the festive crowds jamming the trains from Waterloo to Twickenham, his boots strung around his neck. He made it within minutes of kick-off and introduced himself to Stoop. 'How do you like your passes, old man?' Stoop enquired of his new inside-centre. Bert replied, in his broad-as-Bodmin accent, 'Juss thraw ball out, boy, an' I'll catch 'um.' Stoop's eyebrow arched. So out they went; and within a minute, of course, Stoop and Solomon had helped conspire and conjure up that superlative opening try.

Just on half-time, Stoop again fed Solomon at speed. As the RFU's centenary history had it sixty years later: 'Solomon, 40 yards out, sold the Welsh champion, Bancroft, an outrageous dummy before running on, untouched, to score at the Welsh posts.' It settled the match. England won by 11–6 – their first victory over Wales since 1898. England went on to win the championship, and Wales were not to win at Twickenham for another twenty-three years.

'I say, old boy,' enquired the amazed and impressed Stoop when Bert returned to the halfway line after his spectacular run, 'which school did you say you were at?' Bert lied. Instead of the truth, which was Trewirgie Boys' School, he found himself saying, 'Trewirgie *College*.'

The fib made him ashamed. He had no time for these men, these clip-vowelled dilettantes. At the final whistle, he changed quickly, muttered his farewells, battled his way back to Paddington, waited for the milk train home and never once replied to the unending stream of postcards from Twickenham pleading with him to play for England again. He remained in his Redruth butcher's shop, a true hero among his own.

Stoop's triumph (not to mention Solomon's) against Wales in his first match as captain of England let the sunshine in for a new 'Twickenham-proud' game in the country that 'invented' the whole caboodle in the first place (when William Webb-Ellis chose to run the thing at Rugby School in 1823, or so the legend had it). The day also snapped the blinds up conclusively for Stoop. Suddenly he could see the game's *real* creative possibilities – as the New Zealanders and (less surely yet) South

Africans had, and just as those copper-ladlers the James brothers from Swansea had unconsciously twigged almost twenty years before. As Stoop's solemn – and seething – inside-centre was waiting, hungry and unrecognized, at Paddington GWR terminus that evening for the empty, churn-rattling goods train back to Cornwall, Stoop was at the post-match dinner at a hotel just above the river at Richmond, on the Surrey side. His companion was R. M. Owen, veteran 'half' of the Welsh side who, with his confrère R. Jones – 'the Dancing Dicks', remember? – had each played, did they but know it, their last match for Wales. Owen of the bullet pass, the reverse pass, the change of direction – well, he fancied his time was up. His next birthday would have him thirty-six. He was, said one of his obituarists in 1932 (when he died, dolefully, by his own hand in his Swansea pub), 'utterly obsessed with the possibilities of rugby'.

Now, the player they called 'the pocket oracle' handed down his tablets of half-back play to the young barrister and captain of his winning rivals that afternoon. There was, insisted the Welsh steelworker to the English public schoolboy, a massive difference between the 'scrum-half' and 'fly-half'. Stoop's heart hoorayed as old Owen told him 'a scrum-half is a scrum-half, and a fly-half is a fly-half':

'My advice to a scrum-half is to do away with kicking to touch; or, in fact, any kicking at all. That should be left to the stand-off, who, however, should not forget that the game of football is intended to be played inside, and not outside, the touch-lines. My idea is that the scrum-worker, directly the ball is heeled, should pass direct and as swiftly as possible to the stand-off man, to run or kick before the opposition is on top of him. To do this, a swift and accurate pass should be given from a stooping position. If you're going to pass, do so at once, and from the very spot where you get the ball. If you decide to run, also do so at once, and keep thinking as you run. This again is not to say that mixing up your game by means of ruses that keep the opposition guessing is not of service. That, combined with good passing – waist high and a foot in front of the running man with the opposition drawn up to you before actually parting with the ball.'

Stoop was enchanted that such a testament from a legendary 'half' like Owen – and a scrum-half at that – should underline his own enthusiasms. They had been growing inside him since he was first enraptured by the game as a schoolboy. When, at Oxford still, he joined the London club Harlequins, he had sat, whenever possible, at the feet of Cyril Mowbray 'CM' Wells, the Middlesex cricketer (244 v. Nottinghamshire at Lord's and all that) who had played for Harlequins as a 'half' in the 1880s – and, with delicious relevance, for England six times in the early 1890s *when the James brothers were playing for Wales*. Stoop always gave Wells the credit for the sowing of seeds. If, for England anyway and the set-in-their-ways public schoolboys, CM was before his time, with Stoop it was a question of 'Cometh the hour, cometh the man': England were ready for an auspicious run, just as, with Stoop at the helm, Harlequins at once became the pre-eminent, most revolutionary and refreshing club side in Britain. As A. A. Thomson was to note some years later in *Punch*:

'In his youth, Stoop was a first class scrum-half and a brilliant stand-off. He came in at a time when halves were right- and left-, like soccer halves, and he may well be credited with developing the basic idea of a stand-off half. In strict fact, C. M. Wells, the old Harlequin half and Middlesex cricketer, was the first to see the advantage in attack of one half-back's standing well away from the scrummage. Stoop elaborated and perfected the idea. Incidentally, his theory that a stand-off should really stand a good distance wide of the scrum would, if put into determined practice, help to deal with what seems to be rugger's sharpest menace today. That is the problem of the enemy wing forward who jumps on the scrum-half, wrecks the attack and is thereby said to be wrecking the open game altogether. Granted the sort of quick heeling the Harlequins were trained to give, the long swift pass of a Sibree, Stoop's club, and very definite, scrum-half, and Stoop's matchless determination at the other end of that pass, the wing forward could at any rate be put in his place. No wing forward ever "sat on" Adrian Stoop to any great extent. But it was not only as a player, outstanding as he was, that Stoop will be in our flowing cups freshly remembered, but as a master strategist, a fertile deviser of tactics, and, in any genuine meaning of a hard-worked phrase, a leader of men.'

Thus are open-side, 'flanking' wing-forwards first addressed by a Twickenham man! If we are making out a case for Adrian Stoop to be England's 'inventor' of the tactical structures of the modern game – and it is a very strong one – then here it is.

Stoop was a bit of a first-generation moneyed pukka wallah. He had one, fashioned, blazer for the pre-match photograph, and another, looser, for drinks before the black-tie dance in the evening. And always a cravat on match day. He was born in London on 27 March 1883. His mother was of Scots-Irish stock, his father a Dutchman who became naturalized British. The boy was introduced to rugby football at his first senior school, Dover College, at twelve. By fourteen he was at Rugby School, where, some three score and ten years before, the game which had already become young Stoop's over-riding passion was said to have been 'invented' on Bigside, the parkland alongside the school buildings. Stoop made the Rugby XV in his final year – the first of the century – before going up to Oxford. He was to write later:

'As a means of inculcating self-reliance and a sense of honour it would be difficult to contrive a better games system than that in vogue at Rugby School at the end of the century. All games, apart from on Bigside, were inter-house matches, in every game a boy was playing for his side, never for his own glorification. There were no referees, except in the actual house matches, and con-sequently no "playing to the whistle" which is often a euphemism for taking advantage of the referee's mistake.

The rules were few and simple. If a player knocked on or passed forward, the captain of the opposing team shouted "forward", and a scrum was taken. When an opponent carrying the ball was grasped or lying on the ground, you placed your hands on the ball and said "held", and the ball was played with the foot. A player lying on the ground was not allowed to pass. An offside player did not play the ball. If it accidentally touched him there was a scrum. Anyone guilty of sharp practices was suitably dealt with by his opponents, and taken to task by his captain. Such cases were very rare.

'There were no penalty kicks. The traditions were: tackle hard and low, run straight, and never heel in your own half of the field. In the line-out the forwards immediately put the ball down and used their feet. Every forward pushed in the scrum till the ball was out; then it was the duty of the half-back to shout "out right" or "out left", when the whole defending scrum broke in the direction indicated. When a scrum was formed it was "first up, first down". There was a left half-back and a right half-back, and each worked the scrum and threw in from touch in his half of the field. No master had any part in these games, and all coaching was done by the captain. In my house we had regular scrum practices in a small yard. These traditions prevailed throughout the school, and I do not remember ever practising a tactical manoeuvre. The first time I played on Bigside was in the big school match of the year against Cheltenham. I had no practice with the other members of the XV, who were all strangers to me, but we won the match. I assume that the game was so uniform throughout the school that no practice was necessary.'

In all, Stoop was capped fifteen times for England. He was captain (as well as Hon. Secretary) of Harlequins from 1906 till the outbreak of war in 1914. He was elected Harlequins' president in 1920 and remained so till 1949. The club now plays at a neat modern stadium just across the road from the arena at Twickenham: it is called 'the Stoop'. In an article on coaching, an activity to which he was devoted in his 'retirement', Stoop set down his fly-half's thesis:

'The scrum-half should concentrate on speed first and accuracy next. His pass must never travel behind his partner nor more than chest-high. A quick pass which travels in front of his partner can be picked up by a three-quarter and may lead to a try. He must tell his forwards where the ball is in a loose scrum, and as soon as the ball is out should shout "out left" or "out right" to help them to break quickly. When the ball is no use to him he should tell the forwards to keep it, but never call on them to heel. That is the job of the scrum leader.

'The fly-half in attack should stand wide of the scrum. A quick pass across the field will beat any wing forward, whereas if the fly-half is standing directly behind the scrum the wing forward can cut him off at a jogtrot. If he wishes to work the blind side, the mere fact of standing wide puts his opponent out of action. In common with the threequarters, when waiting for the ball he should stand with his hands resting on his knees, so that he may be in an attitude which will allow him to pick up a half-volley. He should have a reserve of speed when he takes the ball. As his threequarters need room in which to manoeuvre, he should try to swing in and pass out within two strides of taking the ball. This is a very difficult accomplishment to attain. It is generally necessary to change feet as the ball is taken. He should watch the ball into his hands, and then glance at the opposition. He will be able to see his three-quarter out of the corner of his eye. My test of a fly-half is the amount of room he gives his wing on the touch-line.'

As for Stoop practising what he preached, H. T. B. Wakelam, the first ever BBC 'wireless' commentator on rugby, wrote in his history of the club, *Harlequin Story*:

'As a player Stoop had almost every possible attribute – perfect hands (from long practice), great speed off the mark, allied with a very quick brain and power to sum up an immediate situation, perfect control over his passes, always truly aimed, hard and straight to their proper objective, a fine defence (sometimes maligned, quite unjustly, because of the "team" method he used), and quite exceptional control of the ball at his feet on the ground. He could also use both feet in his kicking, which was accurate, if necessary long, and always astute.'

Sewell, as ever, probably hit the button: 'Perhaps Stoop's sometimes caustic mode of expression did not please everybody, but that's the usual fate of all who say what they mean and mean what they say.' And he added, 'Beyond all doubt very many people went to Twickenham just to see Stoop play', much as at cricket they assembled to see WG, Ranji, Trumper or Jessop.

At once came another such. Stoop's last match for England was the 3–8 defeat by Scotland at Inverleith on 16 March 1912 (when Stoop's men were stopped in their tracks as they confidently went for the Triple Crown: how many times has that happened to the haughty English in Scotland?). On 4 January 1913, when the South African tourists came to Twickenham, the fly-half was a twenty-two-year-old Royal Navy sailor, William John Abbott Davies. Stoop's No. 10 shirt was filled at once by the gods.

Sure, the relentlessly brilliant South Africans – inspired by a full-back of genius, 'Boy' Morkel, and a gifted fly-half 'who was head and shoulders above any other on the trip', Fred Luyt – beat England by 9–3; but for Davies it was his only losing international in the next twenty-two he played. On this tour, however, the Springboks laid the Brits to waste, clean-sweeping the four internationals by 66 points to England's solitary 3. When they embarked for home, their captain, Billy Millar, probably summed up the position accurately when he reported: 'I do not think we could say that we had learnt any new lessons from the tour. We could now, justifiably, consider ourselves on a plane with any rugby country in the world. And I am confident that I do not exaggerate when I say that we were the teachers, rather than the pupils. Rugby in South Africa has now reached a decidedly high level, and the standard of play in the minor provinces has improved beyond recognition. Rugby has become a national game in every sense of the word.'

Not so in Australia. Rugby Union's all-time high had been in 1907, when 52,000 watched the All Blacks at Sydney cricket ground. In that same year (after an injured Union player had been refused compensation for medical expenses by the Union), a meeting at the Sydney shop of the cricketer Victor Trumper passed a unanimous resolution to fund a professional 'league'. It took off at once, and was soon challenging the 'Victorian Rules' home-made 'Gaelic' game in popularity. Indeed, when the booming guns began to be heard across the seas, the patriotic Rugby Union at once suspended all further Union matches. The Rugby League did not – and it was to be another seventy years before the Union game restored itself to full health in Australia.

As W. J. A. Davies was posted to the *Iron Duke*, the Australian Expedition Force was being piped off from Sydney Harbour. Among them was 'The Sportsmen's Battalion', consisting of 1,000 rugby players. The *Sydney Argus* saluted them next day: 'How can other men prefer playing normal games at home to this far more noble sport. These volunteers are the type of Australians that love adventure, that know no fear, that could not be mere spectators. For these men no circumstances were strong enough to make them stay at home. They wanted to have a first-hand knowledge of the war, to feel the thrill of battle, to play a part in history's greatest tragedy, to see the world and feel they were doing their duty. They represent the kind of man who wants to be in the game rather than have his excitement second-hand.'

6

Expecting the unexpected

In May 1915 the *South Wales Daily News* printed a letter from a Private George Noyes, of the Welsh Regiment, who was being detained at the Kaiser's pleasure in a prisoner-of-war camp at Altdamm, Germany. Private Noyes was keen to let readers know that the Welsh had beaten the Yorkshire Light Infantry by 6–0 and, in the final, the Rest-of-Prisoners by 9–0. 'There are 16 Cardiff men incarcerated here,' he wrote, 'and we would very much like a rugby ball sent out. The troops are all in good health, except longing for the dear old home again.'

It would be three years till they saw home again. Fortunate blighters. The ghastly toll, in all, of eight and a half million would not. Twelve Welsh international players did not make it through the mass slaughter; the same number of capped New Zealanders were killed, including, on the Somme, young Bob Black, of the Otago Mounted Rifles, the fly-half who had won his solitary (and, for him personalized) jersey in the final Test Match of the Australian tour only weeks before war was declared.

Thirty capped rugby internationals never came home to Scotland; twenty-six England players were killed. The extent of the carnage can be even more gruesomely underlined by the fact that of the thirty young sportsmen who had contested the Calcutta Cup match at Inverleith in March 1914, as many as eleven – over a third – were slain (six Scots, five Englishmen). Five Springbok internationals were killed; in the rugby pavilion at Newlands in Cape Town, there remains a plaque to those rugby and cricket players from Cape Province alone who fell: there are 272 names on it.

Ireland lost nine men who had worn the shamrock proudly, including the great Maclear. Two rugby internationals won the Victoria Cross: Arthur Harrison (a pupil at Stoop's Dover College), who had won three caps as a forward in 1914 and was awarded his posthumously after the Zeebrugge raid, and the Irish fly-half in two matches in 1907 and 1911, Frederick Harvey of Lord Strathcona's Horse. Harvey's VC citation read: 'At Guyencourt on March 27, 1917, he was leading his troop, which had already suffered heavy casualties, when they came under fire from a machine-gunner in a wired trench. Lt. Harvey jumped from his horse, ran for the trench, jumped the wire, and put out the machine-gun'. Par for the course for a Lansdowne Road fly-half in the green.

Twenty French international players never came back to their homes. Ironically, however, after suffering such a grievous toll, France embarked on peacetime rugby as a considerable force in the championship, which at once became, seriously, a Five Nations challenge. In France's twenty-eight internationals as fledglings before 1914, her teams had won only once, famously against Scotland in Paris in 1911 – although they came down with a heck of a *coup de foudre* a fortnight later on their first visit to Twickenham, Stoop's England putting six tries past them in a 37–0 job.

Now, in 'Victory Tests' as the war ended, the French lost only by 13–14 and 10–16 to a strong New Zealand Army side; then, when the championship resumed proper on New Year's Day 1920, they were deemed unlucky to lose to Scotland by 0–5. This was followed by narrow defeats (3–8 and 5–6) against England and Wales. In the following season, they beat America to win the Olympic title, and then beat Scotland and Ireland in the Five Nations. The French were on their way – and in 1921 they failed by a whisker to become the first side to beat England at Twickenham since the South Africans in 1912, which had been Davies's first match in the white shirt. Now France drew 11–11, with a stunned Twickenham not very pleased at all. On the wing for *les bleus* that famous day, by the way, was one André Lafond from Bayonne. Seventy-one years later, his grandson Jean-Baptiste was to play a serenely brilliant full-back's game at Twickenham which deserved, and again unluckily failed, to beat the massively confident English Grand Slammers of the early 1990s on its own.

Possibly thanks to Davies's perfection of half-back play, which the French had witnessed four times now – plus the New Zealanders' own original tutelage after the war with their first five-eighths – their game-plans all came together now, for they found for the first time a rich seam of natural and singularly creative fly-halves. (Mind you, before the war, Stoop had remarked acidly that 'the trouble with the French is that they keep picking 15 fly-halves and no-one else'.) They had a champion in the pack, 'Poulet' Lassere, a Cognac producer, a real warring cockerel of a wing-forward who had played at centre pre-war. He must have been a forerunner to the grand French JPR – Jean-Pierre Rives. Lassere had been a French Flying Corps ace in the four-year German match.

Another stalwart regular was the full-back Jean Clement, a gamekeeper from Valence. Griffiths' history describes how 'his Charlie Chaplin appearance belied his footballing ability, for he was an imperturbable defender with an extraordinary sense of anticipation'. In 1923 Clement asked to be dropped, saying he had 'lost form'. He was, although, apparently he hadn't.

But between Clement and Lassere, three luminous fly-halves succeeded each other to organize and inspire French back play: first Eugene Billac, a Basque from Bayonne who delighted in creative running, till the apparently even more ingenious Jep Pascot, of Perpignan, replaced him. It seems wholly suitable that these two fly-halves were the first specialists to stamp their identity on the position – because rugby in France was, to all serious intents, developed in Bayonne and Perpignan. In the early years of the twentieth century a Welshman from Penarth called Roe had settled in Bayonne and taught the town rugby side the running and passing game he had known in his native Wales (Bayonne, still coached by Roe, went up to Paris in 1913 and won the national club championship by 33–8). Simultaneously, at the other end of the Pyrenees, another Welshman called Griffiths became the first captain of the Perpignan rugby club, and he too quickly encouraged the game to be 'spoke' in his native fluency. (When it comes to fly-half history, you cannot ignore the Welsh for long.)

And after Billac and Pascot, from Bayonne and Perpignan respectively, came the fly-half to whom French rugby romantics still keep alight their perpetual candle of thanksgiving. Between 1924 and 1927, although still losing many more matches than they won, international rugby in France was blessed by the dominating charisma and presence at fly-half of the dashing young chevalier Yves Du Manoir, who was a pilot officer in the French Flying Corps. His flamboyant natural gifts also brought him international fame as a racing car driver, swimmer, canoeist and tennis player. 'But most of all he was the perfection of the chivalrous rugby player', noted one contemporary writer. An advertisement encouraging schoolboys to take up sport in France was captioned simply: 'Model your sport on Du Manoir, boys, and overnight you will become a man.'

A year after Du Manoir stepped down from rugby for France (after the match against Scotland in Edinburgh in 1927), he was piloting a light aeroplane over the packed Colombes stadium in Paris in a solo fly-past of welcome just before the kick-off when the Scottish team had come over for the return match. The engine failed and it crashed. He was still only twenty-three. A mourning nation erected a statue to him outside the gates of Colombes. (There has since been the occasional spontaneous need to erect statues to famous sportsmen:

C. K. Nayudu outside his home cricket ground at Indore in India; Fred Perry at Wimbledon; and Graham Gooch and Gareth Edwards respectively look down in bronze from plinths in the middle of the hideous new shopping centres at Chelmsford and Cardiff. But, one fancies, Du Manoir's at Colombes was the first – and most heartfelt – to be raised.)

That Scottish team which Du Manoir had so joyously played (and lost) against on three successive occasions was Scotland's first great one in history. It won the Grand Slam in 1925 in exuberant fashion – its pack being fiery enough to supply a decent amount of possession to a thrilling set of threequarters, who scored fifteen tries between themselves alone through the season. The link between the two was at fly-half, where Herbert Waddell, both Glasgow 'Accie' and Fettesian in his early twenties, showed precocious aptitude for the game and the position. By the time he retired in 1930, with fifteen caps, most of Scotland knew him only as 'Napoleon'.

But just as Waddell was about to stake out his territory for Scotland, an even more distinguished field-marshal, south of the border, was handing in his seals of state – although in this case 'Nelson' would have been a more apt nickname. Waddell's debutant's curtsey for Scotland was in the losing match against France on New Year's Day 1924. Eight months before, the day after April Fools', England's by now magisterial fly-half and captain W. J. A. Davies had played the last match of his then record twenty-two for England – also against France and on his honeymoon: he dropped a sumptuous last-minute goal with his last ever serious kick on a rugby field.

Davies's ten years as England's fly-half – in which he was never on the losing side in a championship match – spanned not only the Great War but also international rugby's Middle Age and Age of Elegance. In Britain the likes of Bush and Trew and Stoop had only just finished putting the finishing touches and a shiny veneer on fly-half play when Davies first pulled on the white shirt in

1913. By the time Davies (and the likes of Du Manoir and Waddell too) retired, international rugby fly-halves were still full of the creative joys, still revelling in running and passing, and using the punt only as a sharp, offensive weapon, not as a monstrous ground-gainer for your forwards to win another lineout.

In fact the only mundane thing about Davies was the nickname he answered to – 'Dave', wouldn't you know? He had begun the war serving on the *Iron Duke* in the Grand Fleet, and finished it on the *Queen Elizabeth* as a Lieutenant-Commander on the staff of the Commander in Chief. Where Stoop, his predecessor, had been more delicate-featured and happier to use his balletic guiles to dance out of the way of marauding defenders, Davies was fashioned out of teakier stuff and, as often as not when he was collared, his tacklers came out of it more painfully. His comparatively dapper build belied immense strength. He was an exceptional ball-player athlete with a blaze of a short sprint which, crucially, he used to full effect only sparingly. Yet his grandest attribute seems to have been his innate rugby nous. He was made to be a fly-half, they used to say – and the fly-half was invented to be a Davies.

In fact he was born only to be a sailor – into a naval family posted at the time in Pembroke, so he could have played for Wales. His first games of rugby were as an 'inside-half' at the naval engineers' training college at Keyham, in Devonport. In 1910, he graduated to the Royal Naval College at Greenwich, where he was soon Victor Ludorum, and in 1911, still only twenty, he was chosen to play at fly for the Navy against the Army at Twickenham.

In his last match for England he was two months short of his thirty-fourth birthday. He was succeeded as captain by Wavell (later Lord) Wakefield, who called Davies 'the artist and philosopher of my rugby learning'. In the four seasons when the younger Wakefield was captained by Davies, England once shared the championship and twice won it outright. Davies lived till 1967, and before his own death at 85 in 1983, the delightful old warhorse

No prisoners for old Bill – as Hook ushers through Ken Jones, of Wales, at Twickenham.

Alpha/Sport & General Press Agency

Campo, Campissimo! David Campese bamboozles Barbarians.

Popperfoto/Bob Thomas Sports Photography

Danie Gerber celebrates the end of South Africa's exile in the first international match of the Springbok's comeback tour against France at Lyon, 1992. Allsport

Gareth against France. The *allez* cats were Edwards's favourite 'enemies'.

Alpha/Sport & General Press Agency

Ken Catchpole against England at Twickenham...speedy hands, but surer feet.

Alpha/Sport & General Press Agency

Bob Scott…another boomer from Baldy.
Hulton Getty

Boldness was always Serge Blanco's best friend and confrère. Popperfoto/Bob Thomas Sports Photography

Frank Hancock, born in Wiveliscombe, Somerset, as captain of Cardiff 1885–6. An early fly-half visionary, who worked on the coaling boats and later became a brewer. Western Mail & Daily Echo

The first match in which England experimented with the Welsh example of playing four threequarters, a formation advocated by the half-back and dashing county cricketer Cyril Wells, whose philosophies over fly-half play were to inspire the young Adrian Stoop. This was the only rugby international ever

Grand Match.

ENGLAND *v.* WALES

At the Upper Park, Birkenhead,

On SATURDAY, JANUARY 6th, 1894.

ENGLAND.	WALES.
Full Back :	*Full Back :*
J. F. BYRNE, Midland Counties	W. J. BANCROFT, Swansea
Three-quarters :	*Three-quarters :*
C. A. HOOPER, Gloucestershire, left	W. M CUTCHEON, Oldham, rght
* R. LOCKWOOD, Yrkshire, left cntre	†A. J. GOULD, Newport, right centre
S. MURFITT, Durham, right centre	‡J. C. REES, Oxford, left centre
F. FIRTH, Yorkshire, right	N. BIGGS, Cardiff, left
Half Backs :	*Half Backs :*
C. M. WELLS, Surrey, left	P. PHILLIPS, Newport, right
E. W. TAYLOR, Nrthmbrland, right	F. C. PARFITT, do left
Forwards :	*Forwards :*
J. TOOTHILL, Yorkshire	A. W. BOUCHER, Newport
H. BRADSHAW, do	W. WATTS, do
T. BROADLEY, do	T. C. GRAHAM, do
H. SPEED, do	J. HANNEN, do
W. E. TUCKER, Cambridge	J. C. B. NICHOLL, Cambridge
J. HALL, Durham	F. MILLS, Swansea
A. ALLPORT, Surrey	A. F. HILL, Cardiff
F. SOANE, do	D. J. DANIELL, Llanelly

* English captain.   † Welsh captain.   ‡ Doubtful

played in Birkenhead. (Rees may have been 'doubtful' for Wales, but he still turned out.) England won by 24–3. Note England's large contingent from the north – within a year, on the founding of 'Rugby League's' breakaway Northern Union, almost half the side had 'gone over'. Lockwood went to Wakefield Trinity, Morfitt (not Murfitt) to Hull KR, Firth to Halifax, Toothill and Broadley to Bradford, Bradshaw to Leeds, and Speed to Castleford.

Courtesy of David Fox

The true founders of the feast? Swansea's 'curly-haired marmosets' were, to opponents, 'the little varmints'. David James (*left*) lived till 1929, but his brother Evan died of tuberculosis less than three years after acutely embarrassing the England XV in 1899.

Percy Bush (*left, on the ground*), His Majesty's vice-consul and regal mesmerist at rugby who spread the Welsh gospel Down Under.

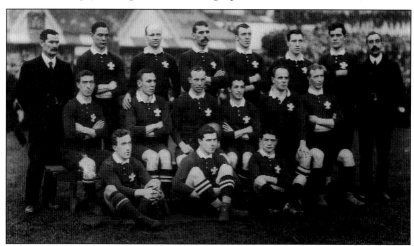

England 0, New Zealand 15 at Crystal Palace, 2 December 1905. *The Illustrated London News* artist Ernest Frater graphically captures England's desperation against the colonial 'Originals' for whom James Hunter tosses a pass to his All Black colleague Fred Roberts, who has Bob Deans (*far right*) unmarked outside him. Each of the three blazingly worked the 'five-eighths' system alongside its creative perpetrator, Billy Stead, the Southland cobbler turned journalist, who is seen in the background between the English tackler and Roberts. The Illustrated London News Picture Library

Basil Maclear during his one season at fly-half for Ireland. He is third from the left in the back row before the famous victory over Wales at Belfast in March 1906 – when the white-gloved Dublin fusilier went about downing the Welsh 'three at a time'. Willow Murray

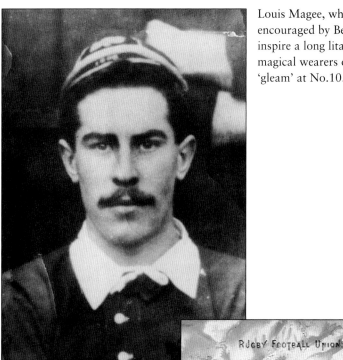

Louis Magee, who was encouraged by Ben Tuke to inspire a long litany of magical wearers of the 'gleam' at No.10. Louis Magee

RUGBY FOOTBALL UNION.

35, SURREY STREET,

STRAND. W.C.

28th February 1905

Dear Sir

You have been chosen to play for England against Scotland at Richmond on Saturday March 18th

Kindly let me know at Once by Enclosed Telegram if you can play.

Yours truly

Percival Coles

A. D. Stoop Esq.

Secretary

Young Adrian Stoop 'nudges the selectors' for the first time. England lost and he was dropped.

Museum of Rugby

Adrian Stoop and James Peters (*front, on the ground*) at Inverleith before England's victory over Scotland on St Patrick's Day, 1906. It was Peters's first international match, and Stoop's second. They were still officially alternating the half-back roles. In this match it was Peters who put on the 'delightful running show'. Museum of Rugby

Fred Luyt, the farmer's son from the Cape who became a lawyer and a Springbok fly-half 'above all others'.

The Illustrated London News Picture Library

The first Wallabies play their opening match on English soil – beating Devon
(*hooped shirts*) by 24–3 two days after landing at Plymouth in 1908. They
brought with them a snake as a mascot (it died on the morning of this match),
new-fangled scrum-caps, and pale blue jerseys embroidered with a Waratah
badge, floral emblem of New South Wales. In the internationals they beat
England and lost narrowly to Wales – and they also won the 1908 Olympic
Games Rugby Tournament final in London, beating the English county
champions Cornwall by 32–3. On their return home, thirteen of the side joined
Rugby League for a guarantee of £100 each. Hulton Getty

The indomitable W.J.A. Davies, matelot and maestro (*standing third from left in the third row from the front*), with the England and South Africa teams at Twickenham before the Springboks' victory in 1913.

OPPOSITE: England 19, Scotland 0 at Twickenham, 1924 – to clinch a second successive Grand Slam for the 'lilywhites', this time captained by Wakefield (*breaking from the lineout, fifth from the left*). Scotland have it, but as Bryce, the Scottish scrum-half, is scragged by the England hooker Robson, he has thrown a difficult pass to Waddell, who bends to collect it as the English back-row forwards, Blakiston and Conway, hasten towards him with intent. Drysdale, dreadnought Scottish full-back, stands behind his best friend, Waddell, but shows no inclination to fill the gap between Waddell and his inside-centre, Aitken. The referee alongside the Scottish fly-half is Tommy Vile, former Welsh scrum-half who was to become High Sheriff of Monmouthshire.

Eugene Davy's grand and extended international career comes down to earth as he is upended by England's Northamptonshire farmer, Weston, at Twickenham in 1933, his final season with the shamrock at his breast.

OPPOSITE: Note the *Daily Telegraph* advertisement (*top left*). Col. Trevor CBE was at his enraptured 'best' after the easy victory by the 'Invincibles' from New Zealand. The Twickenham programme printers were obviously in a nice muddle over the eccentricities of the All Blacks' formation – diplomatically making sure not to list Kittermaster, the new England fly at No.10, on the same line as Nicholls, New Zealand's first 'five-eighths'. Museum of Rugby

OFFICIAL PROGRAMME: TWOPENCE

COLE COURT HOTEL, TWICKENHAM

LUNCHEONS and TEAS served at separate Tables in Banquet and Ball Rooms

The Nearest Licensed Hotel to the Rugby Football Ground.

Excellent Cuisine. :: Tables can be Reserved.

Phone, Richmond 2673

ENGLAND v. NEW ZEALAND

Saturday, January 3rd, 1925.   Kick-off 2.30 p.m.

England				New Zealanders	
No.					No.
15	*J. BROUGH (Silloth)	BACK	A. E. FREETHY, Esq. (Wales)	G. NEPIA	1
14	*R. HAMILTON-WICKES (Harlequins)	RIGHT WING THREE-QTR.		J. STEEL	2
13	*V. G. DAVIES (Harlequins)	RIGHT CENTRE THREE QTR.		A. E. COOKE	11
12	*L. J. CORBETT (Bristol)	LEFT CENTRE THREE-QTR.		K. S. SVENSON	6
11	J. C. GIBBS (Harlequins)	LEFT WING THREE QTR.			
		FIVE-EIGHTH		N. P. McGREGOR	9
		FIVE-EIGHTH		M. NICHOLLS	12
10	H. J. KITTERMASTER (Oxford)	STAND OFF HALF			
9	*A. T. YOUNG (Cambridge)	SCRUM HALF		J. C. MILL	14
		WING FORWARD		J. H. PARKER	15
1	W. W. WAKEFIELD (Harlequins)	FORWARD		Q. DONALD	20
2	*R. COVE-SMITH (Old Merchant Taylors)	FORWARD		W. R. IRVINE	18
3	*A. T. VOYCE (Gloucester)	FORWARD		M. J. BROWNLIE	21
4	*A. F. BLAKISTON (Liverpool)	FORWARD		R. R. MASTERS	26
5	*G. S. CONWAY (Rugby)	FORWARD		C. J. BROWNLIE	27
6	*J. S. TUCKER (Bristol)	FORWARD		A. WHITE	22
7	R. J. HILLARD (Oxford)	FORWARD		J. RICHARDSON	23
8	*R. EDWARDS (Newport)	FORWARD			

*Internationals.

ABOVE: Showing the strength of the 'All Black' system: the 'All Black' half (No. 14) gets the ball out to the five-eighths before the opposing halves can interfere, while Porter (No. 16), who put the ball in the scrummage, stands ready to help.

BELOW: Showing the weakness of the English system: An English scrum-half collared, while the 'All Black' wing-forward, Porter (*on right*), dribbles away, backed up by Richardson (*centre*) and Brownlie (*extreme left*).

The Illustrated London News almost in puzzled awe at the All Blacks five-eighths. The Illustrated London News Picture Library

Bennie Osler and his 1931 Springboks being welcomed by the Mayor of Southampton when the *Windsor Castle* liner docked at the beginning of their tour. After South Africa's Grand Slam, however, British rugby's farewell to Osler was to be less warm. Hulton Getty

Roger Spong, the British Lions' finest fly-half export since Percy Bush, weighs up Middlesex's options in a county championship match against Hampshire in 1932. The Illustrated London News Picture Library

'Wakers' lovingly recalled aspects of his genius:

'Three pictures remain with me, and in one of them the game had been going against us. Our forwards had been so hard pressed that we were almost done, when suddenly Dave swings a long kick into touch 50 yards in the enemy's country, so that we could trot down for a merciful rest. Often when he has done that I have been thankful to be on his side, for somehow he seemed always to know instinctively when his forwards must have relief. Some backs have to be told when their pack is tiring; but Dave could see for himself, and just at the right moment he would bring off those two or three restful kicks, which were so badly needed.

'Then again, after he had monotonously passed to his centres until the opposition expected no threat from him, I saw him suddenly lengthen his stride and cut straight through, swerving always from left to right, leaning backwards, his knees well up, poised in every movement for a sudden change of scheme or direction. To the uninitiated it looked so easy, this breakaway of his; but the gap through which he went he had worked and waited for most cunningly. And finally there was his dropping of goals, that little run, that balanced pause, and then the ball curving over between the posts to pull another game out of the fire.'

Another contemporary, A. A. Thomson, born just four years after Davies, in 1894, also noted his hero's rare ability to meld a sometimes exuberant individualism with a devoted diligence towards the immediate needs of the team:

'Davies was one of those rare creatures who seemed to combine the virtues of both camps: an individualist, certainly, but a glorious partner as well. He completely lacked the individualist's temptation towards selfishness, and he never played to the gallery in his life. He had more beautiful "hands" than anything seen beside the Shalimar. Though he occasionally dropped a match-winning goal, he did not suffer, as some goal-droppers do, from an obsession that they were sent into the world for that sole purpose and he would never sacrifice to a speculative drop at goal a pass that might have brought a convertible try. I remember an enthusiastic sailor once saying to me on the touchline: "He always does the unexpected, but then you expect him to!" He did not have a kick-ahead fixation as some critics said Benny Osler had; his kicking was long, judicious and purposeful, and it was an attacking rather than a defensive weapon. By its means he could nurse weary forwards as a mother nurses tired children.'

For the first match of the 1922 season, against Wales at Cardiff, Davies had to cry off with a strained leg. (A namesake, the Old Marlburian V. G. Davies, deputized none too happily; without WJA, England were trounced by 28–6.) Three weeks later, he was fit to face Ireland at Lansdowne Road. Thomson recalled it as:

'One of those stupendous games in which no quarter is asked or given. When Ireland scored first, not long after the beginning of the game, the huge Irish crowd nearly went hysterical and the game went on, never slackening its speed for an instant, to the accompaniment of an unbroken roar. England equalized, then scored again and again; Ireland defended grimly, but the English forwards were the mighty line, the most formidable in history, and there was no holding the English backs. Particularly was it impossible to hold Davies. It was this urbane elusiveness – he had a maddening air of looking as bland as a bishop or at least as dapper as a dean when everybody else was dishevelled and plastered with mud – that gave rise to one of the classic interjections of the game. As Davies wove an apparently unimpeded way through the Irish defence, an exasperated spectator was moved to exclaim in his agony: "If you can't catch that boyo, for the love of mike ruffle his hair!" G. V. Stephenson, the Irish centre, brooded over this plea for a whole year and then, the following season in the corresponding match at Leicester, took the opportunity when tackling Davies hard, to ruffle his hair "good and proper". Davies laughed, as well he might. England won both matches.'

As this century draws to its end and the worldwide

game of rugby football becomes an ever more clamorous business, there is one veteran journalist and author, J. B. G. 'Bryn' Thomas, still able to reflect on the age of elegance and chivalry. Bryn was longtime sports editor of the *Western Mail*. In well over sixty years of reporting rugby on every continent, he must have seen more rugby men and matches than any man in all history – dear old E. H. D. Sewell's friend and rival, 'Astral' Freddie Dartrell, of the *News Chronicle*, notwithstanding. Bryn, the doyen of the sports box and with over thirty revealing books under his belt (to date), was commissioned in the Royal Navy in the Second World War, and in his *Great Rugger Players* he recalled his fellow officer from the previous conflagration:

'Like all great sportsmen, he had a kind word for everyone, and his greatness did not affect his attitude towards the Game or his fellow men. Technically Davies was a great footballer. In defence or attack he always had the right sense of emergency, and time to spare when carrying out any basic skill. In all games the ease with which a player executes a movement is the sign of his greatness. Davies could stop a forward rush and get to his feet all in the same movement; and this led to a wrong accusation that he would never go down and stay on the ball until his forwards were able to re-group themselves. He was a student of the Game, and his conscientious study and keen application gave him the advantage over all his opponents. It is true that he played in great English sides; but on succeeding to the position left vacant by the great Adrian Stoop, he developed his own skill and that of his fellows to a high degree. He was quick to realize that the outside-half position was passing through a period of change with the advent of the lively back-row forward, and he gave to the Game a new style, which, if it had been followed by his younger contemporaries, would have done much to off-set the dominance and power of the between-the-wars spoiling wing-forwards.'

Like his own compatriots of the Early and Middle Ages

of half-back play – the genie James brothers with each other, Jones and Trew with the nonpareil scrum-half Owen – JBG would be first (as Davies himself would – and, to be sure, always was) to acknowledge the fly-half's debt to his friend, fellow sailor and indispensable scrum-half C. A. Kershaw, known simply as 'K'.

In his pre-war games for England, Davies had been partnered by Francis Oakeley, another matelot – Osborne and Dartmouth, and a former midshipman of HMS *Invincible*. Oakeley, reported Dromio, was 'an all-round attacking and defensive player who gave a good pass from the scrum, but was also capable of scoring'. Just seven months after his and England's final pre-war match, the glorious 39–13 romp against France at Colombes on 13 April 1914, Oakeley was posted as 'killed in action or drowned at sea' in one of the Navy's prototype HM submarines. All the Admiralty could wire his parents was that their son's death occurred 'some time between November and December'.

Contemporary reports cast Oakeley, as some middle-aged Twickenham readers might twig, in the dauntless mudlark role at the heels of the pack that the irrepressible Dick Jeeps was to play fifty-odd years later; Kershaw, in contrast, was altogether crisper and tidier, more of a Richard Hill or Steve Smith type. He was five years younger than Davies. They met a few weeks after the Armistice, when they played inter-fleet games together at Portsmouth. Davies called it the 'goodliest fellowship'. Like Gareth Edwards and Barry John half a century later, they 'talked the same language' – though, unlike those two, it was only English and Rugby, not *Welsh*, English and Rugby.

Kershaw combined a long, hard-thrown pass which gave Davies ample room to move against the suddenly too-fast-released, ambushing wing-forwards. But as Townsend Collins in the *South Wales Argus* recognized with generosity when Davies and Kershaw had twice organized the beating of Wales in 1921 and 1923, 'Kershaw was so very clever at "inside" that his aggressive defence so checked, hindered, or smothered his Welsh opposite that it completely broke up our attempts at combination. Kershaw was clever too, in holding the attention of our wing-forwards, and by so doing, helped infinitely his partner.'

Davies and Kershaw retired simultaneously and threw a party to celebrate Davies's brand-new partnership – in marriage: it was the first day of his honeymoon. The two of them had italicized the truism that few fly-halves had, or would, cut much of a dash without a regular and worthy confrère as his inside partner. As Thomson wrote, 'Kershaw's passes were swift, long and fierce and maybe nobody but Davies could have taken them. He would pick up a ball anyhow, anywhere, and was both as fast as a winger and as thrustful as a first-class centre.'

Kershaw's originality, indeed his daring, had a strong effect on the whole of scrum-half play, just as the high intelligence of Stoop had revolutionized English fly-half play immediately before the First World War. And Davies carried it to even greater heights.

Unlike his predecessor at scrum-half, poor Oakeley, Kershaw survived the war in HM submarines (for his actions in the Baltic he won the Cross of St Stanislaus); he retired as a Lieutenant Commander but was recalled as a Captain in 1939 and was on the Admiralty planning staff for the D-Day landings. He died in 1972 at seventy-five, the same age but five years later than his soul-mate and senior partner Davies, who by 1939 was the Admiralty's assistant director of warship production. In 1946 he became superintendent of warship production on the Clyde. Although the flags and the bunting were often displayed, Davies overall was a bit of a resolute old Iron Duke himself. After his last match, he received a telegram from Windsor Castle: '. . . His Majesty feels sure that you must have created a record by this fitting termination to your brilliant career in international football.'

If Twickenham, now well into double figures, had settled into being permanent winter HQ and officers' mess to England's middle classes – tweed caps, travelling rugs, hipflasks, camelhair coats, and British accents from every outpost of magisterial Empire – Edinburgh's grand new stadium, Murrayfield, was now to be, in its own way, just as definitively evocative. It was opened for the clamorous match against England in 1925, when Scotland appropriately made certain of the Grand Slam for the first time in history. The only sadness, some said that night, was that the old arena at Inverleith, where Scotland had traditionally played – which, for all its personality, reminded more southerly visitors of Tennyson's line 'Far on the windy plains of windy Troy' – was not able to play host to the triumph after all that it had seen down the years.

Not that Murrayfield was, or is, sheltered from the zapping northern zephyrs. Bernard Levin, an old hand at the city's *summer* arts festival, once complimented Edinburgh's ancient founding fathers and city architect 'on inventing hang-gliding long before the sport was given its name'. Thick plaid travelling-rugs at Murrayfield, too – but here worn as skirts as solemn-walking men down from the hills with china-white complexions and pale knobbled knees stride up from the city to the match, more often than not, hand in hand with tam-o'-shanter schoolboys. There always seem more clustering, mustering schoolboys with expectant faces on the way to Murrayfield's rugger. Eric Linklater, in *Magnus Merriman*, wrote of the same sort of thing:

'In bright blustery March weather, Princes Street is full of tall men from the Borders, brave men from the North, and burly men from the West who have made their names famous in school or university, in county or burgh, for prowess in athletic games. It is not footballers only who come, for on this day all other games do homage to Rugby and admit its headship over them, so that cricketers and tennis players, players of hockey and racquets and fives and golf, boxing men and rowing men and swimmers and cross-country runners, putters of the weight and throwers of the hammer, hurdlers, high and low jumpers, pole vaulters and runners on skis, as well as mountaineers and men who shoot grouse and stalk the red stag and fish for salmon – all these come to see Scotland's team match wit and brawn against wit and brawn of England. To see them walking in clear spring weather is almost as exhilarating as the game itself.'

Scotland's young fly-half Waddell was lucky, of course, to have outside him in that mid-1920s threequarter line the likes of the Oxford quartet, Wallace, Aitken, Macpherson and the flying winger Smith. Drysdale was at full-back – Heriot's dreadnought but neat with it – and at scrum-half the disciplined Glaswegian Jimmy Nelson.

Waddell's game had been hardened, if nothing else, on the glum and injury-wracked 1924 British tour to South Africa. With the hard grounds and even harder tackling, at times, those tourists could scarcely raise fifteen men; in the match against Border at East London, for instance, they had to recruit a spectator from the crowd as an A. N. Other. He was a Scot and went down in the newspapers as 'A. McTavish'. Still, Griffiths' fulsome history of the British Lions (which they had not yet – quite – become, of course) notes that 'Waddell's pluckiest game of the series was at Johannesburg where the British were heavily beaten . . . but Waddell's composure and tenacity in adversity reflected the stout independence of his character . . . and there must have been many occasions when Waddell yearned for the smooth service he enjoyed at school, club, and international level from Nelson.'

Sewell saw that match in Johannesburg and remarked, 'it was memorable to me for two reasons: first that I can recall no international game in which the definitely better pair of halves were on the losing side; second that when the South African referee, V. H. Neser, awarded a penalty against the visitors he sang out more than once, "*Our* kick!"' Sewell added, 'To my regret I did not see enough of H. Waddell's footer on that trip, for he has the deserved reputation of being a great student of the game, which is not always the case with many of its greatest exponents. A most accomplished kicker he certainly was.' (The fly-half Waddell had 'outplayed' that afternoon in

Johannesburg was one B. L. Osler. Watch this space.)

Beneath Waddell's deceptive air of casualness there was, said Thomson, 'a personality clever as paint, a brain ever scheming for the original kind of opening'; and the writer was there that Murrayfield curtain-up when Waddell's most celebrated moment came in the 1925 Calcutta Cup match:

'The game went on in a rising fever temperature of excitement and each minute seemed like ten. First one side and then the other kept fighting its way to within a few feet of the line, only to fail by fumbling the ball or by falling from sheer exhaustion. Once Eddie Myers, the talented Bradford and England stand-off half [who had taken over Davies's shirt], got clear away and appeared to be sailing, unimpeded, over an unguarded line, when Aitken, whipping in like the wind from nowhere, cut him down.

'The climax of the drama came when Waddell, ever a menace near goal, made one of his almost historic drop-kicks. It soared up in the nearest of near-misses but, within the next few moments, almost before the crowd's long-drawn sigh of disappointment had died away, he had the ball again and this time it went between the posts with mathematical judgment. With the tenacity of a desperate rock-climber, Scotland hung grimly on to her three-point lead and the tide of excitement did not ebb until the actual last kick of the match. With this Holliday, the Cumberland and England full-back, made an attempt to drop a goal, as brilliant as any of Waddell's and almost as successful. But not quite. Some seventy thousand Scottish hearts were in seventy thousand Scottish mouths at that long-drawn palpitating moment, but the ball passed the wrong side of the post and Scotland's lead of fourteen points to eleven stood as the final reckoning. You have seen the crews of Varsity boats drop, dead to the world, over their oars, as they shoot past the winning post at Mortlake, but never have there been so many players as in this match who were utterly exhausted. It was a magnificent example of men giving heart and soul to the game.'

Although Waddell played for Scotland – with decreasing regularity – till 1930, that drop-kick in 1925 would be his everlasting memorial for the Scots. They would have readily set it in granite at the top of Princes Street. Waddell was a stockbroker. His son, Gordon, was Scotland's fly-half thirty years after him. Herbert was President of his beloved Barbarians through the 1970s and 80s. In 1972, at Cardiff, when the Barbarians scored that resplendent 120-yard, seven-man try against the All Blacks, finished by Gareth Edwards but conceived and hatched by the audacious counter-attack of the fly-half, Phil Bennett, Waddell, aged seventy, was in the committee box alongside the seventy-five-year-old Lord Wavell Wakefield. The Scot and fly-half turned to the old English forward and shouted in his ear, above the acclamation of the throng, 'Wakers, old friend, I will now die a happy man.'

Scotland were not to manage another Grand Slam, incredibly, for almost sixty years. They were an exhilarating force then and won the thing twice in an appropriate grand manner, clinching the deed both times in an obviously similar atmosphere of fervour, against a ratty French side in 1984, and against a swaggeringly cocksure England six years later. As celebration, I tracked down the survivor of Murrayfield, 1925; he was Herbert Waddell's best friend, the full-back Dan Drysdale, as old as the century and living in contented retirement in (of all places) a mellow honeycomb of a cottage down west, in a blissful village in England's warm and cuddly Wessex. The eyes may have been rheumy, but they still gleamed, beady as a kestrel's, when I asked him about his friend and those last frenzied minutes:

'Ah, Herbie was so cool, you know. Nothing got on the top of him. He wouldn't let it. He could drop goals in his sleep. We all thought that first one in the dying minutes was going over – it was a beautifully struck kick. But no bother to Herbie – he just gets the ball back at once and pops it over. Then immediately England surge back on us and their fellow misses a drop-kick by a whisker. We scarcely scrambled it clear as they came in a swarm and I remember felling their sprinter, Smallwood – legs like pistons, chest out, head back – only yards from the line. Then they mounted one last charge. L. J. Corbett it was, in the centre. He was a good player, a Bristol man. He came ripping through the midfield. I thought I'd missed him, then recovered, overtook him, and cut him down just feet from the line, and a dozen yards from touch. We were still on the floor when the whistle blew. We were both at the end of our tether. The only reason I got him was because he was half-dead – and I was only a quarter-dead!'

What else could he remember? 'Well, afterwards, at a supper in the Queen Street Assembly Halls, the Scottish RU quite uncharacteristically ordered champagne for us. They have not done it since, I would think. Overall that night our biggest problem was steering clear of the throng in the foyer of the North British Hotel – there was a fever running through the city. There was also the job of keeping warm in that cavernous Victorian relic. I was sharing with Herbie, of course. The night was so cold we asked a chambermaid to make up a fire in our room. A week later we each got a bill from the Scottish RU, for ninepence.'

Waddell was one of the most colourful blooms of the 1920s. But the garden then was lush and plush with richness at fly-half. The ambushing wing-forwards had not begun their serious corralling, centres and wings were living healthily and with relish off the fat of the land, and fly-halves had no mean thoughts about simply leathering the thing out of sight to give away a distant lineout. New Zealand's superlative five-eighth, Mark Nicholls, had thrilled Britain on the All Blacks tour of 1924–5 with a whole succession of resoundingly peerless displays. Two years later, there was about as much pleasure given when a team from Australia's New South Wales ('the Waratahs') toured, similarly inspired at 'fly' by the former Oxford Blue Tom Lawton – whose grandson, also Tom, was a trenchant and skilful hooker for the dominant Wallabies of the 1980s.

Wales had a wretched time in the 1920s; for season after season as much the whipping boys almost as France. They seemed to have forgotten the knack of whistling up a Merlin to wear the scarlet cloak marked '10'. But Ireland, with many fewer resources, managed fly-halves like Willie Cunningham, a dentist who in 1923 tossed away his boots and emigrated to South Africa, only to be called up to fly more than a few blinders for the injury-stricken British side which limped around the veldt a year later. Then Ireland had the dynasty-founding Frank Hewitt, who was a schoolboy of seventeen when he made his début at centre-threequarter against Wales in Cardiff in 1924; and he only played nine times, the rest at fly, before retiring from the game when he was still twenty-one. His brother Tom also had much too brief a career, playing centre or wing also nine times. Frank Hewitt was said to have retired for religious reasons. The story goes that another player tried to persuade him to change his mind. Frank said, 'You do not find Jesus Christ on the rugby field.' 'Maybe not,' came the retort (could it have been Ernie Crawford?), 'but you hear an awful lot about him!'

Sean Diffley, in his grand little history, *The Men In Green*, reckons that between the wars Ireland produced only one truly outstanding fly – the burly Eugene Davy who played thirty-four times (sometimes in the centre) from 1925 to 1934: 'Davy may not have had the neat footwork of a Jack Kyle or a Mike Gibson but he was immensely strong and fast. He ran full tilt into his passes and was virtually unstoppable with his short bursts near the line. In addition Davy was a noted tackler in the days when the outside-half was fully responsible for his immediate opponent.'

Davy was fortunate to have a scrum-half of the calibre of Mark Sugden, a genuine hall-of-famer for his position. Sugden was master of the dummy pass, and Davy once explained: 'Sometimes when Mark dummied you thought the ball was in flight, that it had left his fingertips. At other times his dummy was so perfect that I thought

I had the ball myself – once I even beat my man with a jink, essayed a punt with a mighty swing of my boot ... only to realize Mark was long gone off with the ball.'

For England, there was the daunting task of filling the boots of Davies at fly-half. Myers, 'tough, squat, and northern', made a fair fist of it. He was replaced by the lugubrious Harry Kittermaster, a Harlequin and school-master at Sherborne. The first of his seven appearances, against the 1925 All Blacks at Twickenham, was by far his most luminous. England lost by 11–17 – but in Kittermaster, for a rosy moment, they thought they had discovered a world-beater, and seventy years later his score was still finding its way into the anthologies, as here in Bryn Thomas's classic *52 Famous Tries*:

'A scrum was formed inside the England "25" and England won the ball for scrum-half Young to send Kittermaster away. The ball travelled accurately through the hands of Corbett and Davies in the centre to reach Hamilton-Wickes on the wing. Once in possession, the colourful wing put his head back and set off along the touch-line in a gallant endeavour to outwit the all-embracing New Zealand covering defence.

'With a series of swerves and side-steps he beat three defenders cutting across to stop him and got up to Nepia. When faced by this superb young nineteen-year-old, the greatest full-back of his day, Hamilton-Wickes sent the ball inside to the supporting Kittermaster who, having launched the movement with a good break, was deter-mined to finish it. The tall, serious-looking outside-half had a long way to go to the line when he received the ball, but such was his determination that he was able to gain on his pursuers. His legs stretched out firmly and defiantly in honour of his country's rugby.

'The large crowd, thrilled by England's brave recovery, although there was little chance of victory, roared loudly as Kittermaster raced for his objective between the New Zealand posts. Eventually he dived over for a great try to complete a movement that must have travelled all of 90 yards.

'The applause was deafening.'

So, you might say, was the silence which, with the coming of the 1930s, was to greet a very different sort of fly-half indeed.

7

One deceives, the other humiliates

Domestically in Britain, the 1920s could be exactly 'halved' into England's Davies era and Waddell's for Scotland. But two neon-winking asterisks between them were the visits of the All Blacks in 1924, inspired by the carrot-topped wizard at five-eighths, Nicholls, and, three years later, the Waratahs from New South Wales (in those days, to all intents, *the* Australian national team at Rugby Union) in which fly-half Lawton had so enchanted his old Oxford friends – and all who revelled in the running and passing game. As the 1930s began, everything seemed poised with an expectancy that another generation of half-backs could carry the game to even more refreshing levels.

After the New Zealanders had finished their programme – if their 1905 pioneers had been 'the Originals', these were 'the Invincibles' – Colonel Philip Trevor, rugby man for the *Daily Telegraph*, summed up:

'A great side has just brought to a close a wonderful tour and established a great record which has the one essential feature of being a real record. It cannot be beaten ... Nepia stands alone among modern full-backs. His pluck is equal to his play, and that is saying a great deal. Nicholls is the brains of the side and Cooke has no rival ... I should imagine that Maurice Brownlie is quite the best forward in the world ... What are the essentials they have taught us? Chiefly, I think, the value, the combined value, of pace and inter-understanding. Obviously, initial pace is of infinitely more consequence than subsequent pace. "Do it at once" is the essential motto of modern rugby football and these New Zealanders are very much moderns, with everything (once the ball is won) stemming from, and revolving around, the outside half-back who is the "creator". Which is exactly as it should be.'

You don't say, Colonel Phil. But neither he nor British rugby knew what lay in wait for them. For the Springboks were coming. And bringing Benjamin Louwrens Osler with them.

The South Africans, in hindsight anyway, had had an uneasy start to the 1920s. Not at rugby itself – they were still, with the All Blacks, pre-eminent at that. But on the Springboks' 1921 tour to New Zealand they had played (as was, and is, the custom) a home side Maori XV. The match was at Napier and, as ever against that tough, proud breed, it was a rumbustiously contested game. The Springboks won by a whisker in a taut, exciting finish.

Within an hour happened something which (although a storm in an after-match pint pot at the time) was to be a prophecy for half a century on. When South Africa were banished from world sport in the 1960s and 70s for the iniquities of apartheid on their playing fields (and elsewhere), this match at Napier could be seen to have lit a faraway fuse.

The travelling journalist for the South African news agency on that tour was C. W. F. Blackett. After the match at Napier he went to the local cable office to file home his story. It so appalled the telegraph operator on duty that, having tapped out the long message in 'cable-ese' to Cape Town, she surreptitiously took it to a local New Zealand journalist she knew would be playing at the town's billiard hall. In no time he had cabled it to every paper in New Zealand. These are just a few passages which the unfortunately named white journalist Blackett had filed to Cape Town:

'Most unfortunate match ever played ... Bad enough having [Springboks] play officially designated New

Zealand natives; but spectacle thousands Europeans frantically cheering on band of coloured men to defeat members of own race was too much for Springboks, who frankly disgusted. That was not the worst. The crowd was most unsportsmanlike experienced on tour, especially section who lost all control of their feelings . . . On many occasions, Africans [white Springboks] were hurt. Crowd without waiting for possibility of immediate recovery shouted "Take him off!" . . . Maoris flung their weight about regardless of niceties of game.'

If that first, brief public intimation of inherent racism (long before apartheid was officially enshrined in the statute) was, in time, to sully and make enemies of friends in the brotherhood of rugby, so too (in a far less important way, of course) was the arrival on the scene in the myrtle-green jersey, labelled '10', of the arrogantly self-esteemed strutter with the singularly outrageous talent at one aspect of rugby football – Bennie Osler.

Osler was born in the Cape in 1901, the penultimate year of the Boer War. He learned his rugby at Rondebosch High School, whence he read law at Stellenbosch, and first played in the national colours against the brave but woe-begone British tourists of 1924. He dropped a goal in the first Test at Durban – 'with the casual gesture of a smoker flicking the ash from his cigarette', said the *Cape Argus* – to tick off the first points of the 46 he would register over the next ten years, but made no particularly clear announcement of the mark he was to make on the game; to be sure, Sewell wrote of that tour that Waddell had out-played him. But as his siege-gun punts lengthened in the thin air, so too did the Springboks' tactic of reliance on their magnificently grinding and disciplined pack supply-ing endless ammo just for Osler's boot. It could gain more ground, and far more safely and precisely, than could men running fast through a midfield minefield with ball in hand. Osler's forwards provided him with the armchair; in return he offered his eight big men a comfortable sofa.

Halfway through his long tenure at No. 10, Osler found a rare, strong and inventive neighbour at scrum-half,

Danie Craven, nine years younger and another Stellenbosch graduate. The pairing cemented the tactic. (Craven, the grandson of a Yorkshire chancer and diamond prospector, was to become even more infamous in the whole wide world of sport with his varied and mostly phoney, ever-changing, campaigns of placation, disinformation and injured innocence during South Africa's isolation half a century on.) Craven was undoubtedly a superlative scrum-half – it is said he invented the dive-pass – and just the man to spread the jam on Osler's kicking ploy.

In easily the most knowing obituary to Osler, on his death at fifty-nine in 1960, Craven recalled how Osler's merciless and unceasing touchline bombardment roused rugby-loving crowds to noisy rejoinder the world over:

'On some particular occasion in England the jeers were becoming especially rowdy. Bennie comes up and says to me with a little smile, "Daantjie, let me have the next ball nice and quick, eh? I don't want to let these folks down." I whip the ball out to Benny. Bang! a long touch. Another crescendo of boos. From the lineout, me to Bennie, bang! another perfect touch. The crowd, obviously resigned to the inevitable, are less noisy this time. "That's taught them," smiles Bennie, "they are beginning to mind their manners."'

The second most telling tribute on Osler's death came from that diligent student of Springbok rugby history Ace Parker, sports editor of the *Cape Argus*. Parker admitted that Osler's almost pathological emphasis on kicking from hand attracted controversy 'as a candle draws moths'. Nevertheless, he said, there was genius there – 'though some preferred to use the phrase "evil genius" for his smothering and stifling of threequarter play – and it could not easily or reasonably be disputed that Bennie Osler was and remains the greatest individual match-winner and tactical master that South African rugby has produced . . . especially as I do not think for a moment that the standard of play at an international level today [1960] is as high as it was in Osler's time.'

It was all very well, one fancies, for Osler to attempt to beat New Zealand on faraway paddocks with the exclusive use of his boot; but when he came to England for the 1931–2 tour, the purists of rugger-as-she-should-be-played-because-we-invented-it gave pained and bitter rebuke, however diplomatically phrased (well, rugby was already a chummy, aspic-soaked freemasonry) – like Stoop's observation that Osler had become 'The Great Dictator who has liked to evolve a fly-half game all his own which subordinates the individual merits and ability of his threequarters to the type of game he favours, or thinks reasonable at a particular time in the match.'

A pre-Craven 'grand old man of Springbok rugby', W. F. Schreiner, was a selector for forty years and missed few of Osler's important matches:

'I saw no one to equal Bennie Osler in the art of executing the drop-kick. There's no doubt Bennie kicked too much, especially towards the end of his career. As he got older and became the target for opposing loose forwards he made increasing use of his feet to look after himself. But for three seasons, from 1924 to 1927, Osler's fly-half play for U.C.T., Western Province and also for South Africa was as good as any I've seen. Osler himself often said that he enjoyed his football most when at the University of Cape Town from 1920 to 1925. When he saw the chance of an opening he had the lightning quickness off the mark possessed by all great fly-halves.'

Parker himself bears out this earlier *joie de vivre*:

'Bennie, with whom I had many an interesting discussion, himself told me: "I played the worst rugby of my entire career on that tour of Britain. It's true that our backline, as a whole, didn't come up to expectations, but I was the big culprit. Frankly, I just couldn't get going. Friends have tried to cover up for me, but the truth is that I was right off form. I regained my touch against the Wallabies in 1933." A remarkably harsh self-criticism, for he still won many games on the 1931–2 tour with the tactical control he exercised.'

(That 1933 series was the Springboks' first against

Australia, who were slowly regrouping their Rugby Union game in the face of the popularity of Rugby League and Australian 'Rules' football. Before the second Test, at 'anglicized' Durban, Osler apparently said he was sick and tired of all the caustic criticisms of his kicking, so he intended to open out at every single opportunity and see if his threequarters could confirm their boasts if only they were given the ball. He did, scarcely hoofing a thing. But with astonishing and gorgeous irony, it was the Australians who ran riot, scoring four grand tries to win by 21–6 in only their second ever Test against South Africa. For the next match, Osler re-polished his boots.)

What Osler did with such a monotonous dull thump of leather on leather was to confirm a trend, which grew apace in the 1930s, that the winning was all. At the end of the 1931–2 tour – in which the Springboks prevailed in each of the four internationals by grinding the opposition down ruthlessly before feeding Osler's instep – the by now esteemed correspondent of *The Times*, O. L. Owen, tried to be fair in his summing-up:

'How far Osler was, in fact, the master-mind and director-general of operations may be open to argument, but not the way in which he habitually used his superb kicking to plant the ball exactly on the spots most awkward for the other side. This he managed to do equally well in attack and in clearing his lines. No one could fail to admire his poise and technique – the tactics were another question.

'Many reasons have been given for the steadfast determination of the South Africans to rely upon their half-backs in conjunction with the forwards, rather than the three-quarters, who, in fact, soon acquired the status of mere opportunist auxiliaries. In some respects there was nothing new about that – it merely emphasized what was the general trend everywhere.

'It may well have been the remarkable skill of Osler in doing so, and of course, the fact that he also was captain, which brought down upon his head the bulk of the criticism . . . Many people felt, and always will feel, that a really great side can be attractive as well as invincible. Nor was it only the onlooker who found much of the play incorrigibly dull on this occasion. Many of the South African backs, who clearly were better than their own halves allowed them to be, must have felt it dull and disappointing, too. Ironically, and pertinently enough, their one clear chance to show what they could achieve in the open occurred during their only defeat, by a Midland fifteen at Leicester, where Osler himself was not playing.

Dear old Sewell in the *Standard* typically blew a more down-to-earth good-riddance raspberry as the Springboks' *Union Castle* liner edged down the Solent for home. EHD, bless him, was not an editorialist who found handy the phrase 'on the other hand . . .':

'I saw [Osler] many a time on tour, including the first match at Bristol on a very fine almost windless day but on a very grassy pitch.

'Not only was his kicking, whether drop or punt – and these were said to be his specialities – never in the class of dozens of other players in Big Rugger, but it was seldom even in the first-class.

'I forget whether he did eventually succeed in dropping a goal in that first match, but I know I gave up counting after the seventh failure to do so.

'He played in 17 games of the 26, practically always behind the winning pack, and dropped four goals! Though drop-kicking was his trump card – when he didn't punt.

'Which is rather more than I expected he would, even though when within about 35 yards of the posts his sole idea of the game of a stand-off half was to let a very likely looking three-quarter line go hang while he chanced a pot-shot.

'No South African wing ever looked like getting a try after normal passing advance in an International game, although the South African pack had their opponents beaten for the ball to a frazzle in all four. And the South African wings were so obviously fast and good.

'Never in my seeing has there been such a conspicuous

failure as "a stand-off" half in Big Rugger as was B. Osler in 1931–32.

'I have been invited to contribute a chapter to a magazine of South African Rugby. I did so. I was not surprised that they did not publish it.'

If Benjamin Louwrens Osler *was* something new under the sun – it proves only that, half a century later, Hendrik Egnatius Botha was a chip off the old block in the No. 10 shirt of myrtle green trimmed with yellow. For his relentless, blinkered (and unquestionably outstanding – though I daresay Sewell would still have demurred) kicking, Naas Botha in the 1980s and 90s must have had even more vilification heaped on him than Osler. I was sitting next to the eminence Carwyn James when I first set eyes on Botha at the beginning of the 1980 Lions tour to the Republic. Naas was twenty-two, blond and handsome, but his reputation had preceded him. He began the match as he obviously intended to continue it – and every other one in which he was to play – with a string of great booming touchfinders. After about the seventh had shelled into the distance, Carwyn sighed and lit another Senior Service with slightly quivering hand. 'Youngsters', he said, 'can only emulate him for this magnificent kicking. If the South African conveyor belt is really still turning out kicking fly-halves in the Osler mould, then I can only weep for them and the game.'

For 'emulation' is very much part of a game's development. As the ever shrewd 'Ace' Parker had noted in his comprehensive history, *The Springboks*: 'Osler's influence on the game in South Africa, during the decade which he dominated, was profound. Whenever a bunch of hero-worshipping schoolboys gathered with an oval ball they practised drop-kicks, shouting "I'm Bennie Osler". His success influenced imitators who did not possess anything like his skill.'

That last sentence of Parker's had an already relevant resonance in Britain of the early 1930s. Scarcely had the Springboks left for home than every fly-half in

Christendom was appealing 'Bags I be Bennie Osler'.

The Five Nations Championship itself seemed happy enough to lose impetus and settle into a lethargy for two or three decades – interrupted by a five-year war – which had a whole succession of unimaginative fly-halves competing in turn to shout loudest that new rugby song, 'I'll find touch, you'll find touch, we'll find touch together . . .' The 1930s were salvaged to some extent, however (as the New Zealanders continued on their own way with five-eighths and 'spare' wing-forwards), by an unconcerned Englishman, a solemn Scot, and particularly by two glistening Welshmen.

Kicking fly-halves, with every swing of their leg, diluted the game's possibilities. Centres and wing-threequarters, when they were not covering or chasing balls that might miss touch, stood around like so many Othellos, 'with occupation gone'. The trouble was, even when laboriously executed, the kicking game was (for the side who had the best pack and best kicker, anyway) a successful one. In the 1930s, a popular schoolboy comic of the *Hotspur/Rover* family ran a succession of serial yarns on sport. The one on cricket was entitled 'It's Runs that Count'; the one on soccer 'It's Goals that Count'. I doubt if the headline-writer was actually trying to make a point about the state of the fifteen-a-siders, but when it came to rugger's turn the series was called 'It's Results that Count'.

A few fly-halves did try to evoke the traditional handling days when, as carefree and exhilarating fly-half philosophies went, you could 'Stoop' to conquer. Wales thought they had unearthed a good 'un from the dried-up mine in Dickie Ralph, but it was the beginning of the 'starving thirties' down there, and he hotfooted to Rugby League and a Challenge Cup final medal with Leeds. Scotland had serious hopes for a short time of Harry Lind, a Dunfermline architect.

For Ireland, Davy, after his years of stout work, was in his thirties now and his stockbroking firm needed him, so they gave the shirt to Dr Paul Finbar Murray, a converted scrum-half, but he could only rise to the occasion with a glittering display in the matches at (it's true, it's true, check it) Murrayfield against the Scots, where Ireland won on the three successive times Murray played there. (Dr Paul's son, John, another medic, played one game for Ireland at fly-half in 1963: the Greens were hammered, and he at once emigrated to Canada.) After Murray *père*'s brilliance at Murrayfield but nowhere else, he reverted to scrum-half, and a fellow Blackrock boy came in; but in his first match at 'fly', L. B. McMahon potted just one of thirteen kicks at goal – and the great, if arthritic, Davy was summoned back to steady the ship for the next three seasons.

England found a truly dynamic fly-half. But Roger Spong played only nine internationals – and two tours, to Argentina and New Zealand, where he was, by all accounts, sensational – before concentrating on his directorships with his family businesses, which covered most things between hardware shops and aircraft engine manufacture. Like other, celebrated fly-halves, Spong was fortunate with his scrum-half, Wilf Sobey – especially so, because they were at school together and then regular club partners for Old Milhillians when OBs' rugger was challengingly top-hole stuff. Townsend Collins, Welsh to the core, gave best in his *Rugby Recollections*:

'Spong and Sobey played their own parts with skill and courage (both qualities are needed to elude or endure the attentions of wing forwards), but their aim was team success. They were an ideal partnership, and greatly helpful to their threequarters. Spong was a very strong runner (so strong that when he played for the British Team in the Argentine he was called "The Railway Train"); but his greater strength was that he linked up with the men behind him – he did not run away from them, and break the chain of combination, as so many clever runners do. One of the most constructive outside halves who ever played for England, he has made less impression upon the memory of football followers because he played for his country so rarely.'

Both Old Millhillians went on the British – now the

119

'Lions' – tour of New Zealand in 1930. Sobey was badly crocked at once, but Spong, as Griffiths' diligent history recalls, 'soldiered on and captured the admiration of the New Zealand public with his powerful running, pace and nippiness. Indeed many old-timers in New Zealand who have seen the succession of British fly-halves place Spong at the top of their list of outstanding pivots, granting the stocky Englishman higher playing status than Jack Kyle and Barry John of the post-war Lions. On tour Spong scored five tries (and another in the unofficial rout of Western Australia), was the architect of countless others and was the spearhead of the Lions' attack in all of the international matches.'

In fact, Spong's excellence could have directly influenced New Zealand to change their still stubbornly singular insistence on the five-eighths ploys and the extra 'rover' wing-forward. As their faithful chronicler T. P. McLean recorded in *The All Blacks*:

'It was at the dinner following the second match against Taranaki that Baxter ['Bim', the Lions' manager] proclaimed openly that the wing-forward, or rover, of the New Zealand team formation was a cheat. Such was his influence, as a former international player and referee, that in 1932 the international Rugby Football Board revised its Laws of Rugby to compel three men to pack in the front row of the scrum – and the rover disappeared.

'Baxter, thereafter, remained more discreet in public, although he might well have criticized the play of the rover, Cliff Porter, in the Wellington match, the fifth of the tour, in which the Lions were beaten. Confronted by Roger Spong, a bouncy ball of a man with sensationally quick reactions, who could break inside or out, and was an attacking fly-half of highest quality, Porter, pinching a yard here and a couple of yards there, set about his opponent mercilessly. In the first Test, too, he continued his constructive-obstructive tactics against Spong, who was not intimidated. Plainly, though, he regarded Porter's play as unsporting. Many Kiwis thought the same.'

Spong remained devoted to the Old Millhillians club

and was chairman till his death in March 1980 – exactly ten days after Bill Beaumont's side had settled England's first Grand Slam in nearly a quarter of a century.

For Scotland, Wilson Shaw was another saving grace for fly-half play in the 1930s. Collins remarked that the Glasgow High School former pupil was like 'a trout at a fly so slick was he off the mark and "through" any gap that offered. The selectors blundered badly several times in wasting him – to the joy of all Scotland's opponents – either in the centre or on the wing.' Shaw scored a spectacularly timed try to beat England at Twickenham in 1938; as Bryn Thomas dramatically recorded:

'It was still anybody's game right up until 2 minutes from the end. Referee Ivor David of Wales, having charge of his first representative match of a long and successful career, looked at his watch. There were just 2 minutes – surely one side or the other would score again! It was Shaw who got the vital score, for he gathered in the loose before any Englishman could kill the ball and went away to the right, dodging and swerving and no one could lay a hand on him. English defenders dived and fell in his weaving path, but none could stop him and eventually he raced round Parker to cross the English line and score the try of the match. Thousands of Scots in the large crowd threw their hats into the air, for they were satisfied now that England could not overhaul Scotland.

'As Wilson Shaw trotted back, a small, modest figure, one realized that he had achieved his zenith in the game. This had been his greatest match and the realization of a boyhood ambition. Every Scot when starting to play must dream of the honour that one day he may lead Scotland to victory at Twickenham. So few victories have been won there by the invaders from the north that any player leading a Scottish fifteen to victory can be sure of everlasting fame.'

21–16: five tries to one. Shaw was chaired from the field by exuberant men swathed in tartan and, understandably, the brew on their breath. The Triple Crown, 'that height of bliss'. The Scottish team had been written off throughout that winter; but, as *The Scotsman* noted with its famous, almost imperceptible twitch of an eyebrow, 'Scottish rugby XVs come into existence solely to confound their critics.' The following year, with Shaw again hived off to the wing because of his speed, Scotland most assuredly did not confound their critics, and lost the lot. Nor were they to do any more confounding for a long time, and a world war, to come.

Shaw, a chemist, went off to concoct important war potions for ICI, and must have afforded himself another of his famously occasional smiles when a book was published, *Rugby Football*, by the man who had marked him, at fly-half, in the Welsh leg of that 1938 Triple Crown triumph:

'To many people it was one of the mysteries of the Game that R. W. Shaw was ever exiled to the wing; there can be few, if any, who are quicker off the mark than Shaw. To be sure, a wing-threequarter should be fast, but, in the modern Game, the fastest man over 15 or 20 yards should be the fly-half.

'When Scotland played England at Twickenham in March 1936, there was the curious spectacle of Lind and Dick in the centre with Shaw on the wing and Grieve at fly-half. Scotland had nothing to lose in this game and everything to gain. With two players like Lind and Dick in the centre, a fly-half of the type of Shaw was exactly what was wanted; instead, Grieve was played, thereby slowing up the attack and reducing the value of Lind and Dick by about half, whilst Shaw spent a drab afternoon marking Sever. One can only note with unqualified approval Shaw's welcome return to the fly-half position, culminating in one of the most sensational and thrilling Calcutta Cup battles ever staged at Twickenham.'

The writer, and generous former rival, was Cliff Jones, of Wales, more than likely the most glittering fly-half to arrive in thirty years or more. Cometh the hour and all that ... The entrance of this defender of the same coruscating faith preached all those years ago by the earliest disciples and saints, like the Jameses and Percy Bush, was to split all Wales down the middle just as its humpety little sea-monster mountain range does its map. For there also came another relishingly expectant 'Dai Baptist' wanting to point the way back to sanity and the hopscotch-swerve. He was W. T. H. Davies, who answered to 'Willie'. Jones or Davies, Cliff or Willie? It was not (well, not *all* that much) that Cliff was Llandovery School (posh public, like) and Cambridge, *and* Cardiff, and Willie was Welsh-speaking, Gowerton County School on the Gower, and Swansea. West is west and east is east. No, it wasn't that Cliff was perceived by some to be a chauffeur-driven, cravat-wearing great Gatsby, dining on cocktails and caviare at Clare College, Cambridge, on the very same evenings when, back in the depressed and industrially vandalized Wales of the thirties, 'our' Willie was hungrily combing the beaches and sea-rim rocks of his native shore to find enough Penclawdd cockles for his tea.

When it comes to their rugby, the Welsh are not like that. Are they?

Anyway, having waited so long to find one saviour for fly-half play, it was just typical – and typical Welsh fly-halves, like London buses – that two magnificent red-liveried jobs arrive at exactly the same time. But rugby itself, rugby the world over, sighed a heartfelt thanks.

A few decades later, the Irish were to have the same sort of debate and division over the respective merits of Ollie Campbell and Tony Ward; so too the English, with Rob Andrew and Stuart Barnes. Both outstanding fly-halves, but chalk and cheese, church and chapel – and, in Wales of the 1930s, never better explained than by the play-wright and novelist Alun Richards, in *A Touch of Glory*:

'Both were match winners, and it seems that the elusive running and body swerve of Davies was in contention against the sudden acceleration and sidestepping of Jones who was certainly the most publicized player of his day. They, like all those before and after them, fell into categories and from the beginning there seems to have been a difference both in style and in temperament. There is the natural instinctive runner and the "made" player whose effort appears greater, who in some ways is more exciting to watch since he is a duellist and brings a conscious act of deception to bear when beating a man. On the one hand there is grace, the nervous intuitive instincts of a sleek and darting forest animal; on the other there is a mental calculation and usually a greater point of identification and admiration. The sidestepper at his best gives off a kind of "Look, no hands!" attitude. One has a cool, insouciant grace, the other is wound up like a spring. One deceives, the other humiliates. This first group I call the High Church outside-halves, the second, the Chapel outside-halves.'

When Davies's eel-like swerves brought him dramatically down-stage when still a schoolboy in 1935, Jones was already settled as the prodigy in the Welsh XV, having been first capped at the start of the 1934 season while still in his freshman's year at Cambridge. He was a stocky 5 ft 8 in. and 11 stone 'square', and Wales had known for some time that, for a fly-half, he had 'the lot' – a darting speed, a slip-catcher's hands, a monkey's agility, and a trenchant killer instinct. Jones won the first of his three Blues within months of going up to Cambridge in 1933 – partnered at inside-centre by the no-nonsense, long-striding North Walian Wilfred Wooller. The two precocious talents went straight into the Welsh team only five weeks after their first Varsity Match – which was won, as it happens, by Oxford, 5–3. (The two of them were to organize massive revenge the following year: Cambridge 29, Oxford 4.)

Jones had begun his education at Porth County School, where he adored the soccer (numerous fly-halves have been thankful for an apprenticeship with the round ball) and was devoted to Cardiff City FC, a First Division force at the time. When he went to Wales's senior public school, Llandovery, in 1928, the still celebrated T. P. Williams had just become rugby master. Williams became known as Welsh rugby's 'pope' and had been inspired at Oxford by the University's threequarter line, which, of course, had helped *en bloc* to win Scotland's Grand Slam

124

in 1925. He at once recognized in young Jones something rare. Many years later, Jones recalled his Llandovery days:

'Out almost every day with a half-back partner, taking passes in all positions, down at your feet, above your head, in all weathers . . . Pope would train me to a speed off the mark – just like a pony in a circus at the end of a long bridle. He'd have me running around him and he'd put the ball further and further in front of me, making me stretch because he maintained that speed over fifteen yards was the greatest thing in rugby football.'

Such a grooming was dramatically confirmed by the authors of *Fields of Praise*:

'Williams worked on the youngster's raw ability, cultivating it, refining it, improving it, like a diamond cutter with an amethyst. One thing he forbade him to do, and that was to drop goals. Jones never made up the lee-way, but his other skills more than compensated: the fly-paper hands, the mastery of the teasing, short punt, the electrifying sidestep. To copy-book moves he brought an audacity, an inspired impudence that transformed mechanical efficiency into match-winning unorthodoxy. He wedded the irrepressibility of Bush to the precision of Bowcott [Harry, the incumbent fly-half for Wales], and the off-spring of Rhondda ebullience and Llandovery meticulousness was pure gold, the magical product of inborn talent and a rugby alchemist. In a relatively short international career of thirteen caps, won between 1934 and 1938, he established himself as one of the greatest outside-halves of all time.'

Such a heady claim was suddenly being promised, too, by excited devotees at St Helen's, that ancient, evocative amphitheatre alongside Dylan's 'brooding, boat-bobbing bay'. It was 1935 and Swansea were due to 'entertain' the mighty All Blacks for the fifth match of their tour. (Naturally the New Zealanders were unbeaten thus far – indeed, no British side had beaten them since Wales, controversially, in 1905.) Two cousins, Haydn Tanner and Willie Davies, were still attending the local Gowerton County School. Haydn was a scrum-half, Willie a fly.

They were both in the Welsh Schoolboys XV. The Swansea club sent a deputation to Gowerton's sports master, W. E. 'Bill' Bowen, pleading that the two boys be allowed to face the All Blacks. Eventually, being persuaded that the teenagers would not be daunted by such immense adult opposition, Bowen relented. There have been a number of famously passionate days down the years at St Helen's – at cricket as well as rugby (Sir Garfield Soberts hit his 36 in an over there; and in 1992 the Australian rugby world champions were beaten by Swansea), but, I daresay, none so famously passionate as 28 September 1935. Swansea beat the All Blacks by 11–3 – inspired and ignited by two pale and skinny teenage schoolboys. As Howard Marshall purred in the following morning's *Daily Telegraph*:

'How well the wiry Tanner played, slipping away on his own – where, by the way, was the New Zealand backrow defence? – giving beautiful passes to Davies and kicking with judgement and precision. The 19-year-old Davies has surely a touch of genius, that instinctive eye for the opening which marks the perfectly balanced, running with changes of pace and direction sufficient to carry him through the smallest gap like an elusive ghost.'

A clamour rose from the west that if the two boys could do it for Swansea, they could surely do the same for Wales itself when they met the All Blacks in three months' time, at Cardiff on the Saturday before Christmas. Jones had already won six caps while still up at Cambridge, but in the final match of the 1934–5 season Wales had been badly (or, rather, heroically) beaten by fourteen Irishmen in Belfast by 9–3. The new Irish fly-half, Victor Hewitt – yet another member of the almost incredible Instonians' dynasty of Irish caps – had, by all accounts, handsomely outplayed Jones that day. For the All Blacks, the Welsh selectors gave a vote of confidence to Jones, but picked Tanner for the first of his record twenty-five caps over a span of fourteen years.

On an afternoon of frenzied excitement at the Arms Park, Tanner and Jones were among those who played 'blinders' as Wales won by just 13–12 – 'that lovely, lovely, point,' said Arthur Rees, the Welsh pack-leader – the winning try fashioned in the final minute by the regally powerful Wooller.

Still, in the following season the continuing Jones–Davies debate was allowed to flourish in full view, for Jones broke his collarbone and Davies stepped up to partner his cousin, Tanner. The two half-backs displayed some scintillating stuff behind a beaten pack, just as, according to all reports, they did through the 1938–9 season after Jones's premature retirement. It was honours even, and sometimes, to this day, in those warm, snug but dingy pubs you can still meet a couple of greybeard leek-eaters arguing the toss fondly over the supreme merits of Cliff Jones and Willie Davies.

Davies was offered an attractive teaching post at Bradford Grammar School – and soon embarked on a glittering career in Rugby League with Bradford Northern and Great Britain. He entranced the Wembley throng in the 1947 Cup Final. Jones retired to practise law and begin his rare collection of antiques, and, of course, to write his 'little' book *Rugby Football*, which ran to an astonishing six editions. Tanner also wrote a best-seller with exactly the same title. So the 'great rivalry' ended, in print, as a mutual admiration society. This is what Cliff wrote about Willie:

'The fly-half must, first and foremost, cultivate speed off the mark; a fly-half at school should practise, day in, day out, running over short distances as fast as he can. His handling must be the most reliable thing about him – he must be perfectly balanced so that he can take the ball, at top speed, no matter where it comes to him. The fly-half must be able to pass the ball smoothly – and here again balance is all-important. Remember to swing the body away from the direction of the pass (i.e. into the on-coming tackle, if any), so as to help withstand the shock of the tackle, and, when selling a dummy, to give the impression of a rending apart of man and ball.

'The perfect outside-half is one who combines the best

qualities of the orthodox and sound with those of the fast and unorthodox; he who can make speed off the mark, but the rhythm of whose running in no way disturbs the general effect of the attack. In this category there has been in recent years but one player, W. T. H. Davies of Swansea and Wales; he most nearly resembled the classical stand-off half. His running was smooth, and he made his openings with a body-swerve and, the greatest asset of all, change of pace. For the most part, he had to make his name in games of a relentless character – each match for him had been a "Derby" match. Had he been playing in English Rugby, instead of in South Wales, it is idle to deny that he would have achieved even greater fame than had been his lot.'

And this is what Haydn wrote about Willie and Cliff (you feel, don't you, that given the choice, and the knowledge that blood is thicker than tact, Haydn had the softest spot for cousin Willie?):

'W. T. H. Davies (Swansea) was the outstanding example of perfect rhythm and it was a joy to watch him run with the ball. He could also be a brilliant individualist and run through the opposition without any apparent effort. Davies was a very deceptive and beautiful runner and his sense of balance was perfect. He was able to give the impression he was running at half speed, his action was so easy and yet he was moving very fast indeed – he has run one hundred yards in ten and one-fifth secs., which is a good indication of how fast he can run.

'The other type of outside-half is the one who is very fast off the mark and can side-step three or four players within a few yards. The speed they do this is amazing. They are usually described as the brilliant individualists and usually score the tries themselves. Two outstanding examples pre-war, Cliff Jones and Wilson Shaw, must rank among the greatest ever.'

Half a century later, at the end of 1992, I went down to Cardiff to toast Wilf Wooller on the eve of his eightieth birthday; on the day itself, as well as a family party with oodles of grandchildren, the grand and still bellicose old giant sat down to a special lunch with, among others, Arthur Rees of that 'lovely, lovely, point' fifty-seven years before. I asked Wilf the inevitable question. Unusually, he had to ponder long and hard. Finally . . .

'The best fly-half I ever played with was Cliff. And if it wasn't for Barry John, Cliff was the best I ever saw . . . No, it has to be Cliff – the best I ever played with and the best I ever saw. Barry was truly remarkable, almost perfect, totally unflappable, but Cliff played in a different time. Mind you, Cliff was more of a twinkletoes, more of a crackerjack sidestepper than a "glider" like Barry. Cliff could sidestep off both feet and was very, very fast indeed. And let's be sensible about Cliff's day – the defence gave us no room, coming up in a line; Cliff would have to take Haydn's pass absolutely flat out and make his decision in a split second. Nowadays they are giving themselves these blinking "options" all over the place. Yes, Cliff was probably the first of them all.'

And the brand new octogenarian allowed, just for a flicker, his still kestrel-sharp eyes to mist over with rheumy remembrance of a vibrant, barnstorming youth – and those heady, haloed days before the guns exploded round the world again, and he was to be incarcerated for five dreadful years in a Japanese prisoner-of-war camp.

8

'Have a wonderful cap, Cliffie'

There were many contrasts between the first and second world wars. In the grotesque quagmire of the first, over three quarters of a million British people were slaughtered; in the second, fewer than a quarter of a million. Sport was officially encouraged to continue, as 'morale boosting', in the second, whereas it had been banned as 'unpatriotic' in the first. The Rugby Union and Rugby League players took part in 'mixed' games. 'Somewhere in the Pacific', South Africa won a 'test' match against Britain, played with a medicine ball on the half-deck of the troopship *New Amsterdam*. In 1940 the 1st Battalion, the XV of the Welsh Regiment, based in Palestine, were flown by the RAF to play a New Zealand XV in front of a crowd of 'many thousands' in Cairo (NZ 11, Wales 9). And when the War Cabinet in London was planning a particularly hazardous operation which involved flying a small but heroically crack detachment in and out of occupied Crete in a night, the PM, Winston Churchill, was reported suggesting, in those squishy sibilants of his, 'Get shome of those rugger-playing chapsh, they'll manage thish short of shtuff.'

A series of unofficial 'Victory' internationals were played in the New Year of 1946 – the same year that Cliff Jones's 'little' book went into its third update and reprint, in which, invited to contribute an 'Afterword', the legendary old-timer Percy Bush, then approaching seventy, wrote a trenchant blast with scarcely a nod of deference to his author. He lambasted all modern rugby players for 'training on cocktail parties and dances', and bewailed the absence of genuine fly-halves: 'What I deplore above all is the utter lack of originality shown by the moderns, except in very isolated cases. There are very few Adrian Stoops these days – the "fly" who brought English football back to its rightful place by the daring originality, and brilliant execution, of his movements.'

Old Percy was way off beam, and I daresay even he would have admitted it had he been present across the water at Lansdowne Road on a crisp winter afternoon when Ireland played the first of its 'Victory' internationals against England. In the programme, the traditional potted biogs did not include Ireland's doughty second-row forward of the immediate pre-war season, for Lieutenant-Colonel Blair Mayne was possibly somewhat tired after winning a record four DSOs, plus the Légion d'Honneur, during the intervening six years (alas, after all that, Mayne was soon to lose his life in a car accident). But on that auspicious day in 1946 the programme did introduce a new name in the home side's No. 10 shirt. It read:

'J. W. KYLE. Age 19. The discovery of the season. John Wilson Kyle was on the Ulster Schools XV two years ago and proved himself to be in the top class by his great display for Ulster against the Kiwi Servicemen in November, subsequently confirming that form against the Army. A particularly straight strong runner, he looks to have a brilliant future.'

And how. Within a year of the Championship proper starting the following season – with Ireland's match against France, now happily restored after being haughtily blackballed for most of the 1930s for suspected professionalism – the pale, freckled medical student with the crinkly ginger hair had inspired Ireland to their first Triple Crown and Grand Slam in all of seventy-four years of trying.

Jack Kyle went on to enchant the very length and breadth of the game, and to win forty-seven caps for

Ireland, a record for any fly-half in history – or, rather, one that stood for thirty-four years till it was overtaken in 1992 by Rob Andrew of England.

Now here's a funny thing. Not many people know this. On the very same weekend in that winter in which Andrew overtook Kyle's record, two famous rugby men, by complete coincidence, happened to be in the lovely old city of Toulouse, deep in the rugby-loving warm south of France. For all they know they might have even rubbed shoulders, literally, on the busy main boulevard, or sat in the same bar for a refresher, or at next-door tables in a restaurant. Rob Andrew was in Toulouse that weekend attending an interview, trying to arrange a new job there and get some experience of French rugby at the vibrant city club. Dr Jack Kyle was in Toulouse visiting his daughter, a bonny language student at Toulouse University. Neither would have recognized the other. 'To be perfectly honest,' admitted young Andrew when I told him of the coincidence later, 'I'd only heard of Jack Kyle for the first time a couple of weeks ago when all this fuss began of me breaking some ancient fly-half record – us modern players aren't too hot on the game's history, I'm afraid, though I'm surprised I haven't been introduced to him at the odd function here or there down the years.'

Not at all surprising in fact – for the full length of Andrew's twenty-nine-year-old life, Jack Kyle had been ministering to the sick in the mission stations of the Third World. So on the eve of Andrew's record-breaking match, against Wales, on 7 March 1992, I picked up the blower and dialled a large bunch of numbers in Africa. If you are mutually patient at being cut off for two minutes every second minute, the old bush telegraph rings out loud and clear with the still crackingly broad and effervescent Ulster accent: 'Tell young Rob my very heartiest congratulations. Wonderful, fantastic. If anything was made to be broken it was my prehistoric old record and it's a real joy that such a fine player as Rob should now take over from me in the indelible record books.'

But how, in the middle of the African bush, could he

possibly know Andrew was a 'fine' player? 'You're never going to believe this, but I was actually able to watch the France–England game live. A friend out here has just got himself one of those magical satellite things, and I can't tell you the thrill it was to watch that international a couple of weeks ago. This is a heck of a team England have found, isn't it? Also tell Rob congratulations to them all – though I hope he won't mind an old Irishman, for the sake of us underdogs everywhere, hoping the Welshmen might just have the beating of them tomorrow, although I fancy that's a far-off possibility.'

Up to a year ago, when they gave him a partner, the sixty-year-old was the only surgeon in the 500-bed hospital at Chingola, hard on Zambia's copperbelt border with Zaire's old Katanga. 'Do I specialize? No hope. Just like my rugby, I'm Jack of all trades, master of none. I'm just like an old country surgeon in rural Ireland sixty or seventy years ago – everything from tonsils, appendices and broken limbs to operations much more dramatic and desperate, though no surgery remotely sophisticated, I'm afraid.'

In the thirty-five years since Kyle's last international, Rugby Union has changed immeasurably. So has an international player's 'work-load', as well as his 'spin-off' rewards. Andrew is happy to say how his enjoyment of rugby and his commitment to it have helped chart and fashion his whole career. As his fame has increased, so has the delightful and modest Yorkshireman's 'profile' and business potential. Top firms like top men. Rob's two brothers farm with their father the family's broad acres near Scotch Corner, while Rob's sport has taken him relentlessly from school to universities at Durham and Cambridge, into chartered surveying with a leading London property firm, thence to France in the very vanguard of Britain's 1992 commitments to Europe. Rob's business suits are as beautifully cut as his rugby has usually been knife-sharp and freshly keen-edged.

In contrast, bellowing down the line to Dr Jack you imagine him in the sweat-stained, lived-in linen garb of a

Graham Greene hero and, in the background, all the sensuous, susurating sounds of sundown in Africa. When Andrew was born, in 1963, Kyle was in the process of being distressingly thrown out of his first medical mission station. 'I always had a hankering for abroad and somewhere that might have needed me. I was first in Sumatra for two or three years, till President Sukarno started his confrontations and had us all thrown out.'

He is astonished when he hears the nature of Andrew's enforced commitment to England and practice – three return flights from Toulouse to Heathrow in the week, for training on Wednesday and Sunday and then, after two days' work, back on Wednesday to stay with the team till today's match.

'They obviously have to give their lives and souls to it now. In all my forty-seven games with Ireland, those of us who were available might just have thrown a ball about for an hour or so on the Friday afternoon. Planned tactics never came into it. I must have partnered eight or nine scrum-halves in my time, and we'd just run out saying "Let's do our best and see how it goes"' – he starts attempting to count them off – 'dear Ernie [Strathdee], Johnny [O'Meara] of course, Hugh [de Lacy], lovely Andy [Mulligan] . . .'

The last name reminds him of something. 'Last year the 1951 Springboks had a fortieth reunion party and somehow they traced me up here. I was delighted to be asked down to South Africa as some sort of guest of honour out of the blue. I could only think of telling Andy's tale of an Irish pre-match dressing-room talk given by my brother-in-law, Noel Henderson, when he was captain of Ireland: "Right, lads, let's decide how we're going to play this game. What d'you think, Jack?"

'"A few wee punts at the line might be dandy, and maybe young Mulligan here can try a few darts on his own. What about you, Tony [O'Reilly]?"

' "Jasus, the programme here says a midget's marking me. Just give me the ball and let me have a run at him. What do you think, Cec [Pedlow]?"

134

'"I think a subtle mix of runnin', jinkin' an' kickin' should just work out fine."

'So, picking up the ball to go out, Noel summed up: "Right, lads, that's decided – Jack's puntin', Andy's dartin', Tony's runnin', and Cecil's doin' all three."'

The laughter barrels up from Africa and bounces, booming, off the satellite and down to Britain.

From school, I remember, we were taken to see him once, playing for Stanley's XV against Oxford at Iffley Road on a rainswept wintery day in the middle 1950s. Our Benedictine schoolmaster monks had already fired us with Kyle's legend, yet for an hour he did nothing much, just neatly finding touch or generously feeding his line. Then, of a sudden, with a dip of his hips and an electric change of gear he left the floundering cover as rooted as trees and glistened thirty-five yards over the sodden turf to score, almost apologetically, under the posts.

That, apparently, was Kyle's mesmerizing knack – a patience for the potent moment, even if one came but once a match. They say Kyle never strained, never once panicked; you would always see him fast asleep on the bus as it arrived through the throng for the match – like Sir Frank Worrell, so calm they would have to wake him to go out and bat in a Test match.

Like Andrew, Kyle was a slightly built fly-half who tackled fearlessly. Having read the books, I wanted to ask him about his scintillating try for the Lions against the All Blacks at Auckland, not to mention the one at Dunedin in 1950, or another against France at Ravenhill; or what about the time he beat Wales on his own at Cardiff; or the tackle on the flying Springbok Van Schoor; or another secateurs job on the rampaging Englishman Ritson-Thomas at Lansdowne Road in 1951.

'Och,' he dismisses with a chortle such particulars. 'One remembers vaguely, but it's all way back in the mists of long ago. What I do sometimes find myself doing out here in Africa when I rest my head on a pillow occasionally is reflect on the rewards of comradeship a simple game gave a lad who was growing up. As boys we were told, "sport is about the friends you will make", and now I'm an old guy I realize how true that was. Our fathers, mind you, would tell us that studying was the thing and we couldn't be wholly ruled by rugby football. And I don't really think we were: rugby then, even at the highest level, was a recreation for a passing passage or two, and when it was over we went happily enough back to our books.

'Tell young Rob that he too will find that out soon enough – that records, and being "better than the next man", ultimately means nothing in the end, and that the extreme of satisfaction is simply being part of the whole communal, confraternal set-up. Like for me to be asked down to the 1951 Springboks' anniversary party in Johannesburg – and suddenly in that same room were old adversaries and now, by definition, the warmest of friends . . . like Cliff Morgan, the best fly-half there can ever have been, thrusting, darting, always unexpected; Michael Steele-Bodger, wicked in the tackle; and Jeff Butterfield, with Bleddyn Williams the most complete centre imaginable . . .'

Bob Scott of New Zealand, 'a consummate artist', was the best full-back Kyle ever played against, he said, and Ken Jones, the Newport express, the most dangerous winger . . . The Springboks' spending so much time to trace him for their celebrations is relevant. Kyle's genius goes totally for granted in the whole wide parish of the game. He toured New Zealand with the Lions in 1950 and mesmerized them. Forty years on, my old All Black hero, the dynamic Bob Scott, was still in no doubt: 'Kyle was extra special on and off the field. Of all of them there has never been, nor ever was, anyone to touch him.' Few men can have watched, with a critical eye, more rugby than T. P. McLean, the All Blacks' historian: 'Kyle's football always had the air of genius about it, whether he was shuffling past a marker, grubber-kicking, or fooling the opposition into a false sense of security.'

Mike Gibson, from the same club, NIFC, and a successor to Kyle as Ireland's fly-half before they moved him to centre, was brought up on tales of 'Uncle' Jack, and he once explained his famous and 'mesmeric' cool: 'This stemmed from the silicon chips (the Irish invented everything to do with potatoes) which enabled him to take himself down almost into a state of hypothermia. While in this state he could often go to sleep, which he often did in the dressing-room before a match, and which he appeared to do on the field. Thus he became virtually anonymous. This lulled his opponents. Then, when least expected, he would pop out of the trapdoor in the middle of the stage and win the match.'

The famous try at Ravenhill in 1953 was a thirty-yarder, a mazy, crazy jig at full pelt which, after Kyle had touched down, had six prostrate and cursing Frenchmen still down there getting a worm's-eye view of his old brown boots as he wandered unconcernedly back past them to the halfway line. A. A. Thomson watched that match for *The Times*, and a fortnight later wrote a tribute to Kyle, headlined 'Deserving of the name Genius':

'He is the all-round stand-off half, in the sense that Stoop and Davies and Waddell were all-rounders; that is, he can get his centres going, he can make openings and dart through himself, and he can defend stoutly, clearing his lines and "saving" his forwards. The modern stand-off, and, again, I do not wish to be ill-natured, often concentrates on the last of these duties, to the neglect of the other two, but Kyle has always performed all three duties either separately or in bewildering combination. However much it might seem that Ireland was the bottom dog, you never knew when Kyle might not slip round the blind side of the scrum or change the direction of the game with an astonishing diagonal kick, snatching the initiative where no initiative was before. He has an extraordinarily deceptive way of persuading opponents that he was about to do something wholly different from what in fact he did. If you thought he would kick he would pass, if you thought he would pass he would kick, and if you hesitated, he would dart by like a trout in a pool and either score a dazzling try on his own or put in a curling, puzzling cross-kick from which one of his wingers would eventually touch down. Even if he never plays again, he will continue to be reckoned the most gifted wearer of the green jersey since rugger began.'

Kyle's resplendent score against the New Zealand icon Scott, at Dunedin in the first Test of the 1950 Lions tour (a draw, 9–9), was watched from the touchline by the Lions' reserve full-back, another Ulsterman, George Norton, who tells it like it was:

'New Zealand got the ball on the halfway and the fly-half kicked ahead. Kyle jumped and got it in the air with his hand over his head. He began from a standing start. You know the way he went, biz-z-z like a motor cycle starting up. He beat the out-half and inside-centre who were coming at him. He was now down at the twenty-five with Bob Scott the full-back coming at him from one side and Charington, the New Zealand wing, a hefty Maori character, coming at him from the other. Somehow or other Kyle gave Scott the idea that he was going outside him but instead went inside against all the rules and succeeded in also beating Charington, who should have been able to sandwich him with Scott. Charington chased him and caught him by the collar as he reached the line, but Jack shook himself off like a terrier and scored.'

According to a friend of mine, the Irish writer Ulick O'Connor, after that match in Dunedin an old Maori asked to be shown into the dressing room. There were tears in his eyes. 'You're greater than Cookie,' he said to Kyle (Bert Cooke was the legendary All Black centre and five-eighths of the twenties).

Some said Kyle's one weakness was that he had no drop-kick. Kyle would just shrug, and momentarily a split-second smile might quiver at his lips. But for his innate modesty, he should have given the same answer as Sydney Barnes (cricket's immortal bowler), when he was upbraided by some dolt for 'not having a googly in his repertoire'. Said Barnes, 'I've never needed it.'

In March 1956, during Kyle's penultimate season with the shamrock at his breast, the *Irish Press* published a piece on the Wednesday before the crucial Welsh match in

Dublin written by someone neurotically worried about Kyle's lack of 'the drop' – he had yet to kick one in forty internationals. Come the match, and it is desperate stuff: Wales, on course for the Grand Slam, leading by 3–0 with twenty minutes to go. Ireland manage a brief flurry, but Owen, the full-back in red, clears his lines with a boomer. But it just fails to make touch around the ten-yard line. Kyle catches it as the Welsh bear down. 'I hear a fellow behind me in the crowd, "Have a wee shot, Jack." Why not, indeed? So I give it a go.' The ball soars high and arrow-true, and it is still rising as it bisects the uprights, clean as you like from all of forty-five yards. The crowd goes barmy, so do Kyle's chums, and 'Molly Malone' sweetly brings home more bacon by the way of two tries in the final ten minutes and glorious victory by 11–3.

He left as he came as he played – quietly. His last match was the 1958 victory against Scotland. He continued to turn out occasionally for NIFC; in 1960 he was enjoying 'a few wee darts' at full-back in the club's 3rd XV. Then, almost canonized in his own land for his fame at rugby, he just slips away with his wife, and his Gladstone bag, stethoscope and his books – Yeats and Burke and Synge and *The Fair Hills of Ireland* – to minister to the sick and the lame and the downtrodden of the Third World.

Just like that. Why leave? The clue may be in a letter from Dr Kyle printed by the *Irish Times* in 1967, before the 'Troubles' boiled over into bloodshed again. The letter was addressed to a notorious Protestant cleric, challenging him for 'his obsessive ravings', and accusing him of 'sowing seeds that create evil from which springs despicable actions'.

Kyle left his home for more important things than rugby – and rugby knew they were *far* more important. But rugby, the wide world of it, could not forget its gods – witness that Springboks' reunion party in Johannesburg. They just had to have the game's 'Dr Jack, of NIFC, Zambia, and the Universe' as a guest of honour. Cliff Morgan himself told on that night of recall and reverie a tale about 'Ireland's and all rugby's finest fly-half ever to draw breath'. Said Morgan: 'It was 10 March 1951, and, scarcely out of school, I was tremulously walking onto Cardiff Arms Park to play my first international for Wales, against Ireland. I was in a swelter of nerves. I felt a hand gently touch my shoulder. It was the man I was having to mark, the maestro Jack Kyle. He put an arm round me and whispered as fondly and genuinely as an uncle would, "I hope you have a wonderful, wonderful first cap today, Cliffie," he said.'

Thus, like all true romances, was the baton passed on. Kyle played for Ireland from 1947 till 1958; Morgan had a much shorter span, from 1951 till 1958, when he kept on running to blaze a hugely successful, mighty popular and much-loved trail in broadcasting, on every side of the cameras, counter and microphone, forever a-twitch, like a good fly-half, for the relishing and relishable possibilities of life between that 'little red light' which means 'on air' and that companionable green room which means '*en fête*'.

Two Welsh fly-halves had dominated the immediate post-war years, Glyn Davies of Pontypridd and Billy Cleaver, whom Morgan succeeded in the Cardiff team. Cleaver, you might say, was almost a modern – an organizer, a kicker, a nurse to his centres and to his pack. The Fat Controller with his flags of green and red and extremely tidy marshalling yards. Those marvellous Cardiff sides of Cleaver's always ran on time.

Davies was of the heroic lineage, descendant of the Jameses. An adventurer, a sidestepper, left or right, yet still the generous presenter of the perfect pass. He went to Cambridge, was the brother-in-law of Sir Geraint Evans, and, after ten games for Wales, concentrated on being a wine merchant. Young Morgan, from Trebanog high on the wind-ripping Rhondda rim, was in awe of, and inspired by, Glyn Davies. Thirty-seven years after that March day in 1951 when, so to say, Jack Kyle passed the baton (as, even less metaphorically, did Davies, for Morgan had now superseded him in the scarlet), I shared a long, long flight with Cliff. We were returning from the

Seoul Olympic Games. He told me about his heroes – his hero: 'I'm telling you, boy, honestly – Glyn Davies had more fly-half talent in his little finger than any other of his time had in their whole frame.'

Alas, I never saw Davies play. Nor Morgan either, but that beautifully titled – and beautifully fashioned – work *Fields of Praise* paints the picture:

'Cliff always played with the passionate urgency of a man trying to get out again. With the ball held at arm's length in front of him, his tongue out almost as far, his bow legs pumping like pistons, eyes rolling, nostrils flaring, and a range of facial expressions seldom seen north of Milan – whether at the opera house or the soccer stadium – the dark-haired, Celtically-constructed, perky Morgan was, at 5 foot 7 inches and 12 stone, the identikit Welsh outside-half. But no-one could have assembled Cliff; he was an amalgam of the social and cultural forces that had shaped modern Wales and of the currents that were defining Welshness anew in the second half of the twentieth century. His was the Welshness of a non-conformist home where Mam ruled and Sunday was for chapel, which meant that Cliff was humming snatches of oratorio before he was out of the shawl. The rugby crowds of the 1950s – strong, now, on "Blaenwern", "I bob un", "We'll keep a Welcome", and "The Holy City" ("... lift up your gates, and sing") – were the last of the harmonious generations brought up on choir practice and the Band of Hope. If there had been room on the terraces to dance then the incessant rain of the fifties would have completed a mass Welsh imitation of the era's favourite Hollywood musical; and if that international crowd could have managed something from the "Messiah" – as, in the fifties, sections of it still could – the chorus best calculated to inspire Cliff Morgan would have been, "Let us break their bonds asunder". It might have been written with him specifically in mind – South Wales is liberally endowed with Handels – for Cliff's india-rubber face typified the unbelievable springiness of his whole body: a favourite ruse of his for evading the clutches of opponents who had managed actually to lay hands on him was to go limp in their embrace; then, as the tackler momentarily relaxed his grip, Cliff Morgan jumped out of the tackle with an agility that made Harry Houdini look arthritic, and scurried away.'

The modern hymnal is that according to the ex-miner and busby-haired troubadour, Max Boyce, who sings of that secret, underground production plant, 'built beneath the mountains, beneath the coal and clay. It's where we make the outside-halves, that'll play for Wales one day'. Cliff Jones, Morgan's grand predecessor, reckons the 'fly-half factory' was above ground, in the very cobbled streets and lanes and alleys and roads which precariously and precipitously zigged and zagged up the sheer steepness of the hills and down the other side, all with higgledy-piggledy little houses perched on them in wonky, leaning symmetry like in the Gren cartoons – and every pathway teeming with people and cars and carts and sheep and sheepdogs. 'From the moment Mother let me out of the front door as an infant,' said Jones, 'I found myself on the only road up the valley which was teeming with traffic ... you had a pair of tramlines, you had to avoid the tramcars, or the lorries or the pushbikes, and when you crossed the road, you came to the railway line, and if you were lucky enough to cross the railway line and reach safety, you fell into the river!'

Cliff went to Tonyrefail Grammar School. There Mr E. R. Gribble taught metalwork, woodwork – and rugby. He was known to all as 'Ned' – but Cliff speaks of him, in reverent, thankful devotion still, as 'Mr Gribble':

'Simply, he shaped my life. He converted me from being "soccer-mad Joe", as he referred to me, to a game he loved, coached and understood. He saw to it that his charges developed a deep and abiding passion for the game which, he claimed, "Sweats the vice out of you". He was a gale of humanity and he displayed total and utter availability. He had massive judgment and cared for his flock and for standards of performance, skill, behaviour, discipline, and fair play.'

From Mr Gribble's school rugby to village rugby. More than for tales of derring-do behind famous packs and in front of vast crowds, Morgan's eyes glint the brighter, even now, as he recollects in tranquillity his days playing for Coedely Coke Ovens XV at Llantrisant, high on yet another zephyr-zapped hillside:

'Before the game we had to drive a herd of cows from the pitch; there was little we could do about the cow pats. That is how we learned to swerve and sidestep. Those who failed to develop these skills smelled horribly for weeks. At Maesteg, a railway line ran over an embankment behind one of the goal lines. During the game, the engines which were shunting coal from the local pit would stop. In perfect accord with the referee, the driver would blow the engine whistle for every offence. It is a well documented fact that deliveries of coal from Maesteg dropped 70 per cent with every home game.'

Then to Cardiff, in the footsteps of Cleaver. Then, mantle of red handed on by Davies, it was Wales – and tremulously catching the mid-morning Saturday double-decker down from the heights of his hill with his boots, cleaned by his dad, in a brown cardboard case. And getting into conversation with the two miners next to him:

'"'Ow the 'ell will Morgan cope with them big fellas, McCarthy, McKay and O'Brien? 'E's only a titch – too bloody small. I know 'im well, see 'im regular. Bet you 'e's not more than ten stone."

'"Don't talk daft, 'e's more than that, mun. Saw 'im at a do last week. Got big shoulders. I reckon 'e's eleven stone if 'e's an ounce."

'So the argument on my poundage continued. Suddenly the more aggressive of the two turned to me for an opinion.

'"You're saying nothing, boy. What do you think Morgan weighs?"

'"Twelve stone," I offered with confidence.

'"Bloody rubbish!"

'"I tell you he is," I said. He turned to his captive audience . . . "Would you credit it? It's always the same.

Them who knows bugger-all about it do always argue." '

Then it was moist eyes and butterfly-bobbing innards as Cliff and the encircling throng paid homage '*Gwlad, gwlad, pleidiol wyf i'm gwlad*'. After which Jack Kyle came up and embraced him: 'I hope you have a wonderful, wonderful cap today, Cliffie.'

In a frenzied kaleidoscope of greens and reds down there, the game gets going. Wales play well, little Morgan displaying a few nice touches, too. Big Ben Edwards hoofs over a mighty penalty. Wales are on course. 'Funny,' thinks Cliff (growing in confidence with every minute as the match takes its course), 'all those write-ups about me having the daunting job of marking Jack Kyle and he's not doing very much at all. Just gets the ball and passes it on. Perhaps he's getting too old for it?'

Young Cliff's contented reverie is suddenly exploded – with a castaneting click of heels, a quadruple gear-change, and just the flicker of a smile to match the magical flicker of a hip, and Kyle has totally left his marker Morgan looking an absolute mug, and now he's past the full-back and he's plonked the ball down over the line before, even, anyone has time to utter the two words 'typical Kyle'.

Over forty years on, and Morgan will still insist, 'Of all fly-halves I played against, without hesitation I know Jack Kyle was the best. The loveliest of players, the loveliest of men.'

If, at the first time of asking, Jack Kyle had taught Morgan the imperative of any fly-half – concentration – another cruel lesson was not far away. That match against Ireland was on 10 March. On the Saturday before Christmas, Wales faced Basil Kenyon's fourth Springboks, a mighty powerful juggernaut of a side, all strength and discipline and knowing no need for frills. They arrived in Wales roaring hot from defeats of Ireland and (by a then outrageous 44–0) Scotland. The Springboks knew Wales would present the main threat to an unbeaten Test tour, the Dragons being between the Championship and Triple Crown of 1950 and 1952. Morgan had sparkled against the visitors in an early pipe-opener for Cardiff. Now, in the Test, the 'Boks set their hard-hammering senior back-row at the fly-half, notably the bald, big and tremendously combative flanker Basie van Wyk. They severed the young man's lines of communication from the start. Cliff panicked and began to kick. Thus, painfully, he learned another crucial fly-half tenet – 'You must have a sense of not only when, but when *not* to do things':

'My scatter-brained and scattily directed kicking simply cost Wales the game. On that day the Welsh pack, with Dai Davies winning the strike in the scrums and Roy John majestically controlling the line-outs, gave me enough ball for us to dominate. Outside – imagine! – I had Bleddyn Williams, Lewis Jones, Malcolm Thomas and Ken Jones. I ignored them because I failed to play the game that came naturally to me. Only once did I let the ball go and Bleddyn got a try. It was a game we should have won if Wales had been right at fly-half. I was mortified with grief.'

It was a miserable Christmas in Trebanog.

A double agony in front of Morgan's home crowd was that the Springbok fly-half that day, Hansie Brewis, a Transvaal cop, gave a kicking display modelled to perfection on his guide and mentor, the infamous Bennie Osler.

Morgan had to wait for over four years to avenge the day – and he chose to do it at the first time of asking and in front of the largest rugby crowd ever assembled in the history of the world: 95,000 at Ellis Park, Johannesburg, on the first Test match of the Lions tour in 1955. His adversary once again was his tormentor from his immature tutorial, Basie van Wyk, even balder, possibly harder. Only two journalists from Britain (which was two more than on any other Lions tour), J. B. G. Thomas of the *Western Mail* and Vivian Jenkins of the *Sunday Times*, covered the whole trip. That first Test ended, unbelievably almost, 23–22 to the Lions. So Morgan's moment of destiny settled the thing. JBG talks you through it:

'The magical moment came early in the second-half. The Lions had crossed over only 3 points in arrears and attacked from the first whistle that announced the resumption. Unfortunately, O'Reilly was just pushed into touch in the right corner and a line-out ordered, at which Higgins fell awkwardly to suffer a severe injury that kept him out for the rest of the tour. His departure from the field of play demanded an increased effort from the remaining seven Lions' forwards and they did not fail in their task. The ball was won at the next scrum, near the right-hand touch-line, and a good heel enabled Dicky Jeeps, playing like a veteran in his first representative match, to get a long, swift pass away to Morgan.

'The Welshman liked to receive the ball from his partner well in front of him so he could run on to it with opponents in his line of sight. Again, like a good outside-half, he liked to take the ball at speed in attack to give himself an initial start against back-row defenders. He had mastered all this in the years between and with a slight outward jink was through the initial line of defence, racing across the Springbok "25" line diagonally with van Wyk chasing after him. This time Morgan was not the caged terrier, but a roaring lion, far too swift for the covering Springbok. He moved round in a great arc, leaning over as he crossed the South African goal-line, to turn in behind the posts as the despairing van Wyk, Morgan's great rival, came thundering up to admit defeat with a sporting smile. Morgan had avenged himself – and Wales – and set alight a brilliant period of attack by the Lions which eventually brought them the greatest victory by any British team abroad.'

Basie van Wyk never played for the Springboks again.

9

Good things come in twos

That Lions Test Series of 1955 was drawn. So at least they left South Africa as the first British side since 1896 not to be beaten by the Springboks. As it embarked for home on the *Union Castle* line, one of the grand old men of South African sports writing, Charles Lambe, wrote in the Johannesburg *Sunday Express* that 'Cliff Morgan is the best fly-half to have played in South Africa in the past 50 years. I have seen every touring team since 1903, and I have yet to see Morgan's equal.'

Had Percy Bush been on that 1903 tour – he went down to enchant Australia the year after, remember – it would be interesting to have sat in on Lambe's comparisons. Not even Britain's still much-loved rugby-writing doyen caught a glimpse of Bush. Bryn Thomas's solitary scribbling partner with the Lions in 1955, Vivian Jenkins (the handsome Welsh full-back all through the era of Jones and Davies), was eighty-two in 1993 and still fielding every question as calmly as he did the barrage of up-and-unders through the 1930s – and returning them with added interest. Viv still recalls with clarity the boyhood tales he heard of Bush at his father's knee in Bridgend:

'Obviously Bush was a character all of his own, the great sidestepper from whom no-one ever knew what to expect next, either on or off the field. I heard how, once, after a champagne lunch, he scored seventeen points for

Cardiff in the first twenty minutes and then walked off saying "That's enough, boys, I'll leave the rest to you." Another story about him was told me by Oliver Piper, an Irish international forward of the day. "I played against him, for Cork Constitution against Cardiff," he told me, "and we were being given a hammering. But the worst moment of all came when Percy ran clean through the lot of us and then, after crossing the line, ran back into the field again without touching down before waltzing through the lot of us a second time and finally scoring." Oh, to have seen Bush play!'

Aye to that, for my generation, which just missed seeing Morgan in the flesh. But at least we've got flickering celluloid. If Morgan says Kyle was the 'best' fly-half he ever played against, he nominates Mick English, the Irish doctor's immediate successor in the wearing of the green at No. 10, as the most 'awkward and difficult'. 'Mick would come up in defence alongside, or even ahead of, his back row. He never gave you a moment's peace, and he was granite-hard with it.' Mick was a Limerick man. I have heard it said, though others claim it, that Mick was the fellow who summed up the Lansdowne Road philosophies so well: 'The state of Welsh rugby is sometimes serious but never hopeless; the state of Irish rugby is hopeless but never serious.'

I remember how that enchanting amateur feel of Irish rugby was brought home to me once when, happening to be in Limerick, I popped in to pass the time of day at his sports shop in the dear old, slate-grey city with Tony Ward, another Irish 'fly' of the legend. He showed me a letter he had come across, written to Mick English by the late Mai Purcell, a colleague of Mick's on the *Limerick Leader*, on the occasion of his winning his first Irish cap. It went: 'Mickie – I should like to impress on you that I'm spending me whole week's wages, viz £3.00, on the trip to Dublin just to see you play and I beseech you not to make an eejit of yourself on this occasion. I furthermore request that on this auspicious afternoon, mindful of your duties and responsibilities, not only to your club and people of

Limerick but to our country as a whole, that you keep your bloody eye on the ball. Good Luck and God Bless – Mai.'

On that 1955 South African tour was England's Doug Baker, who went as fly-half reserve to Morgan, then ended up playing the most valiant and imaginative rugby of his career as the Test team's full-back – 'Nuggety Duggety', all South Africa called him in admiration. He returned a hero, injured himself in England's trial match the following winter, and was never picked again as the England selectors began another of their scatterbrained bouts of musical-chairs with fly-halves, picking four different ones in the following nine games – M. J. K. Smith, the cricketer (whose solitary rugby cap ensured his joining an exclusive double international club), Ricky Bartlett (who played with poise through a rare Grand Slam year for the Whites in 1957), Martin Regan, a Lancastrian soon to join his native Rugby League, and all four of John Philip Horrocks-Taylor, the Yorkshireman at Cambridge, whom the aforementioned Limerick 'fly', English, missed in the tackle and got up off the ground to apologize to his colleagues in green: 'Jasus, sorry, lads, Horrocks went right, Taylor went left – and I was left tacklin' the friggin' hyphen!'

In fact, fly-halves were coming at you now from all directions thick and fast. (Some not so thick, some especially fast.) If this modest treatise is not to become a tedious list of proper names and count of caps, then some serious editing with the pruning shears is, alas, necessary. Not hindered by a rapidly increasing gloss on the image and possibilities of rugby in the perceptions of the general public – has any international, anywhere, been played away from the TV cameras in the last quarter of a century? – the press was also beginning to take a serious, full-page interest outside the world's two passionate rugby-playing 'parishes', Wales and New Zealand, where it continued to be the national game, wallowing and swathed in fervours. (The Springboks, too, would always claim rugby as their national game: but that's always been their trouble – adjusting to the facts of life. A game cannot be 'national' when two thirds of the population hope and pray with desperate supplication that the 'national' team loses every time, as has been the case, till the 1990s at least, with the African majority in the country and rugby's all-white Springboks.)

Anyway, for the happier remainder of the world, the ever burgeoning 'meejer' interest grew apace through the second half of the century. Such exposure needs 'stars' to feed its unending appetites. In rugby, the game's natural 'stars' were thus cued even more downstage into the fierce light of 'the lime'. More than just a few very likely candidates were auditioned for greatness by the expectant theorists but bombed when they actually had to perform with any consistency. Others seized the opportunity, and (however much they may have cursed the accompanying superduper-stardom that now went with the territory) a few seized it with a coruscating grandeur.

One such was Richard Sharp.

As so often in life – even as we have noted, and with more to come, in this chronicle – good things come in twos. Then, if a choice has to be made between the two, luck makes the decision. For the Five Nations season of 1959, England unearthed a real gem at fly-half in, of all unlikely places, the geography department of Manchester University. I say 'unlikely' only in terms of Rugby League, for one of that grand sport's hotbeds is represented by teams which speckle the rim of Greater Manchester – but in this case doubly so, for the glistening new fly-half introduced to England, Bev Risman, was the son of one of the League game's all-time luminaries, Gus Risman.

So well did the twenty-two-year-old Risman play through the Championship season that he was picked for that summer's tour of New Zealand and Australia. Here he again played with precocious judgement and no little panache in the first two winning Tests at Brisbane and Sydney, and then in the first of the four against the All Blacks (won, outrageously, by New Zealand by 18–17, which worked out as six penalty goals to four tries and a penalty). Then Risman chipped an ankle bone, missed the next two (losing) Tests but returned for the last, when, with the scores level and ten minutes left, he set off on an inspired, solo gallop in which he artfully hoodwinked the blindside cover to score a glorious winning try at the corner-flag.

Home came the hero, Twickenham fully expecting to build England's side around him. At lunchtime the day before the first match of the 1960 season, against Wales, Risman tweaked a hamstring in practice at Roehampton. The selectors dispatched a telegram to the Cornish family home of Richard Sharp, just twenty-one, who had played well as a fresher for Oxford in the University Match the month before. Sharp's father, in turn, sent another to his son at Balliol College – 'Get to Twickenham, pronto', or something snappy to that effect.

The youngster did as bid – and not long after teatime, when it was almost dark, he had seven or eight minutes' throwing a ball about in the wintery gloaming with his scrum-half for the morrow's international, Dick Jeeps, England's longtime captain, just back from his second trip with the Lions (the tour before, remember, he had partnered Morgan). Before that teatime muck-around, young Sharp had not even spoken to the celebrated Mr Jeeps in his life.

Next afternoon, waiting to go out into the old cockpit of cabbagey-green, Sharp remembers that he was surprisingly calm. 'I suppose, as a last-minute replacement, little was expected of me, so I knew I had nothing to lose.' Those were telegram days with a vengeance – and an unending stream of them was being delivered to England's dressing room, just about all addressed to Sharp. He must have had about forty – mostly from Cornwall, many from team-mates at Redruth, where he learned his rugby, many more from complete strangers. There was even one ordering him to 'do a proper job' from the Tiverton Water Works, and one all the way from Malta, from Sharp's National Service sergeant major.

The boy sat reading these messages, seemingly

unconcerned, delighted at their 'birthday-card' aspect. Quarter of an hour before kick-off, Mr Jeeps wandered over and told him, 'Hadn't you better start thinking a bit about the game?'

No need really to tell what happened, is there? The Welsh wing-forward (and Lion) marking Sharp was the grand 'Red Devil' himself, the former Parachute Regiment hero Haydn Morgan. Legend has it that the spindly, blond, nonchalant public schoolboy (Sharp not only was one – Blundells – but also looked to be Central Casting's dead-ringer for the type) made a complete monkey out of the fierce and fuming Morgan that afternoon, although the truth is probably much nearer the fact that the shrewd nous of Jeeps skilfully nursed Sharp away from Morgan's exasperated attentions by tying in the Welshman and releasing only when Sharp looked safe. Nevertheless it was, by any standards, a blindingly accomplished début by Sharp. Fleet Street purred like pussycats and poured on the plaudits as only they can:

SHARP SHATTERS WALES (*Daily Mail*)

BRILLIANT SHARP HARRIES WALES IN DAY TO REMEMBER (*Daily Telegraph*)

ENGLAND KING-PIN SHARP (*Daily Express*)

NO HOLDING CORNISH KING (*Daily Mirror*)

NEW STAR LIGHTS ENGLISH RUGBY (*Observer*)

GIFTED SHARP MAKES TELLING FIRST APPEARANCE (*The Times*)

I was, briefly that winter, a sub-editor on the *Gloucester Citizen*. We had a Saturday evening football 'Pink 'Un', but, being Gloucester, the front-page lead and banner headline always pertained to Rugby Union. I remember that afternoon well, organizing the snippets as the Press Association 'runner' ticker-taped in (or, rather, Twicker-taped in) from the International. I like to think that it was me (no, I'm certain it was, honest) who put up the splash front-pager in the biggest print we could find:

SHARP'S THE WORD FOR TAFFIES

– which, those of a certain generation will recognize fondly, was a play on the well-known confectionery advertisement of the time for the toffee manufacturers, Messrs Sharp.

Anyway . . . Sharp kept his place at the expense of the hitherto dazzling Risman (who returned for a few games in the centre and then followed Dad's footsteps to Rugby League) – and for the rest of that season, further inspired by their skinny new icon with the corn-stook hair and bambi-like, leggy long stride, England won the Championship and Triple Crown at a canter.

Three decades and more on, Sharp has long been snugly settled back with his family in their beloved Cornwall. He wrote shrewd observations for many years in the *Sunday Telegraph*. A charming, quietly companionable man, he is an executive with Cornish China Clay. As the 1980s turned into the 90s, the Cornish County XV dramatically won through to three County Cup finals at Twickenham, and, to be sure, the old hero is far readier to talk local rugby than reminisce about his feats in front of teeming thousands and television cameras. But once he has been allowed fondly to tell tales of his litany of saints he grew up to play with for Cornwall – Bill Phillips, Harold Stevens, Bonzo Johns, Kenny Abrahams, Paddy McGovan, 'my faithful old scrum-half, Peter Michell, now don't forget that's Michell without a "t"' – you can squeeze out of him some recollections of his time with England in the wintery faraway:

'I was so lucky with Dick Jeeps, of course. He knew it all. I suppose it did help that we had complementary styles. We were opposites all right: he was tremendously tough and wiry, strong and combative in the best sense. He was just immense at "tidying up" – and then quite out-standing at giving me quick possession which allowed me – now and again, I suppose – to bust open the middle and do something. Yes, I suppose in a way, just like opening partnerships at cricket, a scrum-half and fly-half must have styles which complement each other – one with the knowledge and patience and calm unflappability, the other looking to possibly play a few strokes. But I'll tell you what was most important of all with Dick and me – we grew to become enormously good friends off the field. I think that's crucial in any sporting "partnership", particularly at half-back in rugby. There's nothing you want to do more, you see, than look after your best mate, is there?'

He named two hall-of-fame fly-halves who were in time to follow him in the pantheon after his retirement:

'Look at Barry John and Phil Bennett – would they have been quite as magical as they were had not their scrum-half, Gareth Edwards, been a best friend off the field? Oh, what wonderful, wonderful skills those two had. David Watkins, too, before them, and my own great schoolboy idol, Cliff Morgan. Tell you what, too, Jonathan Davies could have been the very best of the lot as a Union fly-half if he had been given a pack to play behind, which might have been one of the reasons he chose to "go north". No, if you ask me for the six best fly-halves I've ever seen, it would be impossible not to include at least five – dash it, even six – Welshmen.

'Funnily enough, mind you, I never thought the Welsh match was the hardest each year – for me that was always the French game. What tacklers, what toughies with it. *Real* men like that phenomenal Michel Crauste, who always seemed to be marking me.'

I had taken down to read to Sharp details of his classic try against Scotland in March 1963, a sublime match-winner that settled another championship as well as the Calcutta Cup in his final, farewell match for England. I began to read:

'A scrum between the halfway and Scotland's ten-yard line . . . England heel . . . Clarke to Sharp, openside . . . oh, he dummies Ross the flanker . . . Weston, his centre, is alongside . . . Sharp to Weston, this could be promising . . . oh, no, it isn't – I mean, oh, yes, it is . . . Sharp's still got the ball after that audacious dummy-scissors with Weston . . . now he's straightening up, and there's Phillips outside him . . . Sharp to Phillips, his outside centre . . . oh, by Jove, no, it isn't . . . Sharp still has it and that outrageous dummy has carried him completely clear of the Scots, Henderson and White . . . now it's two against one, for Sharp has his winger Roberts outside him as his raking stride approaches full-back Blaikie, who's just taken over from the great Ken Scotland of course . . . Blaikie's never played against Sharp before . . . but he gets him as Sharp passes to Roberts for a certain try for England . . . Roberts has no-one to beat and he's clear for the corner-flag . . . oh, no, he isn't . . . Sharp's dummied Blaikie . . . and now he can't fail to score under the posts . . . what a try . . . I could see that wonderful solo try by Sharp coming from the moment Simon Clarke fed him fifty yards back . . .'

Or words to that effect . . .

The truth lies in that ganglingly deceptive top-lick of Sharp's, his elastic body-swerve, and the selling of those three operatically resplendent dummies – operatic in as much as Twickenham knew a hummably dramatic and favourite tune was due to strike up on its rowdy insistence of an encore finale. The only ones not in the secret were the straw-clutching Scots defenders.

Well, what about that, then? I ask R. A. W. Sharp, executive with Cornish China Clay, exactly thirty years on. He essays a split-second wince. Then shrugs: 'Yes, I suppose that *looked* the best on fuzzy black-and-white television. Three or four dummies? Well, you could dummy in those days. It was part of the game. Not now; they are all so good and aware and so defensively trained for every eventuality. We were almost neanderthal in terms of preparation and training. My only luck was that I had four years at Oxford which I could devote to half-study, half-rugger. I finished my finals on the Wednesday before an England match.'

C'mon, I said, we're talking hardback books and serial rights in Aberdeen; talk me through that final, curtain-call try against Scotland at Twickenham:

'Okay, it looked good on Pathe Pictorial. But do you want to hear about my favourite-favouritest try for England? It was the year before, against Ireland. I don't know why I am so proud of it, I just was. I'm not being precious in the least – or a middle-aged man feeling romantic. It was just a try that means "rugby" and the comradeship of the whole endeavour. Else why play?'

Jeeps was still captain but in his last season (Sharp was to take over as 'coin-tossing motivator'). 'Ireland as ever were playing a dementedly marvellous match. That dear man, Stan [Hodgson, a Durham maintenance fitter and, later, a doughty Lion in 1962] was at hooker. If it wasn't his first game, it was certainly only his second. He was a truly outstanding hooker was Stan Hodgson. Anyway, he comes up to me, late in the game, everything at fever pitch except him, and says with a hoarse whisper, "Richard, if I manage a heel against-the-head, skip, it's up to you." Stan did. Like lightning it came out. Dick to me, dum-dah-dum, and I was over for the score, under the posts and I think I converted it too. As I ran back to the halfway line for the kick-off everyone was ridiculously clapping – but I knew I had nothing else on my mind than to run to Stan and tap his shoulder (no "embracing" in our day) and say, "Stan, that is your try they are applauding, not mine." I don't know why, but that try gave me more pleasure than any of the others.'

Sharp's finale, his tumultuously acclaimed curtain-call, should have been the British Lions tour of 1962 to South Africa. He was in his pomp. And in the first pipe-openers of the tour the South Africans were made fully aware of it. On the Saturday before the first Test, a stern dress-rehearsal against the always uncompromising Northern Transvaal. The Lions debated whether to keep Sharp under wraps for the Test. In the event, they played him. From his first quick pass from Jeeps, Sharp swayed past his marking wing-forward and over the gain line. Terry O'Connor, of the Daily Mail, was there: 'He so swiftly broke the first line of defence. Mannetjies "little man" Roux, a 5 ft 7 ins centre, sensed the danger and went for

Sharp', tackling high and hitting his head on the Englishman's cheekbone. 'Sharp went on for a few yards before collapsing, his face shattered. Instantaneously, everyone present knew Sharp was out of the first Test – and maybe the series.'

Sharp's England centre, Mike Weston, was playing alongside the fly-half. He recalls the incident: 'Roux was marking me when he turned inside to attack Sharp. I am certain we would have scored if Sharp had passed after his initial burst as there was a two-to-one situation. Instead, he attempted one of his famous individual breaks and could not see Roux coming on his blind side. It was hardly a fair tackle, but Richard never showed any bitterness and even went to tell Roux so when he came out of hospital.'

Weston played in all but one of Sharp's fourteen England games, which makes him a good judge: 'He had all the assets needed. Kicked with both feet, had a deceptive turn of pace, and could drop goals from any position. It was remarkable how quickly he gained speed with such long legs. He was a hell of a nice guy who gained everyone's respect, which is why he proved such a fine captain.'

Not a soul in rugby, I warrant, has ever heard, or uttered, a disparaging word about Richard Sharp, epitome of the civilized English public schoolboy. It is an odd quirk of the complex-riddled British class system, however, that the upper-crust species has to tread a very fine line indeed when it comes to popularity with the rest of the mass out there. Not everybody loves a lord but, sometimes, *everybody* loves a lord. After the grievously wounded but still chivalrous Camelot-dotty Sharp had turned, you certainly could say literally, the other cheek and blamed no-one but 'silly old me' that afternoon in Johannesburg, he came home to write a retirement autobiography of such endearing and self-effacing magnitude that the face-shattering incident with Roux was passed off in just a few sentences, thus:

'I missed six weeks in the middle of the tour and this was a great personal disappointment because it came at a time when I felt so very fit and was enjoying every minute of the rugby. One must learn to put up with such things, however, and there were some much less fortunate than I. David Hewitt, who had been such a great success on tour with the Lions in New Zealand, had to put up with a very troublesome hamstring but he was always very cheerful. Poor Stan Hodgson, too, in that black moment at Bulawayo in the first match, broke his leg and spent most of the tour on crutches.'

This was taking Rugby Union to Dr Schweizer or Mother Teresa levels.

The young man who had been chosen for the Lions as Sharp's deputy fly-half was the son of the grand Herbert of Scotland's 1920s, Gordon Waddell, who had played against Sharp for Cambridge in two Varsity Matches (both won by the light-blues). Now Waddell had to step into the firing line, which he did bravely and with commendable skill in the Tests till Sharp made an understandably hesitant return at the end of the tour. Waddell was a beautiful kicker who understood the percentage game, and he was generally steeped in the best sort of clean primness and class – of the rugby variety certainly. The other variety, however, is trenchantly and, in sports writing's strict allowances, nicely and originally suggested by that astute supporter from Selkirk, the writer and novelist Allan Massie, in his erudite celebration of the thistle, *A Portrait of Scottish Rugby*:

'Waddell was a very fine player indeed; yet he was never popular at Murrayfield. Indeed one could go further and say that he was the only Scottish player in memory to be actively disliked and resented by a large section of the crowd. He was shamefully barracked in at least one Scottish trial. Part of the reason for this rested in old schoolboy animosities. Waddell had been the outstanding member of the great Fettes sides of the Fifties, when the school went five years without defeat from another Scottish school. He hadn't, of course, played throughout this run, but he was taken as the arch-representative of Fettes. He seemed to display the contemptuous arrogance

158

that typified that generation of Fettesians, the sense of belonging to a different order from other schoolboys, and to have carried this attitude into adult life. When Fettes came to play Glenalmond, I recall it being reported that Waddell spoke to nobody, refused lunch, merely drinking a glass of water and swallowing a couple of pills. This now seems evidence of nervous tension; it was regarded as showing-off, a disagreeable swagger, and accordingly condemned.

'Secondly, his early selection – he was in his first year out of school, doing National Service in the Navy, when he was picked for the Calcutta Cup match in 1957 – was resented. It was a piece of favouritism, rank nepotism; he had jumped the queue because his father Herbert was a "big cheese" in the S.R.U. This was pretty fair nonsense, though not necessarily without some substance. The fact that he was Herbert's son no doubt carried a little weight, brought him to a prominence he hadn't perhaps quite earned; it wouldn't have done so, however, if he had not already displayed a remarkable talent and a precocious maturity.'

Scotland in the 1960s also fielded at half-back that sound and inseparable Melrose pair, Alex Hastie at scrum-half and David Chisholm at fly. To this day, it seems you can only mention the two of them in harness – like Frank Sinatra's horse-and-carriage. As I write, I just cannot help myself reciting, rhythmically in Bill McLaren's Borders cadence, 'Whyte with the throw then . . . Stagg palms . . . Hastie gathers . . . to Chisholm on the *burrrst . . .*'

Hastie and Chisholm, Mack and McMabel.

Chisholm was unflashy in the extreme, far more the obsessive tidier than scattergun creator. But he did score one surprisingly imaginative and mazy, even dazzling try, against Australia in 1966 at Murrayfield to beat the tourists. The Wallabies' grand fly-half Phil Hawthorne missed that game. Had he not, it is more than a fair bet the score would have been somewhat different from 11–5, for in the next match, when Australia beat England, he dropped three meticulous goals as if in his sleep. (The only others, all fly-halves, to have potted the hat-trick are the two French wizards, the Dax restaurateur Pierre – 'Monsieur le Drop' – Albaladejo in 1960 and Jean-Patrick Lescarboura, also from Dax, in 1985, and, of course, Benny Osler's chip-off-the-old-block, Naas Botha, in 1981.) In the series, Hawthorne dropped six goals in all and finished with a Wallaby record of 28 points. The next record he was involved in was, on his return home, being bought by Rugby League for the then largest Australian fee.

At Union, Hawthorne had been tremendously fortunate to work with a scrum-half of the calibre of Ken Catchpole, whose speed of pass off either side remains enshrined in the whole game's treasure-chest. Another top-grade fly-half – okay, okay, 'five-eighth' – of the period who offers grateful thanks for being a contemporary of another outstanding scrum-half: Earle Kirton followed the sublimely talented Mac Herewini ('the most brilliant natural footballer New Zealand ever produced', said one of Herewini's illustrious predecessors, Ross Brown) into the black jersey, numbered '10', inheriting from him the outstanding Chris Laidlaw at the base of the scrum. When he retired, Kirton, a dentist, settled in a practice not a million miles away from Twickenham and became a vibrant and original coach to Adrian Stoop's old club, Harlequins. (Kirton, 1993's All Black coach, remains the spiritual guide and mentor in matters of tactics and motivation to the England Grand Slam coach of the 1990s, Dick Best, the former chef.)

Kirton, son of a King Country first-five (and racehorse trainer), first came to Britain on the All Blacks' 1963–4 tour – led by the popular Wilson Whineray. The first time he pulled on the sacred jersey was early in the tour, the third game, against Newport. He was very nervous – 'honest, before it I didn't sleep a wink for three nights beforehand.' It was a stinking night, Dylan's 'bible-black' winter skies of Wales weeping buckets. The fretting young debutant had a stinker to match. He could not catch a thing – 'and I even fly-hacked like a drain.' Newport won famously by 3–0, 'a lucky pot which wonkily grazed the bar as it went over: not that any of us could see it all that well in the filthy gloom.' It was to be the All Blacks' only defeat on the whole tour. Kirton, twenty-two, was blamed and, he still reckons, was pretty well frozen out for the rest of the trip, which, for him alone, was a miserable one.

On the flight home, Kirton sat next to the senior back-rower and future All Black captain, Brian Lochore, and defiantly mentioned that he was going to dedicate his next five years solely to winning an All Black Test cap. 'Son, I think you will be awfully lucky if you do,' said Lochore.

In fact, it took him three years. By 1967, for the next (unbeaten) tour of Britain, Kirton played enchantingly throughout the early games and won his first cap in the opening Test at Twickenham. England were handsomely laid to waste – as Wales, France and Scotland would be as Kirton inspired the line. But none was as important to him as the glistening win, against Monmouthshire this time, on that same old ground down by the river at Newport, Rodney Parade.

First – and he is happy to laugh at himself now – when he entered the clubhouse, Newport had decorated one whole wall with a massive mural depicting their great 1963 victory, that night of young Kirton's shame, and the 'pot' that won the match. 'What made it worse was that this ruddy mural showed it to be a lovely, cloudless, blue-skied day, and the ball, instead of just scraping over the bar, was seen by the artist as sailing over as high as the post itself. I just had to break up in mirth.'

And later, just to prove a point to himself, with Monmouthshire leading in the match by 12–9, at the last Kirton, at full pelt, looped the loop with Wayne Cottrell to manufacture a midfield gap on halfway, and then mazily ran all of fifty yards through the desperate Welsh cover to score what was generally accepted to be the try of the tour. Certainly it was the most rewarding – and atoning – Kirton ever remembers.

He played for the All Blacks for thirteen successive

internationals – on the losing side only once, the last. Reflecting on that first, for him disastrous, tour of Britain as a kid, he reckons the gods 'doubly stuffed me'. First there was his shambles at Newport, then, four matches later, they gave him a second run-out against the students of Cambridge University – 'surely I couldn't fail there to get my confidence back and put my tour on some sort of rails.' So Earle trots out at Grange Road, eager for the first time on the trip. The manchild he was marking was down in the programme as 'C. M. H. Gibson (Campbell College, Belfast, & Queens)'.

Says the engaging Kirton: 'He destroyed me. From his first touch I not only knew I was in for deep, deep trouble that afternoon, but also that I had suddenly been confronted by the most brilliant fly-half I would ever see.'

That was the afternoon Mike Gibson made his awesome first bow on any international stage. He was, of course, to go on and become (till Serge Blanco overtook him) the most capped player in international rugby history, with eighty-one. Alas, however, he played the vast majority of those games for Ireland in the centre or on the wing, so he qualifies here, not, as might have been, with a whole vast chapter to himself, framed in a curly-twirly gold-leaf presentation pack, but with only a passing hurrah in this pageant – but a keenly fascinating and entirely relevant one for all that. When Gibson returned from the second of his four tours with the British Lions, from New Zealand in 1971, he gave a compelling interview to that industrious and always original journalist, Terry O'Connor of the *Daily Mail*, who has seen more international rugby than any writer of his generation. In it, Gibson (already long-established at centre) offered still-new insights into the reasons why most fly-halves are nowhere as good as a very few:

'Be it Coarse or International rugby, study any fly-half. Note his positional play, remembering his role as the initiator of almost all the movements. If his team is under pressure you will frequently see him moving behind the set-piece instead of holding his correct position. This is simply self-protection. The fly-half may gain comfort by directing the play but such positioning reduces the possibilities open to his side. Once he adopts such a position he is compelled to run across the field and the rest of the backs have no option but to follow.

'Another defect concerns his state of mind. A fly-half can become so self-important that he considers he must do something as an individual with each ball he receives. He then neglects his role as a link and so neglects his side. To succeed at the highest level the fly-half also requires absolute concentration. Once his mind wanders or he becomes determined to achieve individual supremacy over a wing forward or his opposite number, his appreciation of any situation wanes, and he becomes less alert to new possibilities.

'The faults of a fly-half are easy to see and often have a greater effect than errors made by his fellow backs, but the principles involved when discussing a fly-half's defects apply equally to the backs as a whole.'

Thus he laid his lore down to the *Daily Mail*. Gibson was possibly the greatest fly-half who never was.

10

Another time, another planet

For England there was Stoop, there was Davies, there was Sharp. More often down the century, as the admired Alan Watkins put it once with such typically perfect fine-tuning in his unmissable column in the *Independent*, 'There are in England usually three or four players who are more or less up to the job, and the selectors cannot make up their minds whom to choose. In Wales, by contrast, a period of competition between two players or, alternatively, of cosmic confusion is succeeded by the emergence of one usually great outside-half.'

Thus the uncertainty about whether to choose Billy Cleaver or Glyn Davies was succeeded by the domination of Cliff Morgan. The reign of Morgan was followed by baronial wars, until the succession descended on David Watkins, who, after a brief struggle, gave way to the mightiest sovereign of all, Barry John. He abdicated, however, when he was only twenty-seven, in favour of Phil Bennett, who, after a successful reign – with the brief interregnum of the late John Bevan – transferred the crown to Gareth Davies. Unhappily the reign of Davies was marred towards its close by the preference for Malcolm Dacey evinced by Bevan (by now a power behind the throne). Davies abdicated in disgust. But the throne left empty by him was not filled by the usurper Dacey. Another Davies, Jonathan, had appeared in the kingdom. 'Lo, we have another king,' the simple folk of Wales cried in exultation and relief.

Alan Watkins, of our certain generation, I'm sure hosannahs with us all that, lo, on the contrary, there could never be another king. (I'm aware it is crass to use words like 'king': but, well, this little guy *was* a monarch.) Barry John came upon Wales, and then the world, like a ghost in the night first to delight and then to enrapture totally. He was an insouciant natural sprite with a pale presence and a frail one (although with deceptively strong hips and thighs). Sometimes, as the gilded spirit glided through ferociously hulking enemies, he made it seem they were actually mesmerized by his presence – that, or they were careering into unseen glass walls down there. He was generous and chivalrous; there was a gaiety about him, and he ran like an elfin Puck, and kicked like a dream, particularly out of hand – garryowens or artful bobblers, great raking things, inch perfect at the corner-flag; or snake-spitting grubbers, or one-bounce off-spinners (or leggers) which tantalized and cruelly taunted end-of-tether full-backs to distraction (and, in one or two cases, to retirement there and then).

Or rather, no, John did not 'cruelly taunt'. Angels made in heaven do not 'cruelly taunt'.

He was from Cefneithin in the west, a mining village shadowed by Mynydd Mawr (the 'great mountain') and triangled by Llanelli, Swansea and Carmarthen. Barry was one of four boys, and the back door of the family's terraced council house opened onto the village 'rec', a scrubby stretch of land which became 'our Wembley, or Arms Park or, in the summers, Lord's'.

His uncles were miners and so was his father, 'with blue scars on their hands and dust in their lungs to show for it', Barry remembers. How could he ever forget. 'In the winter sometimes, Dad wouldn't see daylight till the third day. The lovely thing about the village was that all his mates knew he had six mouths to feed – eight in all – so when the chance came they'd give him their turn for a "dubbla" [double-shift], saying "Here, Will, you need the extra pound more than us." And when he was on "dubbla", we boys would take it in turns to run to the pit with his extra sandwiches for the morning.'

At the village school – 'no, not academic, me, if the pass-mark was 50 I'd get 51 in everything; none of this 70–80 lark for me; I'd just clear the crossbar. Why not, still get your three points, eh?' Soccer was the impromptu game at school. 'The best game to develop skills for rugby, anyway. In a way, I think all fly-halves are frustrated soccer inside-forwards anyway, fantasizing about being at Old Trafford or Anfield or the Maracana – because in both positions you have to be born with the balance, the touch, the decisiveness, the boldness.'

Do not read that and think, 'Blimey, what a swank.' There is not an ounce of conceit in John, nor, they say, has there ever been.

At Gwendraeth Grammar School, he made the under-fifteens at twelve. By sixteen he was playing village rugby for Cefneithin, 'the green-and-golds'. Across the 'rec' from the John household lived a man who played for Llanelli, a few miles down the hill. He was a fly-half, too. And had played for Wales. His name was Carwyn James. At solitary practice sometimes on the rec, little Barry would field the balls for Carwyn. And on Saturdays, 'the whole village would go down to Stradey for the match. Can you imagine, Stradey full to bursting, hundreds of us boys on the "tanner bank" clustered together; it was our Mecca, total heaven. And of all of us, I had the bigger bond with Stradey, with the team, the "Scarlets" – because of Carwyn. Because Carwyn called me "Barry" and I called him "Carwyn". Oh, that lovely bond, that almost blood relationship . . . And in time, I got to standing by myself, just concentrating on Carwyn's play, making little sort-of binoculars with my thumb and forefinger and my hands . . .

'I think for anybody learning it is crucial to watch good players in action, and watching them in a particular way. Even if it is the best player in your village, that will do. I made a point of going to Stradey as often as I could to see Carwyn himself in action. The first time I kept my eyes on him for the first ten minutes of the match: I didn't follow the ball, I followed him, trying to keep up with his thinking and see what he did when he was off the ball. In the next match I covered a different ten-minute period in the same way, so that after a number of matches I knew his games very well, his defensive moves, his counterplay. When you think about it, any one player does not touch the ball much during a match; what he does when he is not in possession is at least as important as what he does when he has the ball.'

And in time, as the gods had obviously long decreed, John succeeded to Stradey's scarlet mantle. And, by Jove, what rugby they were playing, too. In 1966 Australia toured. Early on, they played Llanelli at Stradey. (It was as filthy a day as poor Earle Kirton's had been, further east, at Newport, three years earlier.) John was twenty-one, a student at Trinity College, Carmarthen.

I have just replayed a murky videotape, black-and-white, fuzzy little monochrome figures flittering in the gloaming. The once and former crown prince, Cliff Morgan, was at the commentary microphone:

'. . . This is Barry John again . . . going for the break . . . oh, no . . . can't make it this time . . . yes, he can . . . he's broken one tackle . . . he's broken two . . . he's inside again . . . is he clear? . . . ten yards to go . . . can he get there? . . .what a try!'

On the following Sunday, the old maestro centre (outside them all from Jones to Morgan), Bleddyn Williams, now a journalist, wrote in *The People*: 'A new fly-half star has been born in Wales . . . He reminds me of Willie Davies of Swansea, whose acceleration through the gap made him a pleasure to play with and most difficult to mark.'

So the great Willie – Tanner's cousin – just nudges the freeze-frame again . . .

When Australia arrived back in Wales in December for the Test, John was in. The first telegram of good wishes he opened at college next morning (with a raging hangover: 'there had been the night before, if I may understate, the

167

most almighty celebration') was from the incumbent in the shirt. It said: 'HEARTIEST CONGRATULATIONS, DAVID WATKINS'. Soon, Dai Watkins of Newport, unquestionably one of the sacred line from the James boys and Bush, was to leave Wales for Salford and a memorably resplendent and long career in Rugby League.

'I played so-so in that first international.' (Morgan, in his column, wrote, 'John had a grand first match and looked as though he might run through the Australians at any time.') For the first match of the following season, the selectors partnered him for the first time with Gareth Edwards. What did Pat Taffe say when he first met Arkle? Or Hutton when he first spoke to Washbrook? Or Miller's first 'howdy' to Lindwall? Or Coke's to Cola?

'Gareth phoned me at college and said we'd better have a workout. He said he'd come over to Carmarthen, to the Ystrad playing fields at Johnstown. It was a fearful Sunday morning, freezing rain pelting. Gareth was there. Zippy, zappy, you know, rarin' to go in his smart new-fangled tracksuit and polished boots. Handsome is as handsome does, you know, bless him. I'd not long met Jan [his wife] and we'd been out at a Saturday night party. I was dying for more kip, I was more rumpled than even my "top" and my frayed jeans; my plimsolls were covered in caked mud. Gareth started throwing passes at me. I kept slipping over in the mud and praying to be back in that lovely warm bed. Why not call it a day? We were both speaking only in Welsh, so I thought "that's good enough for me, we're going to be perfect partners".'

Then came one of all sport's most celebrated passages of dialogue.

'With the sleet and rain running off my nose I said: "Look, Gareth, you throw them – I'll catch them. Let's leave it at that and go home." Gareth looked very irritated by this. It must have seemed I was a "playboy, couldn't care less" (which is actually what I felt like – sorry).

'"Don't worry about my passes," said Gareth. "I can get them to you from anywhere. Just make sure you catch them, that's all."

'Then he grinned: "You're as confident and big-headed as I am." We both burst out laughing.'

The partnership, and unending friendship, had been forged. Barry goes on: 'The Welsh-speaking was it. His dad was a miner, so was mine. Inside that first minute of aggro we were already communicating in cultural short-hand – as we continued to do on the rugby field right up to the last game we played with each other. It wasn't like just being in the same rugby team, much more "binding" than that really, more like being shoulder to shoulder with the Welsh bowmen at Agincourt and looking to cop it. You know, "I'd die for you, and you'd die for me." Simply, we wanted to play for each other. Therefore one's prime motivation was to make sure each one helped each other.

'Gareth was unbelievably strong. But supple-strong. He was dedicated. He was an inborn gymnast, a human "monkey". If the elasticity of his body was at full, totally extended stretch, he could still find, with that final, extra twitch-flick of his wrists and fingers, that extra yard on the pass to get you wide and clear.

'Gareth was everything any fly-half could wish for. Why I also loved him was because, till the very end, he worked at it. He was famous beyond belief by then, but from that first day we met – and by now I'd long packed up – he still never ran away from any criticism, and he always worked to put right what he knew he should. He always knew that, if truth be known, on the first day we met on the Ystrad fields, he had the worst pass going. *It was terrible.*'

Barry John bursts into chortles at his remembrance. 'Don't tell Gareth that' – he sniggers on, then straightens his face – 'the truth is that in next to no time, Gareth had the best pass any fly-half could ask for: I should know.'

Where Barry himself moved like a self-regulating pendulum, Edwards brought to scrum-half play, noted the authors of *Fields of Praise*, 'the pent-up, explosive star-burst that Cliff Jones and Cliff Morgan brought to fly-half running'.

The best game Barry John ever played in was the one where Wales confirmed the Grand Slam in 1971. 'In any sport it is not often you get two really talented sides gloriously on song for fully eighty minutes on the very same day. We knew we were up against it. I remember sitting in the changing room at the old stadium in Colombes and being really uneasy. Quite unlike me, although we knew it was the crunch decider all right. Crunch being operative, because these French boys were really something, and as hard as iron with it. As I began to change, still somehow pessimistic, I started to look around that damp and legendary old room; and slowly, I remember, a positive truth dawned on me. There's Gareth pacing up and down, keen for the kick-off and relishing the minutes ticking away; look, there's Gerald, all set to out-dazzle the French: and Mervyn, immense and calm; Bevan and Sid Dawes; JT and Dai Morris. Hey, they're on my side. So is that nut JPR – with him the French should be truly worried, because I know if I don't give him the ball he'll thump *me* . . . hey, all these boys are pulling on red shirts, and I'm putting on a red shirt, so what am I getting all nervous about? It's those French fellows in the next room who should be quaking . . . hey, let's get out there.'

It was a tumultuous collision, and a voluptuous one. Power and glory. Passion and pride. 'The French that day were superb. Wales were superb. When France attacked, Lux was going this way and that, Bertranne all over the shop, Villepreux chipping here, there and everywhere, Berot the fly-half doing daft things, the Spanghero brothers smashing through the middle . . . it was crazy, beautiful, great rugby. We defended, tackled everything – even me, believe it if you dare, when that rock-hard Dauga rolled on me at the corner-flag and broke my nose. I was back on in no time . . .

'Then we started to play a bit . . . Gareth was getting stuck in everywhere, JPR began tearing back at them, and Gerald going like the clappers . . . Back and forth . . . it was the most perfect game of rugby . . . skill and honesty and sportsmanship; muscle, blood and bone, and flights of fantasy . . . the lot.'

It was settled, at the last, by Barry John, lightest and

slightest man on the field. There was a set scrum just out-side France's twenty-five, midfield-right. Young, the hooker, struck against the head. Edwards spun to John, going left, who intuitively sensed Berot (expecting a French heel) was a yard off the pace. John ran straight at the inside-centre, Bertranne, who bought the shimmy of a dummy to Dawes. An imperceptible change of gear did for full-back Villepreux and, in spite of Berot's lightning recovery, Barry was over, halfway between posts and corner. The Grand Slam was won. 'I felt Berot's fingernails running down my back as I crossed the line . . . it was the most important try of my life.'

In the victors' changing-room afterwards, Barry kept repeating, 'It was not my try, it was Jeff Young's over there who won the ball against the head. Once he'd done that, the rest was the easy bit.' Shades of Richard Sharp hooraying his hooker, Stan.

Next stop, New Zealand with the British Lions, who had never won there in the century. They were to be coached by Carwyn James, beloved mentor from across the little scrubland park at Cefneithin. It was, of course, John's second Lions tour. He had gone to South Africa, still a tyro, in 1968; but in the first Test at that great, seething, high-raked amphitheatre in Pretoria, within a few minutes of the start, Gareth fed him and he was through a gap and almost clear when the Springbok flanker, Jan Ellis, just managed to grab the collar of his jersey and hurl him down. He fell badly on the concrete 'turf' and crack! his collarbone was snapped. He played no further part in the tour. It was an accident, but rec-ollections of Richard Sharp were all too easy to summon.

Now in New Zealand three years later, this already rarest of blooms was to burgeon almost to perfection. A clamorous series was won by the British for the first time in the century, and the capstan around which revolved the whole Brit and Irish multinational (a granite-hard, in-ventive and disciplined pack, and flamboyant but unforgiving outsides – the great Gibson, in saluting defer-ence, was at centre) was John and Edwards at half-back.

At training, John and Edwards were allowed to slope off and pootle about playing soccer together. The rest of the team did not mind. (Was James, perhaps, the last leading rugby coach to realize the dangers of utter boredom in training sessions? Also, as Carwyn told me once, 'Twickenham might not like it, but the transfer of skills from one ball game to another is something that should always occupy the mind of a responsible coach': shades of Barry as the self-confessed frustrated inside-forward.)

Barry, running in tries but also taking the kicks now with his soft, slippered and unerring instep, in no time approached the hall-of-fame points record for a New Zealand tour, set by Gerry Brand, the Springbok full-back whose 100 points in the South African tour in 1937 had seemed at the time, they said, unbeatable.

On 6 July, between the first and second Tests, the Lions came to Wellington to play the rated New Zealand Universities side. Barry had played in seven games so far, but in this, his eighth, he needed only six points to equal Brand's mark. Within twenty minutes he had kicked two penalty goals to equal it, then cast around (one can only presume) in his subconscious for something suitable to festoon in colourful gift-wrapping the record itself.

Now it so happened that 'the subconscious' was, you might say, on Barry's mind that day. The night before, after supper John had fallen into a 'nice, deep-rooted philosophical discussion and disputation' with Carwyn and that grand and deep-thinking Irish prop-forward Ray McLoughlin, who was defending his insistence (and probably his position at the sharp, business end of the scrum) that in sport, taking ball-playing skills, balance and fitness for granted, then down-to-earth pragmatism and technical and mechanical excellence were all that was required – and only inside those parameters, plus the unknown variables of luck, bounce and rub-of-green, were some men winners, some losers.

As Barry listened, intrigued, Carwyn begged to differ with Ray – sport, he said, was made up of all those things the Irishman had listed; but then there could be more, much more – in seemingly straightforward rugby, too, as well as possibly more obviously cerebral sports and pastimes. 'Instinct, intuition, call it what you like, and a player can be nervous in the extreme at the precise moment, or ice cold and calculating, but suddenly, unpractised, an almost "accidental profundity" can invade his mind in a split-atom fraction of a second and he will do something he had never thought himself capable of had he planned it for a century.'

That, insisted Carwyn in his turn, was what helped transcend sport to an art form. 'That's what makes one actor, say, or one piece of journalism, or one spouting politician seem streets ahead of the other who has just as much, even more, technical and well-coached ability – *spiritual, subconscious, transcendental, unknowing-where-it-came-from ruddy instinctive intuition.*'

Look at Muhammed Ali, the boxer, said Carwyn, 'he trains for all *conscious* eventualities, sure, but his greatest moments are when his *instinct* takes over, and afterwards he cannot remotely explain why he did what he did; all he knows is he's won dramatically.' In a way, he did what he did so conclusively just because 'the spirit was with him'. Did Ted Dexter walk out at Lord's a few years ago knowing he was going to take on the deadly West Indian fast bowlers Hall and Griffith and scatter them to all points? It wasn't a *plan*. It wasn't pre-determined; the state of the game needed, if anything, a long and sober innings. But suddenly the spirit, the unnamed force, the 'adrenalin' got hold of him, and he had laid them to waste in half an hour. Did Richard Sharp know that try might be 'on' against Scotland before the scrum-half gave him the ball at Twickenham that day? Had he planned those three dummies as he caught the ball, or even one of them? Of course he hadn't. It was beyond his sphere of experience – till the moment it happened. 'Even more than the Scots defenders, in a way, did Richard Sharp *not* quite know what was going to happen next,' says Carwyn.

And so on and so forth, into a pleasant New Zealand night. Ray was not wholly convinced. Barry saw what

Carwyn meant, and after another G-and-T or two they all went off to bed.

Next afternoon, Barry in no time kicked his two penalties to level Brand's record. Nothing so mundane as another penalty to break it, surely? After about half an hour, there was a set-scrum, midfield, on the Universities' twenty-five. The Lions heeled. The reserve scrum-half, the popular Chico Hopkins, shovelled it out to Barry, who caught the ball, stood stock still for a split second, then feinted to drop for goal – the obvious thing.

The loose forwards moved in desperately to charge down the 'pot'. Instead, John glided outside their desperate lunge by an inch or two and made as if to link up with his centres, Dawes and Gibson. He 'showed' the next defender the ball, which gave him that split second to come strongly off his left foot and leave the fellow crash-tackling thin air. Every man-jack of the cover was now either on his heels or on precisely the wrong foot, and as four or five of them screeched either to stop, turn or alter gear, like floundering and cursing cartoon cats, John tip-toed delicately through each of these hair-tearing tulips to pop the ball down over the line.

The *Sunday Telegraph* rugby correspondent, John Reason, who had seen no end of 'special' tries in his long experience, told his readers the following weekend how every man on either team – not only the mesmerized defenders, who had been turned to stone – had been as transfixed in wonder as the crowd: 'The try on Tuesday left the crowd at Athletic Park absolutely dumbfounded. John had touched the ball down between the posts and was trotting back to take the conversion himself before the realisation of what had happened sent the applause crashing round the ground. John confessed afterwards that he thought there must have been an infringement. "I thought Chico must have put the ball in crooked, or something," he said, "I couldn't understand why the crowd was so quiet."'

Many years later, the moment was still vivid for its perpetrator – for he remembered particularly the conversation with Carwyn and Ray the night before. 'Looking back, I know that try owes a lot to that first feint to drop a goal. To this day I don't know why I didn't go for it, I had enough room to pop it over. But from then on I could just "sense intuitively" that not one of the opposition around or ahead of me was balanced and sort-of "ready" for me. So I just continued on – outside one, inside the other – all the way to the posts. I know it's funny, but it was all as if I was in a dream, that I had "placed" the defenders exactly where I wanted them, like poles in the garden to practise swerving. I don't know what you call it? "Transcendental"? "Metaphysical"? I don't really know the exact definition of those words, but it was just marvellously weird, like I was down there re-enacting the slow-motion replay before the actuality itself had happened. As if I was in a dreamy state of "déjà vu", that I was in a game, and doing something that had already taken place at another time.'

Perhaps it had – the night before in the bar – and Barry recalls that as soon as he had dapped the ball down over the line, up in the grandstand at the windy Athletic Ground, Ray McLoughlin, who was a few seats away from Carwyn James, had stayed standing till Carwyn caught his eye. And when he did, he waved acknowledgement to the coach that, okay, he did now fully understand what he had been unable to grasp the night before.

Whether they witnessed that try or not, fully ten years after it the authors of *Fields of Praise*, in their triumphant panegyric to John and the deft, poised, fragile illusion of his running, memorably conjured again the image of that day in Wellington by describing him as 'the dragonfly on the anvil of destruction, who ran in another dimension of time and space'. And fully twenty years after it, Barry over-dined, and certainly over-wined, me in his favourite Chinese restaurant in Cardiff's Tiger Bay. Even well into the happy night, he was still eerily crystal-clear about the day in New Zealand when he scored his try 'in another time, another place' to prove Carwyn's point about a sportsman's instinct and intuition.

I wonder how the experience of such an 'ultimate' vision subconsciously helped John's decision to retire. For within nine months he had gone. Just like that, at the age of twenty-seven and at the height of his sublime powers, as well as the adulation that went with it.

The latter it was that did for him. Wales, that season of 1971–2, had gloriously won three matches, against England, Scotland and France to the tune of 67–21. John kicked four goals against France at the Arms Park, pulled off his red shirt – and that was that: 'I had been up to north Wales where they had asked me to help "open" the extension to a bank. It is difficult to explain, but I felt detached, distant somehow, not part of the society of my own folk. The feeling had been getting stronger from the day we got back from New Zealand in the summer. There were a lot of people at the bank, nice people. But I felt totally alienated. They clapped me. Such well-meaning warmth had become a barrier. I was introduced to the girls who worked in the bank – and, do you know, the head cashier, who was sort of shaking with excitement, well, she curtsied to me. Curtsied. Everyone thought it was funny – but I was suddenly very, very upset. It was confirmation of my total alienation from real life. I drove home thinking I may as well be their puppet, their mascot, their rag-doll. I said to myself "That's it, finish: in future I am going to be *me* again, the real me, with all my faults and weaknesses, and my few plusses" ... and I got home and said to Jan, "That's it, love, the end."'

11

Hopscotch, hot Irish and panache

End it was. All hail and farewell one of the by-products of Barry John's brief but resplendent reign was that, in also chorusing him as 'king', the New Zealanders – mightiest rugby nation down the century – were inspired by the Welshman's exploits on their own paddocks to fill the blatant gap in their armoury to which they had for so long turned a blind eye. The fly-half, pure and simple: the out-and-out No. 10. The notorious All Black 'rover' maverick had been outlawed and officially told to go no more a-roamin' by the whole game in the 1930s; now, to be brutally frank, the homegrown, folksy five-eighths were coming under self-examination. Because of New Zealand's relentless string of successes, when it came to pure fly-half play as everyone else knew it, well, perhaps, like S. F. Barnes and his googly (and Dr Kyle with his drop-kick), the All Blacks simply 'hadn't needed one'.

In the 1920s, Mark Nicholls had all the attributes, and more, of the classic fly-half of legend – and his utter brilliance on the 1928 tour to South Africa, by all accounts, made a complete twerp of Bennie Osler and his one-track kicking. Right up to the 1960s, and Mac Herewini and Earle Kirton, there was the feeling that New Zealand were on the brink of producing a stable of classic outside-halves. But, with the forward juggernaut the 'supreme being', the variation remained writ in the tablets to shovel the ball, when it came, out for the centres to bore holes like craters in midfield and then release to either of two flying wings. Of the 'half-backs', the scrum-half was inevitably the senior partner – Kenny Briscoe, Laidlaw and the rubbery, but cricket-ball hard, bundle of brilliance, the Maori Sid Going.

One 'natural fly' of sheer delight, Bob Burgess, was at No. 10, opposite Barry John, when he scored his try at Wellington against the Universities (Burgess recalled it later: 'a shrug of his shoulders and a roll of his eye, and he spreadeagled us all on the ground: absolute, unqualified magic!'). Later, Burgess enchanted most of Britain with his skill on the 1972–3 All Black tour – blond locks flowing, coltish legs reminiscent of a Richard Sharp. But only occasionally: for the most part on that generally sombre, steamrolling trip, one felt Burgess was under orders to keep his singular talents under wraps and either kick or subordinate his class-act to his inside-partner Going's top-of-the-bill. Burgess was a bright man with a gift of friendship and is still remembered with a great deal of fraternal warmth by his British opponents. He was, they recognized, a brave one, too: even before he was capped by the All Blacks, he turned down the extreme rugby honour for a Kiwi and refused on moral grounds to tour South Africa. After his welcome but, for his part, un-fulfilled tour to Britain – I fancy he might have been a sensation had he joined a British or French club, as was soon to be the custom – Burgess settled down as a lecturer in botany at Massey University. He should know that European rugby still recalls him as a rare, if obviously endangered, bloom.

Burgess was, to all intents, followed at once by another singular craftsman at five-eighths in the All Black shirt – Duncan Robertson, not capped till he was twenty-seven, but full of the unexpected joys and ploys for a short time till the selectors, knowing All Black business to be serious business (and business is business), reverted to type and replaced him with the steadier, sober-sides Doug Bruce for an extended run. When I toured New Zealand with Ciaran Fitzgerald's Lions of 1983, the veteran journalist (and hero) Terry McLean sighed and confided:

'The importance of half-back pairing has never been truly appreciated in New Zealand rugby, and it is one of the grave and consistent weaknesses of our game. Look at the strengths of even our keenest rivals, the Springboks; look at their half-back partnerships against All Black teams in South Africa: in 1928, wispy Pierre de Villiers and Bennie Osler, in 1949, Fonnie du Toit and Hansie Brewis, in 1960, Lockyear and Oxlee, in 1970, Dawie de Villiers and Piet Visagie. Great players all, but, more important, great partnerships. In relation to South Africa, New Zealand has never had partnerships like these. The simple cause is the maddening New Zealand pre-occupation with the five-eighths formation, which was invented in Dunedin before the dawn of the twentieth century and which ought to have been interred donkey's years ago. The greatest teams, it could be claimed, are those which have been strongest in half-back partnerships.'

Or like, among others for another little country big on rugby, the interlocking James brothers, Owen and Bush, Tanner and Jones, Edwards and John . . .

Wales were remarkably lucky – and so were rugby's devotees the world over, come to that – to have Phil Bennett primed and ready to pull on John's shirt. Bennett had played for Wales, on and off, in a number of positions in the backs, either as one-off stopgap or replacement; he had been international rugby's first 'sub', replacing an injured Gerald Davies in 1969. And Gareth was waiting for him at the base of the scrum – for the Lions, too, where Bennett played with sureness, originality and no shortage of coruscating sparkle as Willie-John McBride's side laid the Springboks' veldt, high and low, to pillage and waste in 1974. The great scrum-half admits:

'When Barry went so suddenly, I felt I had lost my right arm. I even thought I should go as well, there and then. But I was two years younger, after all. So along came Phil. At first he had none of Barry's utter and instinctive, almost "lazily competitive" self-confidence – for Barry was a competitor, you know, never think that he wasn't. But Phil became utterly brilliant in his own way. A true all-time "great", absolutely no doubt about it. Funny, I ended up partnering Phil more times for Wales than I did Barry. By the end we had an implicit understanding and Phil was a sheer pleasure to play with – he could catch the worst rubbish you might have to throw at him, he could almost bewitch opponents with his footwork, and has there been a better cover-tackler ever to play fly-half?'

For a slight man, Bennett also had astonishing power with his right-footed kicking – from the ground but, particularly, with his punts. I can close my eyes now and see that great swingeing follow-through of his – standing upright, but his right boot finishing higher than his Celtic-black smear of hair, like the very best downstage hoofer at the Paris Folies.

He was from Felinfoel, a nondescript scrabble of a large village which brews the watery beer of the same name, and just down the high hill from Barry's Cefneithin on the road which drops on into Llanelli. The choice was 'coal or steel'. Phil's father chose the steelworks – the 'Klondyke', they called it. His mother worked at the local car-pressing plant. He was a sickly child, pasty-faced and off-sick and inevitably with a snivelly nose. But mad about sports. And a week's bright-red asterisk was Saturday when Dad, back from his night-shift labours in the furnaces, would have three boiled eggs for breakfast, take off his hobnails and overalls, bath, have a cat-nap . . . then, refreshed and glad at heart, walk the boy down to Stradey, to The Match. Hand in hand on the 'tanner bank' where, Uncle Thomas-John alongside, they would watch the Scarlets play.

One day, when the boy was nine, they took him down to St Helen's for the crunching death-or-glory annual against Swansea, and many years later, in a marvellously touching memoir he wrote with Martyn Williams, Phil recalled:

'The platform at Llanelli General was a sea of red caps, scarves, mufflers and cloth caps. It was a massive pilgrimage which had left villages and homes deserted of menfolk. St Helen's, I thought, could never accommodate this moving mass of miners, steelworkers, teachers, ministers and boys. They were all good-humoured; the bantering, the jokes, the bets, everything adding to the excitement of the afternoon.

'It was a Derby spectacular, hard, rough and uncompromising. Skirmishes on the field started fights on the terraces; the shouting and the noise was incredible and I kept tight hold of my father's jacket. Swansea were leading by 5–3 in the second half, with precious few minutes to go before the end. Suddenly Carwyn James at outside-half made a half-break and passed to his centre Denis Evans, who gave the ball to Goff Howells and by that time there was sufficient room for Goff to round his man in the corner and race for a try underneath the posts. St Helen's went mad! Hats, programmes, bags and newspapers were flung into the air. Some 5,000 Llanelli supporters had witnessed one of those Scarlet miracles.'

The fly-half who had manufactured that winning try for Llanelli was, of course, Carwyn James. If the tot Bennett was nine, it must have been 1958, the year Carwyn was capped for Wales.

So it was fifteen winters later, early in 1973, on a still, and ever will be, celebrated afternoon at Cardiff Arms Park that the names Bennett and James came together in tandem for world consumption (although, by then, Wales – certainly West Wales – knew the pairing of the coach James and the springheeled little fly-half had for some seasons lit dazzling flares for the club at Stradey Park).

Bennett had at once assumed John's mantle for Wales and played in the defeat by New Zealand at the start of the 1972–3 season and in the first match of the Five Nations, when England were well beaten. Bennett's performances in both games did not receive widespread acclamation. Compared to the man he succeeded, Phil was frankly a visible worrypot, much more introverted and obviously insecure about his place. His idolaters at Stradey – the home where he was warm and snug and comfy and, as a result, glistening daring week after week

181

– worried as much as he did whether he could take control in the genuine big time. A week after the match against England, there was staged the traditional farewell match for the tourists against the flamboyant scratch team, the Barbarians, at the Arms Park. Usually the thing is a fiesta, an exhibition, but this time – especially after a more than grumpy tour by the All Blacks – the Barbarians finale was invested with the title 'Fifth Test Carried Over', meaning that the tourists were looking at it as a 'revenge' game for the singular beating the Lions had given them on their own patch less than eighteen months before. Accordingly, the Barbarians picked up the gauntlet and picked a dozen of those Lions – and also, uniquely for the olde-tyme ethos of the club, allowed Carwyn James to have a hand in the pre-match 'coaching'. Bennett was picked as pivot and playmaker. He was very, very nervous. 'Well, I knew I would be out of it, estranged. It wouldn't have been too bad to be on the wing, but so evidently replacing Barry preyed on my mind. I couldn't even find the ground when we were called for training at Penarth.'

Before the start, James quietly said his 'few words' in the dressing room, particularly singling out the 'self-estranged' Bennett.

The ballads. The hymns. The presentations. The expectations. Of a sudden, the rafter-packed throng is momentarily silent – and then, as Bennett kicks off, it is to a great wall of presumptive sound . . .

There is that routine first exchange of push and shove, with the ball almost ignored as the two sets of forwards lock horns and flex muscles and spirits . . . a set scrum, another general affray, then a maul – and the All Blacks have it; the mighty captain, Ian Kirkpatrick, has wrestled it free and is in open ground, blindside going right towards the Westgate. A decent pass, making space, to his right-wing, the ripping Samoan Bryan Williams, who carves up the touchline, past halfway, then steeples up a perfectly angled diagonal kick towards the Baa-Baas' posts, over the cover defence. It lands, exactly midfield, on the twenty-five-yard line, and daps once, twice, invitingly towards the posts as the New Zealanders greedily pursue it en masse. The Barbarians have to turn, pronto. One minute into the grudge match, and this could be seriously dangerous . . . Bennett is first to spot the danger, and first to the difficult bobbler, midway between his posts and the twenty-five, knowing this furious wave of adrenalin-charged All Blacks are bearing down on his back, to be sure, can only be yards away . . .

He gathers the ball, and, as he turns – rather, in the very act of turning – he drives his right foot into the ground fiercely, which causes him to pirouette and face the enemy, one of whom is already there. No, he isn't, he's already done for with that first magical hopscotch step . . . But here's another . . . again a mesmerizing right-foot sidestep . . . and then, unbelievably, another . . . and another.

He is in the clear now, with room to bang the thing into touch and bow low at the wall of applause. But he doesn't. What had Carwyn told him before he went out? So, still inside his twenty-five, he passes to his full-back, the onliest J. P. R. Williams, a yard or two on his left . . .

And thus Phil Bennett, nervous, shy and presuming himself to be overawed in such company, announced himself to the wider world. The try which resulted from that voluptuous and bespoke bit of tailoring by Bennett has been reprised and enthused over more, far more, times than any other single incident in all rugby history. It was scored by Gareth Edwards; it co-starred Williams, John Pullin, John Dawes, Tom David and Derek Quinnell; but it was undoubtedly – and the full cast all agree – Conceived, Produced and Directed by Philip Bennett, of Felinfoel, on the Llanelli–Carmarthen road.

It was nice, too, that one Cliff Morgan, of Trebanog and the BBC, was in the television commentary box to relate the facts. This is what he said: '. . . Kirkpatrick . . . to Bryan Williams . . . this is great stuff . . . Phil Bennett covering . . . chased by Alistair Scown . . . brilliant . . . oh, that's brilliant . . . John Williams . . . Pullin . . . John Dawes, great dummy . . . David, Tom David, the halfway line . . . brilliant, by Quinnell . . . this is Gareth

Edwards . . . a dramatic start . . . WHAT A SCORE!'

To this day, and typically, Bennett himself plays down his part in that explosively memorable twelve-second passage: 'At the time I was intent only on getting out of trouble. I sensed they were right on top of me. Perhaps the whole beautiful, amazing thing wouldn't have happened if I hadn't heard Alistair Scown's menacing footsteps bearing down on me. As it was, it was a bit of a hospital pass I gave to JPR, wasn't it?'

John Williams chips in: 'Well, certainly I nearly lost my head as Bryan Williams lunged at me. But what utter brilliance by Phil. I remain convinced that the whole thing was really Carwyn James's try. Unique to the Barbarians, who disapproved of coaching, they asked him to give us a talk before the game.

'There was a lot of needle in the game; both us and the All Blacks were treating it as an unofficial fifth Test decider after we [the Lions] had beaten them, coached by Carwyn, eighteen months before. Now, before we went out, Carwyn soothed us, calming and relaxed, told us to enjoy it; and I'll never forget his last words, to insist to Phil, who was full of trepidation, hadn't played long for Wales and certainly not for the Lions, to go out and play just like he did for Llanelli – every Saturday – "You're not in the shadows any more, Phil *bach*, go and show the world what Stradey knows."'

Up in the press box, as the applause battered on, sat Carwyn James. He was silent, staring. He took a long, deep, satisfied pull on his Senior Service. He inhaled – and then, as he let the smoke waft out of his nose and mouth, a close observer could notice just a split second snake's-lick of a very private, very contented smile. In his weekly column in the following Friday's *Guardian*, he was to write of the moment, 'rare and unforgettable, when you can play at a level outside the conscious; when everything is instinct, but as clear as a bell because you have practised it so often and, especially, dreamed it – that unique moment when sport, lovely sport, not only achieves, but assumes, an art form.'

And not far away from Carwyn, also a journalist now, sat Barry John – and I daresay the passage down there had inspired him to recall again a night in Wellington with his coach and the stubborn, soon converted, old realist, Ray McLoughlin.

The wider world, having been so dramatically converted to Bennett with that one blinding coruscation of his (which set the Barbarians on to victory in a palpitating match of thrilling excellence), took him to their hearts for the remainder of a luminous career which ended with the captaincy of Wales, as they continued their triumphant parade, and of the British Lions (less happily, for his, and his team's, homesickness was all too apparent on the generally sulky tour to a waterlogged New Zealand in 1977). In that year he had scored a quite scintillating try against Scotland at Murrayfield to clinch a record Triple Crown for Wales – another series of crackerjack sidesteps – although his own favourite score remains the beauty for the Lions in the 1974 Pretoria Test, another solo thing made in heaven and fashioned at Stradey, when he showed the Springboks, Gerald Bosch and Ian McCallum the way to go home.

In this pageant of hall-of-famers, Bennett was a superduper star all right. Not, mind you, that Phil cares a fig still for any reputation he might have, or have not, in rugby's global terms. As long as his stock, and the warm memory of his deeds, remains high in the little land west of Offa's Dyke and east of St David's Bay. No problem there – so that's all that matters to him. Instance this speech of his, made in the dressing room in the dungeons below Twickenham, before the fellows in red clattered out to give the English another – well – clattering:

'Look at what these English have done to Wales. They've taken our coal, our water, our steel, they buy our houses and they only live in them a fortnight every twelve months. What have they given us . . . absolutely nothing. We've been exploited, raped, controlled and punished by the English, and that's who you are playing against this afternoon. Come on, Gar, look at what they're doing to your fishing, buying up the rights all over the place for fat directors with big wallets. Those are your rivers, Gareth, yours and mine, not theirs.'

Bennett inhabits the radio commentary box these days, not the scribblers' desk. I last saw Phil, touchingly, back at his beloved Llanelli in the late 1980s. I was there to report on the first match for the Scarlets being played by yet another custom-built fly-half from Max Boyce's underground conveyor-belt. Jonathan Davies, latest *Wunderkind*, had moved down from Neath. Towards the end of the match, as a raging arc light of the crescent moon beamed down heralding the keenest frost of the winter so far, I warmed up by ambling round the perimeter fence of Stradey. On the west-end corner, huddled against the corrugated iron in his anorak, with his arms round his son's shoulders, stood, unrecognized and still whey-faced and worried-looking, the hero Phil Bennett, the earlier scarlet jinker who had created the winds and the sun.

With Barry John watching from the press box, the new boy in the red shirt, with just the teeniest stutter of foot-work, sent a big wing-forward the wrong way, and plonkingly found a long touch. Phil looked satisfied. It even looked, in the cold, that he might have been purring. At any rate, for sure, the legendary line looked like continuing.

So it did, for rugby as a whole – and bloomingly. But not for Rugby Union. Despairing of the bickering back-biters in the Welsh Union's committee rooms, Davies soon took his sumptuous talents 'north', to Widnes. All he wanted, he said, was a modicum of respect, an occasional 'thanks' or 'well played' from the management, and 'a little bit in return for the talent God gave me – like a doctor or a lawyer uses his skills to buy a little security for his family. All I get from the Welsh RU is 13p a mile for driving sixty miles to training practice.'

The same discontent with the Welsh game's politicos (both track-suited and pin-striped) and the hopeless antics of more than a few alikadoos had affected Bennett's immediate successor, Gareth Davies, another made from the genuine mould of fly-halves – not so restless and shimmyingly neurotic an original genius as Phil or Jonathan, but handsomely clean-cut at every single aspect of his game, which he never failed to play on Quality Street. He too packed up in despair, not to go north but to end up as an executive with the BBC.

Many years later, in 1993, with Welsh rugby fortunes – *sans* fly-half, *sans* teeth – still in a slump, Davies was stung to write to the *Daily Telegraph* disabusing a current Welsh fly-half who had published a sigh that the man in the No. 10 shirt was now no more playmaker and conjuror, but anonymous, faceless courier. Wrote Gareth:

'The boy who can handle, pass and kick naturally is a prime candidate for the No. 10 jersey. With these attributes, it is reckoned he is equipped to be the most dominant player in the side – a decision-maker. I believe that unless these skills are inherent, naturally part of the youngster's game, there is little chance of his succeeding at the highest level.

'Needless to say, I was surprised to hear Adrian Davies, the Cardiff and former Cambridge University fly-half, proclaim that the modern game had developed and changed so much that the fly-half of today is a link, and only an integral part of the team. He also went on to say that pre-match preparation by the whole team, and not dominant individuals, was the main constituent of today's successful sides.

'Apologies, Adrian, but bunkum! And I think he is fully aware of that, for his strength is his tactical awareness and his ability to dominate proceedings on the field. Any fly-half of quality will have more than a modicum of self-belief and confidence, and will want to dictate matters.'

Percy Bush, the 'great dictator', would have trumpeted 'aye' to that.

Gareth Davies was a fine fly-half, but unfulfilled enough to be remembered as no more than a passing (and kicking) angel in this litany of saints. But he was a British

Lion, picked for the injury-wracked, losing and contro-versial tour of South Africa in 1980 – to share the No. 10 jersey or, rather, contest the Test place with a pale, slight sprite of an Irishman, who could kick like a dream, pass with the exquisite certainty of a dunce on *Mastermind*, and tackle with a conclusive finality and scarcely a blink men three times as big as himself. Certainly Seamus Oliver Campbell remains high in the pantheon which these pages acclaim. In the event, neither Campbell nor Davies was able to do himself full justice on that tour to the Republic, well and generously captained by the English forward and totem Bill Beaumont. A shoulder injury meant that Davies played in only four matches; Campbell missed eight of the first nine games with hamstring trouble, having already only got into the tour very much on the back foot, and a limping one at that.

Which two accidents to the chosen fly-halves happened to plonk a nice tin lid on what had been a long-running, intriguing and very Irish o'tale. For when Beaumont's management sent an SOS for a replacement, pronto, they asked for one Anthony Joseph Patrick Ward. Another true great. But whether greater than his friend Ollie, Ireland will never really know . . .

As they say in the serials, *The Story So Far* . . .

Through the 1970s, Ireland had found themselves with, if not by any means magical, more than satisfactory piv-otal duties being done by the long-serving Barry McGann, a decently confident and 'comfy' fly-half with a rotund girth on him and (in spite of boasting that his only tactical 'numbers-calling' to assist his own line and confuse the opposition's was that when he shouted 'outside' he meant 'inside') an innate footballer's brain in him. Barry also had the very devil of a canny kick on him – long, short and medium. Then Mick Quinn had more than a few games, working to roughly the same priorities – get the ball to Gibson as speedily as possible (that erstwhile great 'fly' was, of course, an almost permanent fixture in the centre now or, if not and criminally, on the wing).

And thus Ireland would go on. So they presumed. Till,

out of the blue, they somewhere and somehow unearthed a rare gem. He was a squat, square fearless fellow, with a fly-half's 'Russian-doll' thighs made in heaven for the job; and he had a precocious footballing nous which already seemed as sharp as even McGann's. The reason why no-one in the Dublin rugby establishment had heard of Ward till he burst upon them like a firework was that, although born and schooled in Dublin, he had been in the Irish Schools soccer XI (left-wing outside Liam Brady, no less), and after leaving St Mary's he spent two years while at PE college playing as an amateur for, among others, Shamrock Rovers and Galway City, for the latter in the topmost class of the European Cup.

The carefree gypsy in him, perhaps, turned him back to his rugby. He was such an immediate wow with Munster's lovely Garryowen club that he sailed through the Irish trials for the 1978 international season so swimmingly that they had to put him in for the opening match against Scotland at Lansdowne Road. Well before teatime that day, the old wooden place was jumping. Ward single-handedly beat the Scots, scoring all the points and popping such a nonchalant fizz all round that he looked as if he had been at it for years. Certainly the twenty-three-year-old looked as if he would be wearing the green and organizing the gleam for seasons to come.

Which he did. Well, for two seasons. In 1978 and 1979 he broke records, played like a honey generally, and was each year voted the Five Nations Championship's European Player of the Year. It was heady stuff, and the whole rugby world relished and savoured the articulate and classless young man's huge success, and hugged them-selves in delight with his play. During that first explosive season of Ward's, a friend of mine, the writer John Hopkins, was preparing a diverting textbook on rugby (at last) and thought to ask young Ward to contribute a note on fly-half play. The 'article' was duly delivered. A 'note'? It ran to well over 2,000 words. Adrian Stoop could not have bettered it. Shades, too, of that conversation long before between those two monarchs, Barry John and

189

Mike Gibson, on their way to New Zealand in 1971 – and the very definition of the fly-half of legend. Ward's piece for Hopkins began:

'I don't know whether it's because I'm involved in the position but to me the whole game of rugby revolves around the stand-off. I think he has got to be the kingpin. He's a little field marshal out there. You know you can usually pick out a scrum-half easily. He tends to be jaunty, small, talkative. From meeting a stand-off before a game I'd say that as a race, we have no similar identification mark. But the second a team walk on to a pitch I think you can pick out the stand-off very easily, even if he hasn't got a number on his back. He tends to be the footballer and for some reason to dress and look the part. That is my impression anyway. And he always calls the moves even if one of the centres or wings is captain. Except when I first started playing senior football I have always called the moves. It's a responsibility you must take from the start. He is in the unique position of being able to see everything that happens on the field, from the forwards and the backs.'

In the 1979 Five Nations season, his second, Tony was voted 'man of the match' in three of the four games (in which he clocked up 33 points). Midst all the adulation, I remembered just one squeak of criticism when, at the end of a pulsating drawn match against France, a moment of hesitation caused him to fail with a drop goal which would have given Ireland the championship. That summer, Ireland toured Australia, whose sporting press welcomed Ward as if he was a Hollywood beefcake hero. In his first match in Canberra, Ward obliged them with 19 points, an all-time record for any Irish player in a match. The following week he played a brilliant game as Ireland beat New South Wales. In the team coach on the way to the first Test Match in Brisbane, he was composing his thoughts – 'I know I perhaps didn't look nervous on the field, but in fact I would get very tense till we kicked off' – about the rigorous afternoon to come. 'I was in the back of the bus and Pat Whelan said, "Prepare yourself, Tony."

I said, "I don't believe you." When we got out of the bus Noel Murphy, the coach, said "Tony, you're out." And all I could say was once again, "I don't believe you."'

He would, he was told, when he saw Ollie (Campbell, the 'reserve' fly-half) lining up the first kick. The Australian press went wild. The Irish press went wilder. And Tony, shattered, demanded a meeting with Murphy to ask what he had been doing wrong. Was it his kicking? Or his breaking? Or what? No answer was given – he was dropped and that was that. Ward rang his mother in Dublin and said he was leaving the team and coming home at once.

He was pleased that his mother and his friends in the team had talked him out of it. And he sat in the grandstand and watched Ollie Campbell equal Ward's newly set record of 19 points – the mischievous gods of coincidence could not have been more precisely taunting than that – in a record Irish international win (27–12). In the second, and last, Test Ollie scored all the nine points which ensured another victory – and the two fly-halves returned home to a jangling front-page furore all over Ireland in which their separate, different and outstanding fly-half play took a back seat as rancour overflowed about the Irish class system, the Leinster–Munster divide, the Dublin middle classes, the lot. And, true enough, the country was split down the middle over the considerable merits of Tony Ward and Ollie Campbell, two lovely young men, each with a lovely talent.

Point and counterpoint. There was even a front-page splash that a boast had been made in the Lansdowne club by a senior member of the rugby establishment, as long ago as the previous April, that Ward was going to get his come-uppance in Australia. Indeed, in Irish rugby, one correspondent wrote:

'The chances of Ward being dropped by an Irish selection committee in Ireland in the past two seasons were drastically slim as to be virtually inconceivable . . . to those of us who know Ward's capabilities well, a tour could only have meant him coming into his own much more. There is but one answer. Minds were made up before the second match of the tour, before the first, probably before the team left Dublin in May, possibly long before even that. And that perhaps represents a serious indictment of the people vested with tour selections . . .'

A couple of pages further on and you could find different flames being fanned when, while suggesting that Ireland might think of playing two five-eighths, the writer is quite definite that 'Campbell has it every way – speed, thrust – he can break either side and link up better with his outsides – resource, and superb kicking ability.'

And so it went on . . . The perceptive, questing Dublin journalist Eamon Dunphy, a former Ireland soccer player, probably summed up the poignant situation best when he wrote:

'Unlike most rugby heroes Ward has an image. This was cultivated when he emerged as a brilliant young player in the 70s. His dark Mediterranean good looks and his imaginative, shimmying game attracted the interest of the popular press and thus of ordinary people. He was soon the best-known rugby player in these islands. He went on English TV shows like *Superstar*, was photographed topless in the *Daily Mirror*; dammit, the man was behaving like a bloody soccer player.'

Dammit, now you come to think of it, the fellow *was* a bloody soccer player.

He was becoming the wrong kind of legend. That sort of thing was an affront to the rugby ethos. All right to get outrageously drunk, to bash down the odd hotel door, even, as one contemporary Irish legend did, to urinate on the banqueting floor while the after-dinner speeches were being delivered. Boys will be boys and are expected to be so, in private, you understand. But currying popularity with the masses is not our way, old boy.

A former president of the Irish RFU, in all seriousness, felt he had made the final and convincing point when he announced publicly that when Ward's provincial team, Munster, had toured London the year before and were

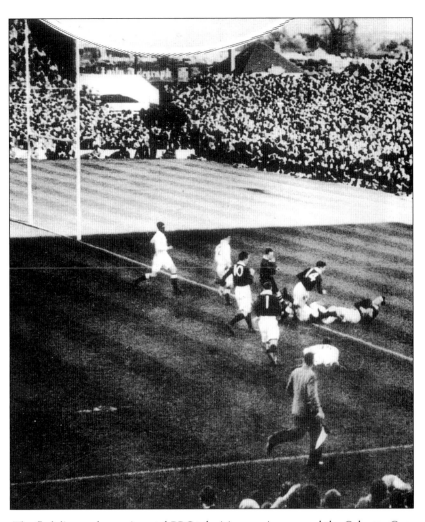

The fledgling and experimental BBC television service covered the Calcutta Cup match of 1938, won by Scotland 21–16. So this opening try of the match, by Scotland's wing, Renwick, was the first ever to be logged by television. England's full-back, Parker, spilt a Garryowen and Shaw (No.10) chipped ahead for Renwick to gather and flop over. This was, of course, 'Shaw's match'. Note, nostalgically, Twickenham's evocative South Bank, favourite 'Kop' for thousands till its replacement by a modern monstrosity before the 1991 World Cup. Also see how the West Stand shadows the turf, the spring sunshine gleaming on the field only beyond the posts. The *News Chronicle*'s broadcast critic excitedly referred to the picture quality on television which 'enabled watchers at home to clearly see the lines of the groundsman's mowing-machine on the pitch'. The Illustrated London News Picture Library

Cliff Jones and Haydn Tanner (*on ground*) in harness for the first time before taking on the All Blacks in 1935. *Seated, far left*, Vivian Jenkins, later journalist; *seated, second right*, Wilfred Wooller. Western Mail & Daily Echo

One of Dr Jack's 'few wee punts at the line' helps destroy England, by 22–0, at Dublin in 1947. Alpha/Sport & General Press Agency

In the Ireland dressing room, 1951…It was another championship for Kyle's men in green which, thanks to their 'subtle mix of runnin', jinkin' an' kickin',' worked out 'just fine'.

Hulton Getty

IRELAND V WALES, Dublin, March 4, 1978.

Tony Ward was in his pomp in this resounding scrap at Lansdowne Road, but all the craic from him was not enough to prevent Wales's victory by 20–16 which ensured a third successive Triple Crown, unique in history. It was Gerald Davies's Five Nations' farewell, and the penultimate match for the immortal half-back pairing of Bennett and Edwards. By now, another luminous No.10, Gibson, had been banished to Ireland's wing.

IRELAND

WALES

REFEREE
G. DOMERCQ (F.F.R.)

TOUCH JUDGES
P. BEATTY (I.R.F.U.)   F. PALMADE (F.F.R.)

		IRELAND				WALES	
FULL BACK	15	A. H. ENSOR WANDERERS	KICK OFF 3.00 p.m.	15	J. P. R. WILLIAMS BRIDGEND		FULL BACK
THREE QUARTERS	14	C. M. H. GIBSON N.I.F.C.	RIGHT WING	14	T. G. R. DAVIES CARDIFF		THREE QUARTERS
	13	A. R. McKIBBIN LONDON IRISH	RIGHT CENTRE	13	R. W. R. GRAVELL LLANELLI		
	12	P. P. McNAUGHTON GREYSTONES	LEFT CENTRE	12	S. P. FENWICK BRIDGEND		
	11	A. C. McLENNAN WANDERERS	LEFT WING	11	J. J. WILLIAMS LLANELLI		
HALF BACKS	10	A. J. P. WARD GARRYOWEN	OUT	10	P. BENNETT LLANELLI CAPTAIN		HALF BACKS
	9	J. J. MOLONEY ST. MARY'S COLLEGE CAPTAIN	SCRUM	9	G. O. EDWARDS CARDIFF		
FORWARDS	8	W. P. DUGGAN BLACKROCK COLLEGE		8	D. L. QUINNELL LLANELLI		FORWARDS
	7	J. F. SLATTERY BLACKROCK COLLEGE		7	T. J. COBNER PONTYPOOL		
	6	S. A. McKINNEY DUNGANNON		6	J. SQUIRE NEWPORT		
	5	H. W. STEELE BALLYMENA		5	G. A. D. WHEEL SWANSEA		
	4	M. I. KEANE LANSDOWNE		4	A. J. MARTIN ABERAVON		
	3	E. M. J. BYRNE BLACKROCK COLLEGE		3	G. PRICE PONTYPOOL		
	2	P. C. WHELAN GARRYOWEN		2	R. W. WINDSOR PONTYPOOL		
	1	P. A. ORR OLD WESLEY		1	A. G. FAULKNER PONTYPOOL		

MARCH 1878. 1978

NEW WEST
LOWER STAND
OPENED
March 4th 1978

LANSDOWNE ROAD

Cliff Morgan breaks, blindside, against South Africa at Cardiff in 1951. He was to punt ahead feebly and allow the Springboks' full-back Buchler yet another chance to counter-attack. 'My kicking that day cost Wales the game', admits Cliff still. The referee is 'Ham' Lambert, a vet who had played both rugby and cricket for Ireland in the 1930s. Western Mail & Daily Echo

The Springbok prop Augustus Koch collars Morgan in the Lions' Test against South Africa at Johannesburg in 1955. Later, Morgan's resplendent try was to settle the match – and an old score. Hulton Getty

Bev Risman's inspired blindside try secures victory, by 9–6, for the Lions in Auckland.

Hulton Getty

Richard Sharp is baulked by Brian Cresswell of Wales, but his lofted kick has already let slip England's marauders. Few can have made a more telling debutant's bow in international rugby than the Oxford undergraduate in 1960.

Alpha/Sport & General Press Agency

'Silly old me'…Sharp's unceremonious exit in Johannesburg, his cheekbone smashed by Roux's tackle. Popperfoto

The nonpareil Mike Gibson returns, briefly, as a fly-half – pursued by Wales at Cardiff in 1977. Colorsport

First season in tandem as Wales beat Scotland at Cardiff in 1968. Edwards (*on the ground*) has passed, John clears the line. 'You throw them, I'll catch them'.
Western Mail & Daily Echo

Ireland's Gibson (12) and Slattery (7) hesitate as their soon-to-be British Lions comrade John begins the dance which led to Wales's glorious 1971 Grand Slam. This was still Cardiff's romantic old Arms Park, with the ancient lamp-standards and the hymns in Welsh and *ex tempore*. John scored half Wales's points in this victory by 23–9. Alpha/Sport & General Press Agency

Carwyn James...
rugby's cerebral soul
and spirit – and, sure,
another Senior Service
and G-and-T, bach.

Colorsport

Light hidden under
botanist's bushel...Bob
Burgess scores against
Mid-Wales, 1972.

Colorsport

'Show the world what Stradey knows'... Such exhortations led to Phil Bennett telling it straight to his British Lions, Bay of Plenty, 1977.

Colorsport

Jonathan Davies, on the one hand, and Franck Mesnel, with two, during France's victory over Wales at Paris in 1987. Popperfoto/Bob Thomas Sports Photography

Ireland's Russian doll and 'little field marshal'. In this match against England at Twickenham in 1978, Tony Ward equalled the all-time Five Nations Championship record with 38 points. Colorsport

Ollie Campbell...humble genius and by far a better handler than record-breaking hoofer. And has any fly-half ever tackled more heroically?

Popperfoto/Bob Thomas Sports Photography

SCOTLAND V AUSTRALIA, Edinburgh, December 8, 1984. Mark Ella's glorious final fling for Australia when he orchestrated a 37–12 victory and a British Grand Slam for the tourists – after which he tossed across the golden No.10 shirt to the 21-year old apprentice Michael Lynagh who, in the centre that day, had nervelessly kicked 21 points in the Murrayfield gloaming.

Le bon génie de la Pampa… But this time Hugo Porta is bottled up by Terry Wright and his opposite number, Grant Fox, during Argentina's World Cup tie against the All Blacks in 1987.

Popperfoto/Bob Thomas Sports Photography

Rob Andrew can only gape in awe behind him as John Rutherford's try seals Scotland's 33–6 rout of England in 1986. The year before, Rob admits to being 'petrified' at marking Rutherford. Colorsport

Craig Chalmers passes the parcel safely in spite of Fergus Aherne's attentions in Scotland's defeat of Ireland in 1992. Allsport

The grandeur of the Slam. Rob Andrew on a high at Twickenham after England's thrilling 1991 victory over France. Colorsport

Stuart Barnes boldly buzzing for England 'B' – and waiting for his turn at the honeypot. Colorsport

'If us guys don't try anything, then what are we out there for? We've got to make things happen'…England's mesmerized centres, Lozowski (13) and Barley (12), can only sit on their heels and stare as Mark Ella's reverse flick sets up Roger Gould at Twickenham in 1984. Colorsport

Two Tens tangle, Wallaby and Barbarian…Michael Lynagh stops Jonathan Davies in his tracks. Popperfoto/Bob Thomas Sports Photography

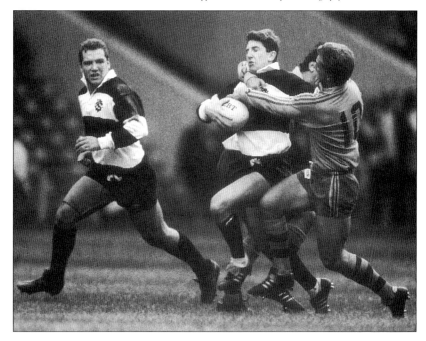

Michael Lynagh's match for immortality…in the World Cup epic in Dublin in 1991. Allsport

Lining it up like a golfer on the green, Grant Fox prepares to sink another side. Colorsport

A rare rugby picture…Jeff Squire must wonder what's coming next as Naas Botha presents a pass to his threequarters at last. Cape Town Test, South Africa 26, British Lions 22, May 1980. Colorsport

invited, on a day off, to watch London Irish play, Ward had declined firmly: 'How can you possibly ask me to watch London Irish play rugby on the same day Manchester United are playing Arsenal at Highbury?'

As the whole debate swirled on, gloriously out of hand, through the winter of 1979–80, young Seaumus Oliver, Dublin's Old Belvedere public schoolboy, kept his own counsel as well as his cool – and in a splendid season in the Five Nations he kicked a record for the whole long history of the tournament. His 46 points carried Ireland to an aggregate of 70, another record, and would have brought home the title but for a disallowed try at the end of a thrilling, fever-pitch defeat in Paris by just 18–19. Tony Ward sat in his sports shop in Limerick watching it all on television. What a waste; but what a rare jewel the Irish rugby establishment had discovered to replace him.

In twenty-two international matches, Campbell was to post a record 217 points on the scoreboard. In seventeen matches, Ward's tally was 98 (although when he did come back for three matches in 1981 – a disappointing experiment, with Campbell moving to centre to accommodate him – it was Campbell who continued to kick the goals).

But Campbell was more than a kicker. Much more. He had a myriad of virtues, concentration and patience packed in his locker, and possibly – as the game approaches the end of the century – only Rob Andrew and Michael Lynagh approach him for the fearlessness of his head-on tackling. Campbell's lassooing, corner-flagging defence, in the manner of Kyle and Morgan and Bennett, was also as thrilling as it was exemplary.

What Ollie did share with his friend and rival, Tony, was a delightful, soft charm, a complete lack of side or conceit, and a genuine generosity about the other's 'superior' talents – which is more than can be said for their supporters, who continued to split every taproom and lounge noisily down the middle by insisting on the overwhelmingly better skills of their particular favourite. Ward v. Campbell was, bejasus, Us v. Them. Campbell v. Ward was, begob, Them v. Us. On the nights the Irish selectors met, the supplicating devotional candles lit in churches round the land doubled and sometimes, so it was said, trebled. Were you an Ollie or a Tony man? I don't know about churches, but certainly the wrong answer could get you thrown out of pubs.

And, to be sure, the difference between the two of them was evident. Tony was the dark, beetle-browed Iberian-Celt of a fly-half, a Morgan or Bennett. Ollie was the other sort of Celt – pale and freckled complexion which goes red, not nutbrown, in the sun. Tony was the swarthy Russian-doll fly-half, as we have seen; Ollie was the vulnerable wraith who could, clickety-click, shorten or lengthen his stride to flit away from – or, when he wanted, get involved in – the hurly-burly. Like Jack Kyle, Campbell had a peppery head of hair. Those Irishmen of a certain generation who watched them both find it impossible to separate their genius at fly-half, one from the other.

Ollie's father, and namesake, was a prop-forward who had taken late to Union after being brought up, as all good Catholic boys should be, on 'the Gaelic'. He first took his son to rugby when he was six – and Dad was playing, at prop, in an Extra-C XV. At eight, Ollie went to Belvedere College (Tony O'Reilly's throwaway line, 'Us Belvedere boys are tops at everything, especially humility', less fits Campbell than anyone I know). In the garden, when the tot got home, or on holidays, Dad would teach him about tackling:

'"The smaller you are, the harder they fall," he'd say. I always remember him telling me to tackle low, to go in low, down by the knees preferably. I can remember doing that in the back garden time and time again, and I got to really enjoy tackling. It's not supposed to be something that fly-halves in general do – I must say it's something that I've never had much problem in doing and it's never really worried me. One of the things I get a great kick out of is making a good tackle, and that is the one single thing that I can remember learning from my dad.'

One late winter afternoon, midweek before an

international weekend, I strolled up to the Old Belvedere ground on Dublin's Anglesea Road. Ollie was practising. Solitary. He did not see me watching, admiring. He kept at it till the lights were winking warm in the city yonder. Kick, kick, kick. Fetch and carry, fetch and carry. Kick, kick, kick. Short ones, long ones, wide ones, narrow ones. Fetch and carry, fetch and carry. Kick, kick, kick. Punting ones, torpedo ones, considered ones and hasty ones. He ends up with one from the halfway line, soccer's centre circle. He claws the mud from studs. With care he lines up his right instep against the ball, his left foot forward and alongside. He looks down at the ball, then up to gauge the distance. The goalposts are far away in the murk. Then, neither hurried nor too cautious, one-two-three-four-five steps back; a little one-and-a-half chassé sideways and left. A glance at the ball, the posts, then back to the ball. Up to his tiptoes just once, then a rhythmic, slightly curving run, eyes down, and . . . woompf! The 'H' is perfectly bisected.

Campbell's kicking was so prodigious that people in high places were talking about changing the rules and the points system. It was not a fair game when Ollie was around. Although he had been a schoolboy fly-half since he was nine, he never kicked at goal – 'not even a twenty-five drop-out' – till he was seventeen. 'After that I got the taste – so started practising. I would work on all types of kicks, drop-kicking and on my punting as well. Diagonal kicking was my favourite and was the kick I employed perhaps eighty per cent of the time up to when I first got my cap. At that time it was the kick that most out-halves used, probably because of Barry John's influence. I felt later that it is a very difficult kick to master, and you have to hit the ball in exactly the right position. Wingers are so aware of it that they hang back for it, so unless it goes to ground it can turn out to be a very bad kick. The grubber is a kick which seems to have gone out of fashion – it's a lovely little kick to use in attack. The one danger of it is that if you don't run up far enough to your opposing fly-half and try it, the chances are that it's going to hit someone's legs and end up behind your centres rather than the opposition centres. So I think the secret of it is to go as far as you can and actually use your body as protection against your opposite number and just slide it through. Once it does get through, it's a very difficult ball to defend against.'

Ah, but enough of kicking, he would say – 'to be honest, I thought my passing was better than my kicking'. He did not for a moment mean it to be, but when he realized that might have sounded the tiniest bit boastful, Ollie blushed and looked embarrassed. Passing, sure; he also had the crucial fly-half's ability imperceptibly to shorten or lengthen his pit-a-pat stride. And he had a slip-fielder's safe hands. I remember that, at one of those marvellously enjoyable (alas, till 1993 days, all too rare) victory hooleys at the Shelbourne on a Saturday night after Ollie had kicked a hatful and also manufactured a couple of tries for others, his regular scrum-half, Robbie McGrath, explained how, at one scrum, they had agreed on signals for an attempted drop-goal by Ollie. In the event McGrath's pass squirted out at Campbell's bootlace; he was completely off balance and unready, yet he picked the thing off his toe, changed total direction and intent in one stride, and took off on a mazy, bewildering run that presented a try to Moss Finn.

When I recalled that fleeting passage to Ollie, fully a couple of years later (on the 1983 Lions tour to New Zealand, where, incidentally, his tackling was utterly heroic as the British Isles took another beating), again he blushed, not at a good memory but at the implied plaudit. Ned van Esbeck, doyen of the *Irish Times*, once explained how the boy had never sought to bargain with his talent: 'Ollie's a humble man. If he were locked up in a room or stuck in a lift with four other men for twenty-four hours they'd all come out of that room none the wiser as to who he was. They wouldn't even know he liked rugby football. His modesty is such that he wouldn't have even mentioned it.'

The British Lions' 1980 tour to South Africa was to be

the last to the Republic for a considerable span. The Lions were beaten convincingly enough in the Test rubber but unquestionably had the excuse of an injury list which at times reached almost ludicrous levels. As we have seen, Gareth Davies and Campbell, the two fly-halves, were injured at once; David Richards, the good, clever Swansea back, manfully held the breach, but as the first Test Match, at Cape Town, approached, Richards was going to be needed in the centre.

My first Lions Test Match was just as I had imagined. The humidity, the fervour, the yellow ball bobbling on the turf of green concrete, the passionate local team let out of their cage after being primed for months (in this case, years) on red meat. Just like I had seen on the newsreels over the years when snippets came back in Technicolor of Ronnie Thompson's side or Tommy Kiernan's or Willie John's.

The fierce contrast of light harshly splitting the pitch as the tropical sun drops fast behind the high raked grandstand. The pointilliste's dream backcloth of dotted face-pinks and shirty primary colours climbing steep from the opposite sun-burned touchline. The section in the shade for the nobs, where leathery-faced Afrikaaners, with defiant, fierce eyes and Goya's-Duke-of-Wellington noses, recline alongside beleaguered Empire Loyalists in old, low, wicker chairs to watch the game, binocular-case straps diagonally slashing across the old school ties of olde England or old Holland. They seem to ignore the long streaks of elegance beside them, the tanned-hide ladies in cool pastel frocks, with bright red nails like newly used daggers on the end of fingers that have never peeled a potato; they probably think Fairy Liquid is a poovy London drink. I saw scarcely one black face in the vast crowd.

But what is this? Who is this? The face is familiar; so is the gait, the tree-thick thighs, and the beetle-black eyebrows and hair. It looks for all the world as if the man in the Lions red marked No. 10 is Tony Ward himself. It is. Less than a week ago the fellow who thought he would

197

never again play for Ireland – let alone the British Isles – was sitting with his dog in a Limerick vet's waiting room when a journalist traced him via his sports shop. 'The Lions have sent an SOS – and they only want you,' he was told.

Now here he was, pulling on a red shirt at famous, infamous Newlands; then bandaging a badly bruised right leg with which he had not been able even to practise kicking for a month. The match was an heroic one: Ward saved the day, if not the match. The Springboks ran out at Newlands to the most mighty, frightening roar I can remember. For half an hour they made the Lions look old and mangy. They scored three tries in this time. Then, defiantly, the British, having dug in, started peeking over their barricades. Led by Ward, whose kicking was truly superb, they carefully whittled away at the South Africans' 16-point score. With ten minutes left it was, incredibly, 16–16. Two minutes later it was 19–16 to the Lions after Ward had dropped a glorious left-footed goal. The place was stunned. We beleaguered band of British press-box bods squeezed each other's thighs and shoulders and nearly dared not look. I do not think I had ever wanted my team to win so much – no, not even Gloucestershire to beat Middlesex in 1947, the first cricket match I ever saw at Cheltenham – as I willed the British Isles to hold out against the dreaded 'Boks.

It was not to be. To their credit, the South Africans rallied from the ropes. They scored a try, to lead 22–19, and, though the amazing Ward pegged them back to level terms again, in injury time the Springboks thrillingly clinched the deal. When the dust had settled there was an eerie stillness: we had witnessed one of the epic rugby matches of all time – and there was no denying that five tries to one was just deserts in any language, even Afrikaans. Tony Ward had scored eighteen points. Not in ninety years of British Lions history had any man scored more points in a Test Match. A week before he had been watching television in slate-grey, misty Munster.

If a combination of jealous Irish selectors and the

gem-like dazzling sharpness of Campbell's play had con-
trived to give Ward many fewer international caps than he
deserved, that palpitating afternoon in Cape Town – plus
more than a few famous ones back home in Limerick for
Munster – keeps the delightful man who loved his soccer
as well as his rugger enshrined in the lore of the
immortals.

On that 1980 tour to South Africa, we were also
honoured to watch a player who is even more of an all-
time hall-of-famer. In their infinite rugby wisdom, the
selectors of the South African Barbarians XV flew Hugo
Porta from the Argentine to play at fly-half against the
Lions on that lovely, wide, sea-fresh arena at King's Park
in Durban. He was a revelation; *it* was a revelation to any
soul uplifted by the creative arts and sciences of the
position. I remember reading the cable Carwyn James,
the visionary, sent back to the *Guardian*. It did not even
bother to start with the score (Barbarians 14, Lions 25) or
another stupendous show by Ward (a close-quarter try
which included three luminous, hopscotch side-steps and
16 points in all). Carwyn's report simply began: 'To study
the craftsmanship of a great player is a privilege. On
Wednesday afternoon, against the Lions, everything that
happened around Hugo Porta was contested at a much
lower level of skill and intellectual awareness. For a critic
or coach or ex-fly-half, it was a question of having one's
faith restored in the aesthetic and artistic possibilities of
backplay . . .'

On that tour, Carwyn's two confrères and drivers were
Clem Thomas, one-time rampaging flank-forward and
bane of fly-halves, now an erudite enthusiast for the
Observer, and John Reason, one-off *Sunday Telegraph*
pamphleteer of the rugby pages and iconoclastic damn-
and-blaster-with-faint-praise of the mundane and
mediocre. That day in Durban, sitting next to Carwyn,
Reason memorably described Porta as the fly-half equiv-
alent of 'a sleepy-eyed Clint Eastwood waiting to erupt
from under his sombrero'.

What true-grit and true-great fly-half should not have

that quality, that patient, knowing, confident serenity?

Later, Reason enlightened and elaborated:

'Porta could play closer to an opponent without being tackled than the top matador working with a bull. Like Barry John but in a subtly different way, he eluded defences by change of pace, by chopping his stride, by lengthening it. He looked predictable, but that he never was. He was a magnificent kicker, too, both out of the hand and at goal, and like all the others, he had that rare gift of being able to improve the options of the players outside him.

'So many fly-halves whom history regards as great have worked the ball to death, and have only given it away when they have made sure that not only is nothing possible for themselves but even worse, even less is possible for the players outside them. Porta broke so many tackles that it could not have been a matter of chance and his distribution of the ball was immaculate.'

After the wickedly pointless killings of Margaret Thatcher's Falklands War she put a stop to British sporting links with Argentina. But two years later, determined to see Porta play once more (and, obviously, for the last time, since he had already been in the autumn of his career that day in Durban), when Argentina made a brief rugby sortie into France, playing an international at Toulouse, I caught a boat-train and went to pay respects. The morning after the match, a few of the French team, which had won well enough the day before, joined the Argentinians for a comradely breakfast and *au revoir*.

Hugo Porta wears the trim, tailored black blazer of the Argentine touring team. His hairstyle is as neat and tidy and precise as his manner; he is sombre, serious and courteous; he looks like the lawyer he is, and on this day the only clue to his hobby is a vicious, horizontal two-inch gash of congealed blood on his right cheekbone, caused by a French boot the day before. At his side, over the *café au lait*, Porta's marker and France's captain sits in admiring comradeship. Jean-Pierre Rives, by comparison, looks like an ageing student trendy, an extra from a remake of *The*

Wild Bunch in which Gucci might have been the designer: sky-blue patent leather jacket and posh gym shoes with an ochre flash to match his cascading hair of Pernod yellow (for which national beverage he is an executive salesman). The only clue to his hobby is the invitation to bend down and feel his denimed knee and see how puffed and swollen it is.

At the De la Salle monastery school in Buenos Aires, Porta played soccer – 'No. 9 or No. 10, of course,' he smiles. Many said he should turn professional. 'But my father insisted I should study. I agreed with him. At my club they play all sports. Rugby was fun. At first I was scrum-half, then in 1970 I was selected for national training. I was fourth-choice scrum-half. Then one day all the fly-halves were injured – they chose me.'

Within a year he was the foregone selection at fly-half, and by the end of the decade he was every right-thinking expert's choice to wear rugby's No. 10 shirt in the World XV to play a Mars Select.

Now well into his thirties, he had, of course, played, the day before, behind a beaten pack; yet in everything he did there was a fluid, thrilling delicacy, a controlling calm and an understanding of the whole panorama of his job. In his youth he must have been built like Barry John, with a slight, schoolboy's frame belied only by thick, steel-strong thighs.

On the ball, and in the crudest company, he displayed too, as John did, an insouciant, puckish, amateur style. Being one himself, he appeals to the sporting romantic. Take this, from the Toulouse local paper on the Sunday morning we were breakfasting: '*Porta est un symbole, un chef, le maestro du carousel, l'homme aux pieds d'or, le bon génie de la Pampa, celui qui a donné au rugby Sud-Américain ses lettres de noblesse ... il donne une merveilleuse sensation d'équilibre et de sérénité ce que représente, a ses yeux, cette "vuelta" dans l'hexagone.*'

In other words, hot stuff.

Better even than the *South Wales Echo* on Barry! Porta never saw John play, but he said he had watched him on film and been enchanted. You mention Gareth, and his eyes glint and he shakes his head in wondrous recollection of the fellow, and says how he would have revelled in being outside a scrum-half like him. He has no doubt about the three most fierce but fair wing-forwards who have marked him. The former French flanker Skrela, and his apprentice – this gentleman over here, Jean-Pierre Rives. 'If he is not tackling you, he is always hounding you, worrying you, leading the charge for his country. He is so fast and energetic, so chivalrous and so proud.' The third was Graham Mourie, New Zealand's farmer-captain – 'so hard like the devil, but so honest with it, and good-humoured; he honours the foe, and I honour him.'

By delightful fluke, back in London only a couple of weeks later I lunched with Graham Mourie in a Kensington pasta house. The great and good man had just handed in his breast-fulls of All Blacks campaign medals by refusing, on the moral grounds which had split New Zealand down the middle, even to consider playing against South Africa. Now he was passing through London on his way to 'a few fun games with the Paris University XV'. He said a major sadness in his decision to retire had been that it meant passing up an opportunity to play against, and mark, 'unquestionably the best "first-five" of his time', Ollie Campbell, on the upcoming Lions tour to New Zealand:

'Campbell's kicking is one thing – it could yet win every match for the Lions [it did not] – but as a first five-eight, look how he commits the flanker to go for him by just holding on to the ball that split second longer. With the ball in his hands he is a marvellous operator. You see, breakaway wing-forward play is actually not necessarily tackling your fly-half, but "shepherding" him, veering him off, making him go the way you want him to.'

The finest fly-half Mourie had played against – he missed Barry John by a year or two – was, 'unquestionably', Hugo Porta.

'He could have been the best at any game he chose: at soccer he would have been a World Cup superstar. He has

202

balance and grace and nous. He could transfer the ball in a trice from one hand to the other, and he always left a free arm slack so he could "sense" a tackle coming and adjust; he felt that on his arm like a cat's whisker. Just phenomenal. Surely no other first-five can ever have had Hugo's instinctive vision, all-round ability, or grace.'

That day in Toulouse a couple of weeks previously, when, thankfully, Porta had at least sketched an outline of his greatness, also heralded a new talent in the play-maker's starring role. It was the first home international for Didier Camberabero. A young man who suffered neither fools nor selectors with much generosity, had he been more diplomatic he would have won many more caps. As it was, his qualities had him making his debutant's entrance against the daunting Porta in 1982 – and still wearing France's No. 10 shirt well over a decade later. Didier was from a half-back dynasty – his father, Guy, was the French fly-half and expert kicker in the 1960s, and his uncle, Lilian, was scrum-half. (They partnered each other through France's first Grand Slam in 1968.) The family owned a *tabac* in La Voulte, in the blissful Ardèche, where the Drôme runs into the Rhône.

Because of its nature – clustered pockets of *la culture rugby* speckling only certain regions – French inter-national rugby has gone in for family representation. In the 1950s and 60s, for instance, another fly-half family was the brothers Lacaze, Pierre and Claude, from Vienne, just a few miles north of La Voulte on the Lyons road. When they were not alternating at full-back – something else the French selectors have made a habit of doing with their natural fly-halves – they were taking it in turns to pop drop-goals over from various ranges. Pierre was six years older; they called him *le papillon*, 'the butterfly', a name assumed by Claude when he took over the fraternal shirt. It was the latter, so the Kiwi legend goes, who in 1961, aged twenty-one, was attempting to clear his lines with a punt in his first match for France, at an even more than usually windy Wellington – gusts of 140 km/h being recorded. The ball left his boot in the correct direction – then stopped, thought about it, and blew back over his head and the try-line, where Kel Tremain flopped on it to score. By all accounts, poor young Claude spent the rest of the match blubbing buckets of tears at the infamy of the gods.

Camberabero *fils* also, to my knowledge anyway, put up a first for an international fly-half. He plays in a wig. It is not a delicate single-strand Frank Sinatra scalp-sewn job like Geoffrey Boycott used to bat in. Oh no: with Gallic abandon Didier goes for the full works – a Davy Crockett bouffant rug in an auburn tint, with a jaunty slash of grey to highlight his front quiff (*un panache* to the trade, apparently). It makes the French fly-half look rather like dear old Dickie Davies, who used to get his Andover barber to run up a streak of grey forelock on his wide, natural, blow-dried busby of a hairdo on his way to the studio at LWT to present the ITV Saturday sports programme.

In another day and age, when international rugby was not so tense and tunnel-visioned, the sight of a fly-half in a wig would have been meat and drink to any openside wing-forward, from the Test team to the Old Clodhoppians Extra B XV. Once in the 1950s England fielded a fly-half – was it OMT's Doug Baker, or Ricky Bartlett (the Harlequin who used to be described in the match programme as 'an insurance broker and pig farmer') – who wore the then new-fangled contact lenses. This was mentioned in the *Irish Independent* on the morning of a match against England at Lansdowne Road. Exclaimed the Garryowen brickhouse Tom Reid, as he read the paper in the dressing room just before taking the field, 'Jasus, boys, just clear a path and let me have a run at the Quin fellow, an' I promise you he'll be out of focus for the rest of the game.'

Camberabero went bald in his late twenties. He says it upset his personality as well as his rugby, and, on reflection, the selectors had been correct to have such little

204

confidence in him. He went to be fitted for his wig in 1990, when he was twenty-nine, at the 'Lombardi Diffusion' salon in Béziers. Once the carpet had been laid – he calls it his *complément capillaire* – he gave up the family *tabac* and accepted a job on the wigmakers' public relations staff. (So he could also be said to be international rugby's first 'sandwich-man', a player with an advertising billboard on his head.) 'My baldness gave me a severe complex', he says. 'It affected my game and my kicking, too. *Le complément* has transformed me completely in a match and since fitting it I now have a composure and inner strength that had been tragically lacking before.'

In 1991 Didier modelled his new hair at Twickenham for the first time. His new confidence had him approaching 350 points in only thirty-five games – easily a French record. But he was always much more than a superlative kicker, for he displayed at once in that hectically glorious match *le panache* to match his hairdo, playing the fulcrum part in the grandest collective try ever seen at the old stadium.

Early on in this Grand Slam finale, England missed a long penalty, and all eyes and senses – certainly those of the England XV – for a moment relaxed and prepared for a twenty-two drop-out. Instead of touching down, the French captain and full-back, Serge Blanco, opened up from behind his lines. Jean-Baptiste Lafond and Philippe Sella took it on and, with England frantically funnelling back, Sella and Camberabero worked a mesmerizing dummy-scissors loop, on their own ten-metre line and the same distance in from touch – going towards the newly opened, high-raked north grandstand. Now Didier showed how he could play, indeed how his hairpiece had helped harness his hooraymanship.

He sniped across the halfway line, losing the gallant, puffing-back forward Jeff Probyn with a voluptuous, almost contemptuous, sidestep. Then, with dainty exactness, he slippered the ball over the head of the retreating and panicking full-back Simon Hodgkinson, caught it himself in full-pelt stride and was now up to England's twenty-two-metre flag. England's bold general, Will Carling, had, remarkably, made it right across the field, but could only fling himself with a lunging shoulder-charge at Camberabero a split second after the French fly-half had dapped the most inch-perfect of cross-kicks to within five metres of the posts. That totally took out the corner-flagging Richard Hill – and left the French wing, Philippe Saint-André, to compose himself, smile, collect and triumphantly launch himself at the line as Jeremy Guscott's all-in, last-gasp dive went for his ankles. The palpitating thing was done. Outlined by Serge. Coloured in by Didier. *Et voilà – le panache.*

There have of late been any number of other hugely gifted fly-halves who needed no hairpiece to conjure up the word *panache*. For instance, Errol Tobias, the black South African from Boland, a lovely prancing runner and all-rounder I watched in 1980, would have played more internationals for other countries unhindered by a statutory racial policy. He was 34 when the Springboks gave him full caps at fly-half in 1984, but then there was the whiff of grudging, tokenist window-dressing about their award. In the World Cup of 1991, Western Samoa's Steve Bachop was rivetingly impressive in the No. 10 jersey, as was the American stalwart and carrot-top Chris O'Brien. When they held the inaugural World Sevens at Murrayfield in the spring of 1993, it was a positive thrill to revel in the arts and sciences of Fiji's magnetic little fly-half, Waisale Serevi, a rare and genuine chip off the old block, for the island's 'father' of rugby, Sir George Cakabau, was a demon fly-half in the 1930s. The Fijian press handout at Murrayfield described Serevi as 'phenomenal, brilliant, superb and unparalleled, with impeccable timing, sizzling breaks, a devastating sidestep and a paralysing dummy. No adjectives are left to describe this little genius'. Well, not by that author, anyway. And such, mind you, was the tenor of superlative emanating from across the Irish Sea only a few weeks before when a brand new fly-half in the green, Eric Elwood, gleamingly led a famous victory over England with such flamboyance that the pubs were awash that night with the utter certainties that they had found another in the line of Magee and Davy, Kyle and Ward and Campbell. We shall see what we shall see . . .

12

Try it, and it works

Now Scotland presented for our delectation the very best of their famous bunch. John Rutherford, of Selkirk, made his nervous entrance in the blue in 1979 and for the following decade was a dominant force for the good in rugby. With that glistening shot of mercury Andy Irvine, the energizing Hastings brothers, and a dauntlessly brave scrum-half, Roy Laidlaw, Scottish teams of the 1980s were built around a thrilling spine. But the wisest head and shoulders belonged invariably at fly-half on John Rutherford. He was an utter pleasure to watch, and must have been confounding to play against. He won forty-two caps, a Scottish record for the position, always in harness with the burrowing mudlark Laidlaw. Rutherford became a thrilling punter in attack, though he did not take the kicks from the 'floor'. In 1981–2, he scored in all five internationals without taking a place-kick; and, all told, he scored seven tries for Scotland – two or three of them luminous, incisive things – and potted a record twelve drop-kicks. He worked intensively at his game and in his maturity, when he had honed it, he was acclaimed all round as the best fly-half in the world game.

On the Lions tour to New Zealand in 1983, I had to return home after a month or so to cover some cricket. Ollie Campbell was the senior fly-half for the Test side, but as the tour continued and the first Test had been lost, I recall taking bets – large ones – with fellow journalists at my farewell supper in Christchurch that, with Rutherford so evidently the outstanding natural footballer in the party, the selectors would have to come to their senses and play him in the Test side at centre. My colleagues scoffed; Rutherford had never played centre in his life. A few days after my return to England and the cricket, I watched smugly on pre-dawn television the next Test from Dunedin – and saw Rutherford, at centre, sublimely score the try of the series.

Like many other fly-halves of the legend, John came from a soccer background. His father, Bill, was on the committee of Selkirk AFC, which played in the East of Scotland league – and Helen, his mother, made the post-match tea, ran the baths and cleaned the kit. But once young John had begun his tots' rugby at the town's youth club, and then been picked as a hooker at Philiphaugh Primary (which was located alongside Selkirk RFC), Dad too was converted to the oval game. By the time John made Selkirk High School, his sport was so pre-eminent that, as well as starring in the volleyball and basket-ball sides, he was turning out at rugby on Saturday mornings, racing home for lunch *en route* to playing soccer in the afternoon for the British Legion Boys XI. He made his first appearance for the Selkirk rugby club in the Gala Sevens (the Borders nursed and cradled the sevens game). John scored three tries in the first tie, and he was away.

Playing for Jed-Forest in that tournament was a spiky, sniping little scrum-half called Laidlaw. In 1974, at neighbouring Melrose, Rutherford and Laidlaw played together for the first time, for Borders' U-21 v. Argentina U-21. The *Southern Reporter* noted: 'Rutherford displayed some fine touches and, with Laidlaw, looked the part, and a lot more will be heard of this pair.' And how – for Scotland they were to partner each other a record thirty-five times, and, of the eight matches they missed as a pair, Scotland lost seven!

On one of those occasions, John was injured and Richard Cramb took his place at fly-half. Norman Mair of the *Scotsman*, who was to become their Boswell, tells, delightfully, how the telepathic understanding of Roy and John was such that it was always said that they could find each other in the dark; and for Roy it was never quite the same with any other stand-off. In Dublin Airport, on the morning after Scotland's defeat at Lansdowne Road in 1988, Roy, in search of the loo, came upon a gaggle of somewhat bedraggled Scottish supporters. One of them looked up. 'Still looking for Richard Cramb?' he enquired, sympathetically.

More than two or three times when Five Nations rugby was staging two matches on the same Saturday, I can recall myself plumping for the one involving Scotland, simply because I knew Rutherford would be on show. For, down the seasons, Rutherford had been so neatly un-hurried, letting slip with his kicks and leadership ploys and cunning runs, his scavenging seagulls in the blue shirts; never rushing, always in control, always perky – no, not perky, that's the word for Welsh fly-halfs. 'Spruce' is nearer the mark for Rutherford. He was always beautifully turned out; always upright in both meanings of the word; energy always disciplined and his intellect always twitching, keen to show off the game's classic traditions.

Norman Mair was luckier than I was. He saw all Rutherford's internationals – and this, just one example from the tens of thousands of paragraphs Norman must have used up on the young man, was his description of another singular try, against England in 1986:

'A pass hurled from Colclough to Andrew's ankles defeated the stand-off. Finlay Calder who, in his support play, would have earned many an approving nod from Graham Mourie himself, plucked the ball off the floor brilliantly and gave it to John Beattie. His lob pass was accepted by Laidlaw who passed to Rutherford. With a devastating sidestep off his left foot, Rutherford beat the covering Mike Harrison on the inside, three other Englishmen being simultaneously jerked on to the wrong foot like puppets on the same string. The stand-off's turn of foot took him to the line for the try with which he equalled Herbert Waddell's remarkable bag of seven tries in only fifteen internationals.'

Yet you do not exactly remember Rutherford for his sidesteps, as you might remark, 'By Jove, what a sidestep Bennett had on him' or 'Do you remember Sharp's dummies?' You recall Rutherford for his instinctive excellence of method, his mastery of every 'stroke' in the fly-half's game. Once his youthful weaknesses as a kicker had been overcome by his diligent and solitary practice, a few whispers gained ground that he was overdoing the boot; but his Selkirk compatriot, the writer Alan Massie, readily puts them to rest:

'There was some criticism even in the midst of the 1984 Grand Slam triumph that he had become a kicking fly-half, disinclined to run the ball as he had done in his earlier days. The criticism was understandable but ill-judged. Rutherford had matured to the point when he played like a general, not the leader of a raiding party. Inevitably, a little of the adventure had gone out of his game; but you play Rugby to win, and all four games were won. In three of them at least, the point was reached when the only way Scotland might lose was through mistakes in midfield.'

When Rutherford retired, in 1988, the Scottish branch of the Variety Club gave a celebratory dinner for him (and Laidlaw) at Glasgow's Albany Hotel. The main speech was delivered by the delightful Jim Telfer, longtime coach to Scotland, and of the Lions of 1983. He began with an apology: 'It may have been that under me his running style was a little curbed but I hope that he will never blame me for this, while feeling that his other strengths were encouraged. Quite frankly, gentlemen, for me, when I coached the Scottish side, John ran the show. He controlled the game and if he played well, we played well.'

Telfer ended a lovely reminiscence with what he would take to the grave, 'with my dreamy mind's eye of John, my vision of him, as the runner he was by nature. Picture any match with John at stand-off. We've just scored a try and the opposition kick-off. It could be for Selkirk, for the

211

South or for Scotland. The ball kicked deep into our twenty-two; John fields, dummies to kick to touch but instead steps off his right foot and takes off, ball in two hands, running left. The counter-attack is on. John as I shall remember him.'

In that 1983 Lions tour to New Zealand, Rutherford showed not the slightest pique that Ollie Campbell was the preferred first choice at fly-half. Not only that, he said, but it was an infinite pleasure to play outside Campbell, at centre:

'I think a fly-half should have great vision, the ability to read a game and the ability to make instant assessments so that he does the correct thing for each situation. He should be able to pass quickly and accurately so that he can get his threequarter line running to fullest advantage, and he should possess a good kick and have variety to his kicking. The perfect fly-half must also have pace, particularly over ten metres, and the running talent to be able to break inside or outside; finally he should be able to pressurize the opposition and be courageous in covering and tackling . . . Ollie had almost everything, in my eyes. He had speed, he had "hands" and he was an adroit and persuasive link from the point of view of the backs outside him. He was a wonderful kicker both from hand and off the deck and, by heaven, he could tackle.'

Had there been another Lions tour during Rutherford's career, he would certainly have been the senior fly-half. As it was, when the next tour came up, to Australia in 1989, Scotland had already found another 'fly' worthy of selection for it – young, coltish Craig Chalmers. At once they unearthed another 'Laidlaw' for him, too, in the spikily abrasive and quite brilliant Gary Armstrong. Scotland's lustrous consistency at half-back in recent times has been an immeasurable bonus for the stability of the side and the sanity of the selectors. In the past two decades, except for the occasional injury, they have needed only to write down four names – Laidlaw and Rutherford, Armstrong and Chalmers – and then fill in the rest of the team around them. By contrast, since the

1979 Calcutta Cup match, Rutherford's first, England incredibly have fielded fourteen different half-backs against Scotland: Bennett, Horton, Davies, Cusworth, Williams, Andrew, Barnes, Young, Smith, Youngs, Harding, Melville, Morris and Hill.

England's pin-stickers, ruinously spoiled for choice, recruited those fourteen from all points of the land. Scotland's quartet of utter quality live less than a quarter-hour's drive from one another in that sublime little Borders triangle of valleys carved by the Tweed and the Teviot. The two fly-halves, Rutherford and Chalmers, are from Selkirk and Melrose; both scrum-halves, Laidlaw and Armstrong, from Jedburgh.

Both the tyros blushingly pooh-pooh the idea that they were on a definite course to emulate the deeds of their famous, neighbourly mentors. 'Compared to Roy and John and all they accomplished together, we are just wee babes still,' says Armstrong. Crucially, of course, they differ from Laidlaw and Rutherford in as much as they are children of Rugby's new system, the new and almost Jesuitical determination of grass-roots coaching administrators to catch them young: 'Give me a child at seven and he's a two-footed kicker for life', and all that.

As is the new way of things, Chalmers, the Melrose Grammar Schoolboy, came, step by considered step, through the ranks of graded, representative colts, school, junior club and under-age international levels, unlike Rutherford who had to muck through self-taught, on instinct and nous.

Yet, if you have got it in the first place, the end justifies the totally different means. Coaching from the cradle and progressing right through 'the system', as Chalmers experienced, and haphazard, intuitive make-do-and-mend, as Rutherford and Laidlaw did, happily can result in identical performances when it matters.

Chalmers was just twenty when he made his shy debutant's curtsey against Wales at Murrayfield the season after Rutherford's acclaimed exit. It was the twenty-two-year-old Armstrong's second cap. It was

213

astonishing. They both scored a try, and both could have been (literally) blueprints from the decade before when John and Roy began. First, Armstrong's awareness, daring and rat-trap snap into the retreating Welsh scrum as it disintegrated over its own line was pure, bonny Laidlaw itself. And later the resplendent, almost opulent, grandstand finish and swerve by Chalmers which adorned Scotland's rampaging six-man try in the corner was almost a Rutherford dream-topping 'special' incarnate.

That first day, I recall fearing for Chalmers as he ran out to face fifteen vengeful, uncompromising wolves in red. He looked so palely delicate, even faun-like. He put no foot wrong and, apart from his try, his unruffled maturity, almost detached insouciance, was quite astonishing, even to those who knew him and had picked him in the first place. I remember the Scottish captain that day, Finley Calder, just shaking his head afterwards, for once almost lost for words: 'Craig was even the calmest and most collected fellow in the changing room before we ran out,' he said.

Not only had the rich seam of the Borders certainly unearthed in Armstrong an inside-half to out-Dorward Dorward – Arthur, the mudlarking scrum-barking terrier of the 1950s – or outshine the all-over polish of Alex Hastie, or, in time, run the records ragged of even Laidlaw himself; it had produced that even more rare and precious commodity, an outside-half from the same topmost drawer whence came the grand Wilson Shaw, the Waddells, Chisholm and the best of the tartan best, John Rutherford. Yet, as is the way of all sport and sportsmen, the 'best' is always there to be bettered and, who knows, by the 1995 World Cup young Craig Chalmers will still be only twenty-six and will have filled out mightily – physically, as well as intellectually and creatively – and by the end of the century, a reprint and reprise of this little history of No. 10s could even have him hailed as the best of the best in any colour. Or again, even before 1995, he could have left the scene, flitted away like a butterfly on a breeze, by choice, as Cliff Jones did, and Richard Sharp and, of course, Barry John – 'travelling that short while toward the sun, leaving the vivid air signed with their honour' – or, no bones about it, the selectors could drop him, ditch him, toss him away without a 'thank you' even. For that, too, is the way of all selectors.

As Englishmen know only too well. Especially English fly-halves. It is a bewildering story, and a long one. It is based, one presumes, on being spoilt for choice, because England's seam of talent – or, if not talent, depth of playing resources – is larger than anybody's. In 1980 Bill Beaumont's England XV won the Five Nations Grand Slam for the first time in twenty-two years. A settled pair of half-backs played in all four matches – John Horton of Bath at fly, a careful, diligent and undemonstrative player with a shrewd kick, and an effervescent scrum-half, Steve Smith. In the shambles of the previous eight seasons, with mind-boggling neuroses, the selectors had picked as many as eighteen different half-back pairings. Did that one, serene, Grand Slam season tell the pin-stickers anything about the very fulcrum of the team needing to be settled? It did not. The next eight – barren – seasons saw twelve half-back pairings.

The fly-half to suffer most through the 1970s was the skilful and most accomplished Yorkshireman, Alan Old, brother of the England cricketer, Chris. In the 1980s, the selectors' knee-jerks particularly upset another Tyke from the broad acres, who played his bewitching rugby for Leicester, Les Cusworth. He was a gnomic, bald, magical little runner and for more than ten seasons was considered by friend and foe alike as the country's most creative and daringly guileful playmaker. In those ten seasons, criminally, he won only twelve caps for England, each in higgledy-piggledy order and given and taken away without selectors' rhyme or reason. Cusworth was thirty-four when he won his last two caps in 1988, delighted at a final chance to trick and treat the midfield. Ten seasons earlier he had been dauntingly thrown in at the deep end against the All Blacks at Twickenham. They said the young man overdid his kicking – and, in turn, they booted him out for three years.

'I suppose I did over-kick. But I had the impression that was expected of me. It was just a huge disappointment, all the family down to see me, and so proud. And I let everyone down. I had to kick and kick, just stick it in front of the forwards. Of course I was nervous.

'Franny Cotton [England's doughty prop-forward] came up beforehand and said in that way of his, "If ever you're goin' to forget anything, laddie, make sure it's not the rule to stick leather on leather." I even did that like a joker, and knew it, but at the end the captain, Bill [Beaumont], came up and put his arm around me and said, "Well done, son, first cap of many." Dear, good, old Bill.'

He was dropped for England's next twelve games, returning for another frying-pan job, against France in Paris in 1982. It was a famous victory (celebrated, you will remember, by Colin Smart's 'Old Spice' toast with after-shave, and captain Steve Smith's immortal quote from the hospital bedside, 'Colin's still unconscious, but when he comes round I can promise you he'll smell okay').

'Of course it was always a terrible blow not to be picked when you just wanted one more chance to prove it. But the disappointments were always muted at Leicester because the club is full of such good, caring folk, and they just inspired me to go on doing the business for them.' (And Leicester continued to win every trophy on offer.)

'So first England drop me for over-kicking. Next time it was for weak tackling, though I don't think I ever really shirked that. But, surely, the fly-half game is to make things happen. No one should blame you for dropping a clanger or two. It's like the brave, bold decisions in real life. Like another of my sayings: "If you've never made a mistake, then you've never made a decision." And fly-half has to be the decision maker, hasn't he?'

Mind you, he says, in his long span in the game – and between international matches, from 1979 to 1988 – he noticed immense changes in the demands of the position: 'For instance, a fly-half just can't control the play like he used to. He's more and more dependent on every single other player, and all he can really hope to do now, defences being so ruthlessly and tightly organized, is to look to create second-phase possession. It's almost the only way to find a chink through any international defence.

'Okay, the fly-half might still call the shots. But every single other man has got to know what the shots are. It's not off the cuff any more. If only you folk on the touch-line realized that good old-fashioned first-phase possession is now a liability more often than not, and to just run at an organized defence for the sake of it and just to see what happens is suicide. The knack now is to restrict play to the exact areas where you have the best chance of scoring – and if that means your fly-half kicking a lot every Saturday, then so be it. You can start playing by the seat of your pants, with off-the-cuff inspiration, once you've worked to get the opposition's defence into lots of ragged tangles.'

No matter the impish Cusworth was harried hither and yon more by selectors than wing-forwards. 'Twelve England caps is twelve England caps and I'm mighty proud of them. I came from very humble beginnings and very proud of them – my father was a miner, my mother a school dinner lady. My dad never went abroad in his life but I've been all round the world playing rugby. He pushed me through Normanton Grammar School to make sure I didn't have to go down the pits, and it was only through him and the school rugby coach, Alan Jubb, that I continued in the game. So when people say twelve caps aren't enough, I just thank my lucky stars.'

Cusworth's last two caps of his proud dozen were awarded under new management. England at last got a grip, put an end to the Buggins's-turn, old-boy sinecures of the selectors' chairmen and management panel, and in 1988 gave the job of manager, 'for the foreseeable future', to Geoff Cooke, a north-country manager, who chose as coach an enlightened and enlightening former England captain, Roger Uttley. They promised the players continuity and fidelity – as long as they worked in return. The results, for England rugby, bordered on the sensational. Eighteen months after the new broom, England were playing Scotland in a Grand Slam finale at Murrayfield – and losing, as much thanks to the Scots' shrewd disciplines and taunting oomph as their own swaggering, collective arrogance (England had progressed so far in less than two years, they did not think they could lose). England then won a record head-to-head Grand Slam in both 1991 and 1992 – and, in between, got to the World Cup final, where they lost to Australia in a thrilling game. Apart from the first two matches under the Cooke–Uttley revolution, when the veteran Cusworth was asked to come in and steady the ship, England's fly-half throughout this triumphant passage was yet another Yorkshireman – soberly calming and undemonstrative Rob Andrew.

Andrew, too, like Cusworth, had experienced the selectors' whimsical vagaries – but, still only twenty-five in 1988, he was easily young enough for rehabilitation by Cooke and Uttley. (Another outstanding young fly-half, Stuart Barnes, of Bath, might have seriously challenged Andrew for the job but, fed up with being promised a game here and there, he opted out and said he would prefer regular matches with his club.)

When Andrew first played for England at Twickenham in 1985, he was perhaps better known as the Cambridge University cricket captain, and one recalls the pleasure that England might have at last stumbled upon the genuine article at outside-half – a self-contained, seemingly self-assured 'natural' with a cricketer's safe pair of hands and, as the soccer men say, 'two feet'.

It turned into a disillusionment as painful for the sensitive young man as for the put-upon English supporters and reporters, who responded to each successive false dawn with a series of increasingly fruity raspberries. Andrew thought most of them were directed at him, and, as his position demands that he make the play and inspire the plot, many of them certainly were. Inevitably, he soon joined that sullen swirl of cast-off England fly-halves wondering where they went wrong and almost relieved not to be looking over their shoulders any more.

'Match after match, you could feel the tensions and frustrations and lack of daring getting to you,' he admitted. 'I know I lacked confidence even in what ability I had. I was riddled with self-doubt. I was England's fly-half – great! But then I'd begin to think "Why me?" when there were so many super players around at other clubs. Did I really deserve to be chosen?'

During one of Andrew's blue periods, when he had been dropped again in 1986, I happened to interview the abrasive Australian coach Alan Jones, and asked him how he would start to build a new England side. The answer surprised a lot of people, myself included.

'I would plan it and pick it totally round Rob Andrew,' he said. 'He is a gentleman and a chivalrous hero, which is important if you are going to have someone to look up to, but he is also a tremendous natural ball player with a rare and innate sense of when to run, when to kick and when to let it out. Yet you English have the audacity to tell him he's not wanted any more; it's inexplicable to us Australians.'

Jones had met Andrew at the Waterloo club near Liverpool when the North XV played Jones's Wallabies. He told the boy, 'You could be a world-beater, son.' Andrew laughed. 'I won't even dare to read tomorrow's Sunday papers, because I know my game will be torn to shreds.' Said Jones, 'You need a season playing in Australia.' A year later, that is exactly what Andrew did. It worked – all Australia said so, after a number of glittering performances.

Andrew had spent that summer of 1986 playing with the Gordon Club in Sydney. It was by way of a sabbatical from cricket. The previous summer he had captained Cambridge at Lord's – a draw, after outplaying Oxford for two days – and then played seven 2nd XI championship games for Yorkshire. He averaged 26 in twelve innings and was wondering if he might follow the likes of

Peter Squires and Alastair Hignell into county cricket each summer and rugby all winter – a pretty impossible ambition now, with first-class rugby's far heavier year-long demands. Still, he had one first-class century to his name, 101 not out at Trent Bridge against Pick, Such (later of England) and Afford in 1984, on the eve of the University Match, where he promptly came out with his eye in and made a duck. The following summer he captained the Combined Universities XI against the Australian tourists at Fenners. He opened the batting against the pacemen, Geoff Lawson and Dave Gilbert, and made 40 out of 58 before the slow left-armer, Murray Bennett, had him caught. Then he took two Australian wickets – those of David Boon and Lawson – in ten overs.

Cricket was always the family game on the farm near Richmond. He was a blazing schoolboy all-rounder at Barnard Castle. Second on the list was soccer and a boggle-eyed devotion to George Best.

It was only rugby at Barnard Castle, of course. Through the 1970s he idolized Phil Bennett for his darting panache; later it was John Rutherford for his insouciant cool. (When he played his third match for England, against Scotland at Twickenham, on 16 March 1985, he admits he was awestruck almost into immobility as they lined up against each other at the first scrum.)

It was at Barnard Castle, years before that, that the youngster met his future rugby international – although neither of them knew it then. Rob Andrew and Rory Underwood, born within four months of each other in 1963, were contemporaries at the school in Teesdale on Durham's Yorkshire border. Through their teens their schoolmasters report that they were both so slight, 'so skinny', that the possibility of their leading an assault on adult rugby's Grand Slam – as well as both becoming the most capped England players in their positions – seemed so remote as to be laughable. Neither made any impact on the selectors of any representative schools' rugby. Yet both were picked for England within three years of leaving Barnard Castle.

Their (since retired) housemaster, Kenneth King, remembers fondly: 'Schoolboy sports stars can be "gods" to the house, but both Robert and Rory wore their success so well, almost bashfully; straightforward, uncomplicated, super blokes, both the very embodiment of the fact that nice guys can finish first.' Their games master and rugby coach, John Oates, looked up copies of the annual school magazine in which, match after match, the reports had variations of 'the intelligence of Andrew and the speed of Underwood again prevailed'.

A mix of 500 boarding and day pupils, Barnard Castle is, everyone says, a happy school run by an affable enthusiast of a schoolmaster, Frank Macnamara, who once played scrum-half for Northumberland. 'If it wasn't for Rob and Rory,' he says, 'the most famous of our recent alumni would be Kevin Whateley', who is Inspector Morse's amiably lugubrious bloodhound in a blue serge suit, Sergeant Lewis.

If the school had been founded fifty years earlier than 1883 – 'for the sons of the middle classes' – it would have been a fair bet it was the model for Dotheboys Hall itself. Dickens wrote the first half of *Nicholas Nickleby* in the top room of the King's Head in the town, whence he carried out his research into the notorious cruel and cheap boarding schools which then infested the area. But Dotheboys it is not – and, equally, Kenneth King is no Wackford Squeers. The old housemaster speaks with the softly querulous and kindly cadence of Robert Donat's Mr Chips in his middle-to-late period. And, like all housemasters, he remembers vividly long-gone generations:

'Robert was, oh, so small, so right from the start he had to think about his games and you could see him doing it as he played, and always he had this innate self-belief in his ability. His cricket was tremendous, and his squash, and in no game ever once did he play slyly and, win or lose, not honour the foe after the game. Robert was so neat and tidy and thoughtful in everything he did.'

Oates recalls: 'Robert, for his age, had given himself a very high skill level. He'd work and work at practice and really love it. Kick, kick, kick, catch, catch, catch. And at each stage of development – and long after school as his sport has progressed – he has never had the slightest smidgen of swagger and always realized that whatever levels you attain there is still a hell of a lot to learn. The same goes for Rory. And what very nice guys with it. Perfectly representative of the ethos of Barnard Castle – character, but of quality not of frills.'

That 'innate self-belief' his old housemaster noticed in the boy who was to break Jack Kyle's all-time fly-half record is a most relevant observation. Once he had been assured of more than 'just one last chance' in the England team by the Cooke–Uttley management in 1988, arrived another jolt to the young man's suddenly found self-esteem.

The fly-halves for the 1989 Lions tour to Australia were named as Paul Dean, the dependable, assured and tactically wise Irish fly-half, whose selection nobody disagreed with, and the callow but abundantly promising Scot, Chalmers, who had, of course, played barely a season since Rutherford's retirement. Andrew took this particularly badly – the supremely gifted Jonathan Davies, of Wales, would unquestionably have been first choice, but his by now total disillusionment with the Union game had already hastened him to the League. So the selection of such a tyro, however precocious, as Chalmers told Andrew that, of four British fly-halves, he was considered bottom of the pile. He resigned himself, bitterly disappointed, to a summer of muckabout cricket.

In the opening match of the Lions tour in Australia, Paul Dean tragically smashed his leg; he would not play first-class rugby again. The Lions sent for Andrew. 'It was like a dream. Elation and no pressure, because I wasn't meant to be there in the first place, was I?' He played his first 'dirt-trackers' match for them in Queensland, at Cairns – and at once made a scorching break, changed up the gears through the gap and created a scintillating collective try. He had broken free of the manacles. The first Test was lost badly; young Chalmers carried the can, and Andrew took his place. The rest is triumphant history. He had played with five different scrum-halves for England; now he was partnered by one of the world's best at the time, Robert Jones of Wales. It was an eye-opener.

'No offence to anyone else, I always partnered very good players, but suddenly the ball was only coming out to me when it was right that it should. And when it did, I found I had that vital fraction of a second in hand to decide what to do. We had only practised together on the Thursday before the Test, but from the first moment somehow we were on the same wavelength. It was instinctive, glorious.' Jones, for his part, enthused about Andrew. 'He was absolutely world-class; a true delight to partner.'

So Andrew came back for a new English season, strutting at last – and would (in his own self-effacing way, that is) continue to do so through two record-breaking Grand Slam seasons and a 'so-near' World Cup campaign which rocketed the whole game to previously unconsidered heights of popularity and interest.

Throughout that march of triumph for England – winning matches they might have lost, often, it seemed, by force of cocksure personality as well as relentless power – Andrew was the calming influence, the tidier, the support-play provider, the nagging kicker, the saving tackler. His game was continually being given a keener edge, too, by club performances of consistent brilliance by his old rival Stuart Barnes (they had played against each other at fly-half in the University Matches of 1982 and '83 – Andrew's Cambridge winning well on both occasions). Now, a whole decade later, Barnes was still hammering on the door of No. 10. England's rugby community was split, reminiscent of Ireland's Ward–Campbell tribal war of a dozen years before.

In early 1993, England's triumphant progress showed signs of spluttering. Unconsidered Canada were beaten, but only uneasily; there was a late, surging rally to take the wreath against South Africa, but only after Naas Botha's unerring boot had shocked them into coordination; France lost at Twickenham, but only just, and undeservedly. Something was wrong with England's self-acclaimed juggernaut, and Stuart Barnes, whose first cap for England (even before Andrew's first) had been all of ten seasons previous, was demanding a chance.

The appealingly restless and noisy Barnes had, remember, on two separate occasions dramatically announced himself fed up with warming his bottom on the replacements' bench and said he did not want to be considered again. Both times he asked for forgiveness and another chance. Certainly things had changed in the England set-up. 'And in the nine years since I first played for England my hair has gone grey,' he laughs.

Barnes is an engaging extrovert, bright as blazer buttons, and as perky and challenging off the pitch as on it. With the grey hairs, he says, has also come a more philosophical approach.

'Of course you have to think of yourself as the better player. That's how fly-halves particularly are meant to think. No offence to Rob, whom I like enormously – who doesn't? – but fly-half play in the modern idiom is all about getting past that gain-line through the heavy traffic, not "lying off" and kicking.

'It may be individually frustrating but I know I'm not going to get back into the first team by having another "head fit" of rebellion and walking off in a stupid strop again. I've done it twice, so by now it's obviously lost its originality, hasn't it? When I came back into the fold I just said I wanted to try and prove I could perform at the highest level. Only I have a bearing on whether I perform or not. It's all totally in my hands as to how I train for a match, how I prepare mentally. What is, however, not in my hands at all is selection. That's why there is absolutely no point in my getting all worked up about it any more.

'At the moment I'm content enough that I proved myself categorically in England "B" matches. Obviously I wouldn't be human if I didn't feel that England have made selection cock-ups concerning fly-halves. I can't help but say otherwise, and that's what all us replacements should be thinking. Counter-arguments that have been used against me, like kicking and lack of vision, do not stand up to scrutiny or examination. Sorry, but that's the sort of decisive thinking that fly-halves are meant to have, isn't it?'

A week later, England were stunned by defeat in Cardiff by Wales, their hat-trick Grand Slam shattered. Rob Andrew was made the scapegoat. Step forward, Stuart Barnes. We would see what we would see.

With just a few hours to kick-off in the 1993 Calcutta Cup Match at Twickenham, the nation was still hearing how Barnes was intent on grabbing his chance. 'Well, everybody knows I'm a gambler, gambling's in my blood. As it should be with any man who is offered the privilege of wearing the No. 10 shirt in an international match for one's country. Of course I'll give it a go. No way will you find me walking off at the final whistle today and comforting myself, like some fly-halves have done, by saying, "That went well, I didn't fumble, I found touch, I didn't do anything wrong." To me, if I said that, it means I would have had a terrible game – because I didn't make anything happen. In modern rugby, there has been a stigma attached to the word "risk". I like to get the ball and simultaneously weigh up the option in a split second's intuition – knowing "Yes, it could go wrong if you try that, but the likelihood is that it won't go wrong – so go for it, boy." But if the likelihood is that it could go wrong – say, under 6–10 – I'm no twerp and I'd steer clear in an international; it is a team game after all and I'm not that egotistical.'

All said in a confiding, matey burr – but you did worry for his utter certainties; after all he was just a few hours away from playing in his first ever Five Nations match. To be sure, I could not remember an England international sportsman – except those ridiculous 'I'll moider de bum' horizontal heavyweight boxers of ours – going out to play with such a swagger of assurance since the great cricketer Ian Botham was in his pomp.

Barnes was born in the London suburbs, but his father

took a job in Wales and the boy was educated at Bassaleg Comprehensive. He played in all the age-level groups for Welsh juniors till, when the time came, he announced for England if they wanted him. He won three Blues at Oxford, where he read modern history. 'I wish to God I'd gone for Eng. lit., but in those days I thought they'd laugh if a little lad coming up from a Welsh comprehensive announced to Oxford dons that he wanted to read literature.' He loves his Conrad and his Hazlitt and his Hardy. Pretty confidently I would say he was the only member of his new England XV, apart from Gloucester's grand totem Mike Teague, who voted for the Labour Party in the 1992 General Election – 'Sure, I'm on the left wing there, too.' After a match, 'a Guinness-and-port, then a few glasses of red, feet up and some good music, bliss.'

So out he runs to take on Scotland. It was quite gloriously resplendent how the man did what the man had said he would. Three particular sprinklings of fairy dust, and quite a bit more besides, and Barnes single-handedly, and with a joyous daring, fashioned three ragingly thrilling tries to allow the English backs to refind and re-establish their reputations. Scotland were laid to waste – and the banner headlines next day recalled those of thirty-three winters before which had garlanded and festooned another outrageous Five Nations debutant in the same jersey, Richard Sharp:

BARNES PUTS SCOTS TO FLIGHT (*Sunday Telegraph*)

BARNES THE FLOWER OF ENGLAND (*Observer*)

BARNES OPENS DOOR TO ENGLISH HEARTS (*Independent*)

SORCERER BARNES WEAVES HIS MAGIC (*Mail on Sunday*)

Rob Andrew watched it all from the replacements' bench – and next day, I daresay, the world's record-breaking fly-half cancelled his Sunday papers – although not for long: by the summer of 1993, when both of them toured New Zealand with the Lions, it was Andrew who won the No. 10 jersey in the Tests.

If Andrew, for all his quiet, neat and fearless talent, presented his game as surreptitiously as T. S. Eliot's self-effacer –

> No, I am not Prince Hamlet nor was meant to be,
> Am an attendant Lord, one that will do
> To swell a progress, start a scene or two –

then Stuart Barnes certainly sees himself (and why not?) in a royal capacity when it comes to fly-half play. It is difficult, from this distance, to realize that Barnes's first one-off cap for England before Andrew succeeded him was won, at Twickenham against Australia on 3 November 1984, in direct confrontation with, arguably, the most regal and majestic No. 10 of all time. If Barry John was called, with reason, 'the king', then Mark Ella was the very 'prince' of fly-halves. Within a month, Ella's 1984 Wallabies inflicted a glorious whitewash on the four British Isles national teams. It was a voluptuous spasm in which the young aboriginal – who, uniquely, scored tries in all four Tests – set coruscating new standards for the position.

And, in doing so, he preached what he practised. I was privileged to follow him throughout the tour. From Twickenham the Wallabies went to Belfast to prepare for the Dublin international. The touring team came in from practice at Ulster's ancient old club, Malone. It was bucketing down. The others returned, pronto, to the team hotel. Mark Ella stayed – to conduct a seminar. It was quite, quite memorable, and one recalls it like it was the day before yesterday.

He looks out at the rain, and shrugs and smiles: 'Sure, at home we only play in the rain two or three times a year. But we have to continue telling ourselves that our running game is suited to all conditions. Okay, it's wet – so you play your natural game and we'll play ours. Of course, we'll keep running the ball and, you'll see, it can be done. You have to make an effort to play good rugby. So often in Britain, I guess, threequarters trot out and say, "Oh, it's raining, so let's just leave it to the forwards to slurp around." If backs don't try anything what are they out there for?'

There are more things in the philosophy of young Mark Ella than are dreamed of by the majority of greybeard, clipboard-screaming coaches in Britain. For almost an hour, the twenty-five-year-old sat on a table in the Malone RFC clubroom and talked without a note to an entranced group of sixty or so of Ulster's leading coaches, schoolmasters and players.

'What I'm about to tell,' he began, 'is not meant to degrade your British style of play at all: I just think it is worth it to compare it with my own attitude towards rugby . . .'

He was received in awed silence, except for the odd scratching of a pen as a coach scribbled notes. Talk about the infant preaching to the wise men in the temple.

His arms were folded across his green national sweater as he extemporized, with insight and no little wit, his brown leather lace-up shoes gently rocking from the table. Behind him the usual clubhouse plaques in signwriter's gilt named the captains and the cups and the caps. The legendary Ernie Crawford played for Malone in the 20s, Jimmy Nelson in the 40s . . . those old-timers would have been awestruck at the aplomb of this young man – even more so by the content of his tutorial.

The dark-skinned handsome native boy from the aboriginal mission station was himself that missionary now. He was born into poverty in La Perouse, which the rich whites of Sydney scornfully call 'Larpa – our Soweto'. They don't look down from the aircraft window for shame when they fly into Sydney airport over Botany Bay. It has been an aborigine compound since Captain Cook hit land.

May and Gordon Ella brought up their twelve children in a shanty hut, which a nailed-up plyboard partition turned into a two-roomed job. The family slept on shared mattresses on the floor; no privacy, no sewerage; there was one cold tap; a bath was a communal trough in the yard; a shower was when it rained, for the roof was a sieve.

Yet it was, the boy will tell you, a home with a lot of love and laughter. May was the adored, feared matriarch; Gordon, whose white grandfather had married an aboriginal girl, was the romantic who loved to catch mullet off the cliffs when he had time away from the factory night shift.

But at least – as ghettoes go – the compensation was the sea down the lane and the sun on their backs. And 'La Pa' had a junior rugby and cricket team, so the children knew more than the rudiments when they were admitted to Matraville HS – since when Mark's brothers, the twins Glen and Gary, first inspired the Australian Schools XV to a thrilling walkabout round the world before graduating, each one, to the full national side.

Mark won his first cap for Australia in 1980. He was twenty. The torch he carried became brighter with every appearance. In 1983 he was elected Young Australian of the Year.

I sat there in Belfast, listening to him, and musing . . . I had seen the languid, outside body swerve of Richard Sharp; the carefree, waiflike, insouciance of Barry John; the hopscotch of Bennett; the vim, dash and control of young Gibson; the dozy skill and awareness of Porta . . . This boy here is in that classic line. But he is a revolutionary within it.

He scarcely fits into the canon. An original. It is worth rereading the description of the old-time Australian player and visionary coach, Cyril Towers. He had written in the Twickenham programme a week before:

'Ella runs from the shoulders down, with the fingers, hands and arms completely relaxed; he takes the ball on one side and passes before the foot comes down again; his concept of the fly-half position is that it is semi-restricted – the attack must begin further out; he is very difficult to

229

think against – if you think ahead of him, he will slip inside, and it's no good thinking four or five moves ahead, because he hasn't invented them yet.'

Ella sits on the clubhouse table. No side, no swank. Only his soft voice, and the coaches' pencils frantically scratching at their notebooks. Many of them must have been coaching rugby for over twenty years. They were not going to miss these revelations from the twenty-five-year-old prophet:

'You Irish have particularly impressed me that you are trying at least. But it's still dull football. You have got out of the habit of entertaining and running the ball – it's an attitude which has evolved over the years. In Australia, we have been playing running football for a long time. I grew up playing that way. But here, the natural ability has been coached out of the players. You are playing too basic a game, concentrating on the physical aspect rather than moving the ball. Everybody says Britain has potentially the best backs but they only turn it on for five minutes in an entire match. That's no good. We have already lost count of the number of occasions teams started to run the ball against us when we are out of sight and the match won. Only then would you Brits move it.'

Above the scrape of the scribbling hieroglyphics, the packed room of rugby elders were murmuring enthused murmurs which seemed to mean a mixture of *mea culpas* and *eureka*.

'Fly-half play', Ella went on, 'was more speed of thought than foot. Look at little me. I'm not fast. I'm not a stepper. I can run a bit, but I've no idea of a jink either off left or right. And you know I can't kick for peanuts. At set-pieces, no, I never run up in defence – simply because no-one actually runs the ball at me; and in Britain they nearly always simply kick. A breakaway wing-forward has honestly never touched me in years – and I think that might be something to do with the secret . . .

'The crucial thing must be the speed of the ball through the hand. The quicker you get it, the quicker you can pass it on.

'The nearer you play to the opposition and the straighter you run, the better. It's common sense. Then, the shorter the pass, the quicker you can decide your options. Then, you can think of varying the length of your passes.'

It was stunning stuff. No note, no prompt. Out of the mouths of babes . . . I wished Percy Bush could have been listening from heaven; or Adrian Stoop. Perhaps they were. Or Carwyn James, the coaching genius and old fly-half, who had, alas, died the year before, mourned by the game. How proud Carwyn would have been of this aborigine boy's clean mind and logic. On he went:

'British coaches must let young players read the game themselves and think for themselves on the field. That is non-existent in British rugby at this time. You are over-coached and the emphasis is far too much on winning – in any way. Your teams would rather defend than attack because it has become natural to them. As much as they are trying to say it's changing, I don't see it. Your teams have no imagination, they have been taught the same old moves with the same old patterns. They continually keep on calling the set moves.'

Nor was he finished, and I hugged myself again for being the only journalist who had bothered to turn up. And all taking place on Dr Jack Kyle's patch and parish. The British fly-half disease, said young Ella, was reliance on the boot. 'Kicking away possession is absolutely crazy. To score a try you have to have the ball in your hands. I say to my scrum-half, "I'm calling the shots, give me the ball however bad it is!" All this British business of kicking for twenty minutes to size up the opposition!

'If in the first twenty minutes my scrum-half puts up one kick himself, then okay, I suppose; if he puts up two, I'll go over and hit him. His job is to get the ball to me any way he can. I call the moves, I distribute to those outside me and then, with the ball in their hands, they can put the pace on it. I know a lot of our fancy moves cause us Wallabies to make mistakes; we try everything and aren't quite getting the points on the board, but at least we try and we'll keep on trying. If not, isn't the whole thing totally boring for everyone concerned? How can you go out there and have the feeling "If I try something, and it doesn't work, we're going to lose"? No, you go out there and say "If I try something and it works, then we're going to win."'

It was still bucketing down outside; no matter, Ella was smiling – and so was every utterly refreshed fellow in the room as they turned another page in their notebooks and queued, to a man, for Mark Ella's autograph.

There is, in fact, not much more one needs to log about Ella's fly-half play. Simply, as he talked that day, so he played.

On the following Saturday, Ireland were well beaten in Dublin – Ella dropping two goals and dapping down a blinding, 'loop-the-loop' try at the corner-flag. Within the next three weeks, Wales and Scotland were both comprehensively smithereened by the Australians by an aggregate score of 65–21. Both times, Ella was an inspiration and a joy.

Then, just like that – still twenty-five, and two years younger even than Barry John had been – he retired. Rugby League, understandably, offered him a fortune; he declined it firmly and positively, with a gracious smile – and became a businessman and an unofficial, worldwide diplomat and distinguished human-rights activist for the cause of aboriginals. I was next to meet him four years later, in 1988, when he was the enchanting manager of the commemorative centenary cricket tour of England by a team of Australian aboriginals. He remembered how he had preached his gospel to the rugby elders of Ulster. 'That was an apocalyptic rainstorm, wasn't it?' he recalled. 'Apocalyptic' in more ways than one, said I. When he retired aged twenty-five, he had played exactly the same number of Tests for Australia, beginning in 1979, against Hugo Porta's Argentina, when he was twenty.

Ten years later, in 1989, he was coaxed out of retirement to play for his club in Sydney, Randwick. In the last minute, he picked up a bobbler, whipped it to a loose forward, looped round and took the pass, fingertipped on to a centre, who flipped it away at speed to the winger, who was tackled five yards from the flag, threw it desperately inside as he fell . . . and Mark Ella took the ball in his stride and, with a shimmy, was over the line and under the posts. Last-ever game – still practising what he preached. A marvel.

The marvel? Of the *whole* century? Deep down, there is a certain case for saying that Ella probably was. He says he 'couldn't kick', but then I heard him say he didn't need, or want, to. He said he couldn't run – 'I'm no stepper' – but he could accelerate and change intent and stride like that Inspector Maigret black Citroën car of the classic series: lowering his suspension and sinking his hips to defy and baffle the cover before vrooming away over the cobbled streets of midfield. Australians still tell of Ella intercepting a Scottish pass at Sydney in 1982 inside his own twenty-two and setting off for the faraway line – chased by the quicksilver and brilliant Scots winger, Roger Baird. Ella knew it was Him v. Carl Lewis – and really no hope – but he kept changing his stride patterns, slowing down, or feinting inside and out while sidestepping thin air; thus Baird (one of the fastest then in rugby) could never 'hit' his own stride, and Ella scored his try – though Roger was never more than a couple of paces behind him for the 'run-in' of fully fifty metres.

Australians have never been quite able to fathom British rugby. Eighty autumns ago the first rugby tourists to Britain from Australia were also bemused. They had been beaten only by four Welsh sides and the Midland Counties in twenty-nine matches when they met England at Blackheath on 9 January 1909. The Aussies won fair and square, but the English accused them of dirty play and the collar-studs in the RFU committee box refused to offer the customary three hurrahs at the final whistle.

The first touring side was packed with Aussie-Irish – the half-backs were the dashing captain McKivat and McCabe; and McCue. Hickey and McArthur were the other leading lights. The tour manager was the rubicund Captain McMahon. A Rugby League team from the colony had already visited England and been dubbed 'the Kangas', as in kangaroo. At the inaugural 1908 banquet in Holborn to welcome the new Union visitors, a smirking English RFU official suggested calling them 'the Rabbits', on account of the plague at the time in New South Wales of the white-tailed bobbers, and also because the Aussie-Irish were reputed to breed like them. McMahon bridled with contempt at the jibe and that night called a team meeting and proposed a vote on three names, 'The Wallaroos' was thrown out first; then 'the Waratahs' (a red flower), because it grew only in New South Wales; finally, says the tour report, 'Wallabies' was agreed on unanimously.

That side played in light blue shirts and navy bags. After they toured again, in 1928, they were told to wear dark green. Only Cambridge are the light blues, ol' boy. Ireland and South Africa, who 'copyrighted' the two shades of green, furiously complained. So Twickenham ordered the change to yellow, 'with green trimmings allowable'; pukey but distinctive.

Those Wallaby sides between, and after, the wars regularly found inspiration from their fly-halves – a succession of grand operators like Tom Lawton, grandfather of the stalwart hooker two generations later: Dick Tooth, the Sydney doctor; Arthur Summons, who would point his right toecap in the direction he wanted the scrum-half's ball; Phil Hawthorne, whom Barry John marked in the Welsh boy's first international match and so hugely admired thereafter; and Paul McLean, richly accomplished at fly or full-back, and one of the astonishing Queensland dynasty, six of whom won Australian caps in the eighty years from 1904 – with, doubtless, more to come. Paul McLean, a prodigious place-kicker, was one of a number of leading Australian players who refused to tour New Zealand in 1982, saying they were 'jaded with rugby', though rumours suggest the reasons were more to do with 'tour expenses', and the appointment of a new coach, Bob Dwyer, from the Sydney club, Randwick, for which Ella played.

This 'rebellion' of established players, in fact, probably went a long way to allowing the birth of Australia's wonderful Grand Slam side of 1984. Dwyer's enforced bunch of keen young tyro replacements acquitted themselves superbly against the All Blacks, and although the coach was soon to lose his job for three years to the gregarious Alan Jones (Rob Andrew's aforesaid mentor), that 1982 tour can certainly be seen as laying the first crucial cornerstones of the glistening decade which was to come for Australian rugby.

13

'Just get us down their end'

Mark Ella, whose first, and winningly stupendous, series had been in 1980, against the perplexed and, in comparison, suddenly ponderous flat-battered All Blacks, unfrighteningly planted the flag for the invigorating new generation at the base camp. In the first match of the 1984 tour to Britain, against England at Twickenham, Ella's scrum-half was Nick Farr-Jones, a pleasantly soft-mannered, intellectual Sydney law student. A couple of months before the team arrived in England, Ella had played inside a well-built, sandy-blond, teenager centre from Queensland – Michael Lynagh, who had confidently kicked three penalty goals in his debutant's match against Fiji in Suva once a few had been missed by the chosen kicker, a versatile greenhorn who had alternated in his first half-dozen Tests at full-back or wing: his name was David Campese.

Thus it was that those four comparatively inexperienced young men – Ella, at twenty-six, was by far the senior – threw down a gauntlet to champion the thrilling possibilities and even the beauty of modern fifteen-man rugby. Having presided over the inaugural announcement, Ella bowed out, content to leave this trio of kids – Campese, Farr-Jones and Lynagh – to re-point the sharp priorities of his own gospel, and then spread the word for inventive and dramatic rugby football. Which they did – and with a missionaries' devotion, which was acclaimed the world over when the three of them led Australia to a resplendent World Cup victory seven years later, in 1991.

Ella's last match for Australia was the Grand Slam finale against Scotland in 1984. The Wallabies, with an exultant show, won by 37–12. Every point was scored by the quartet – a blazing curtain-call try to sign off by Ella, a truly original blindside job off a lineout by Farr-Jones, and two 'Campissimo' originals by the winger. Each one of them was unerringly converted through the Edinburgh gale by young Lynagh, who added for good measure a then Murrayfield record of five whistle-clean penalty goals.

A week later, once the pilot of the triumphant team's Qantas airliner had allowed them to unfasten safety-belts over the English Channel, Ella called the small band of Aussie journos to the bank of seats he had bagged for a sleep, and said, 'Gents, if you're interested, well, I've retired. As simple as that. No more bigtime rugby for me.'

Every question began, 'Why tell us now, when we can't possibly write it up for twenty-four hours?' Said Mark, 'Because I knew it would save me taking my phone off the hook for a month once I got home.'

I looked up what Neville Cardus had written when my particular boyhood hero at cricket, Tom Graveney, retired. Mark Ella's span was far shorter than Graveney's. I substitute only the names of the game and of the man but it still holds good:

'If some destructive process were to eliminate all we know about rugby, only Ella surviving, we could reconstruct from him, from his way of playing and loving rugby and from the man himself, every outline of the game, every essential character and flavour which have contributed to rugby, the form of it and its soul, and its power to inspire.'

Back to Australia's Grand Slam. I remember vividly that morning in Edinburgh on 8 December 1984. The Grand Slam, uniquely for the Wallabies, was very much 'on'. Never before a whitewash – England, Wales, Ireland and, now finally, Scotland. The corridor the tourists had commandeered at the gaunt, grey 'rugby' hotel, the North British, rang strident to the full-blast psyching-up sounds of the Furies and Dire Straits.

The Wallabies had one dilemma to solve before the afternoon's showdown at Murrayfield. Who would take the kicks? The young centre, Lynagh – he had been twenty-one four weeks before – had played a tour of exciting promise, but only in direct ratio to the increasing nervousness of his place-kicking. Indeed, in the previous Test against Wales in Cardiff his aim had been so lamentable that the full-back, Roger Gould, had superseded him – and certainly Gould's 12 kicked points had been responsible for battening down the victory at the Arms Park. Now in Edinburgh, on the eve of the Grand Slammer itself, we had stayed behind after training as Lynagh took a string of place-kicks from every corner of Murrayfield. It was not the 70,000 throng of the morrow, sure, but us knot of a dozen hacks, pencils poised, must have been pretty daunting as we watched the boy in silence. The 'H' of rugby posts can be either Heaven or Hell for a kicker in trouble. Lynagh took sixteen kicks – and fifteen of them sailed massively true through the posts. 'Well done,' I said, as he gathered up his clobber at the touchline. 'Don't congratulate me,' said the young man, 'it's all down to my dad back home.' How come? Well, Lynagh *père* is a well-known sports psychologist, and all through the week, by telephone, he had been 'talking through kicking's mind over matter' with his son. Now the knack had returned – and next day Lynagh was given back his record-breaking kicking duties and helped KO Scotland and put the seal on a memorable tour with a voluptuous 37–12 victory. As he saw the triumphant tourists off, the chivalrous Scottish captain and scrum-half Roy Laidlaw (whose 'inseparable' partner, Rutherford, was injured and missed the match) shook his head in admiration and said, 'They did not so much give us a beating, but a lesson. My only consolation is that some ten- and fifteen-year-olds in Britain might have been inspired to start working on what us Scots have been taught this weekend.'

So Ella took his last, acclaimed curtain-call – and Michael Lynagh picked up his No. 10 jersey and moved downstage into the limelight.

Back in the mists, the Lynaghs had arrived in Australia from Galway. Michael's father, Ian, obviously was steeped in sport, and mother, Marie, was an Australian champion sprinter at schools level. Michael seemed a 'natural' when scarcely out of nappies. He began with soccer, then cricket, and at Brisbane's Gregory Terrace College he was being talked about as a future Test cricketer before he was fifteen. By that age, his golf handicap was already in single figures. In those mid-teens, the family spent a year in the United States, at Oregon, where Ian had been posted on a course – and there the boy revelled in US football and found he had a marvellous touch at 'gridiron' kicking.

Back home at rugby-keen Gregory Terrace, the US experience had fired his enthusiasm for the oval ball – although it was a long time before he could bring himself to admit that perhaps he was not going to emulate his all-time boyhood hero, the Queensland and Australian cricket captain and elegant eminence for years, Greg Chappell. Nevertheless, as Lynagh grew up to become acknowledged as the very best and most complete – if not the most dramatic or thrillingly mercurial – rugby player in the world, the increasingly adjectival laurels with which you could garland him conjured up memories of the upright and upstanding Chappell of the cricket field. Take for instance this valediction by John Arlott in the *Guardian* on Chappell's retirement:

'Above all, he was the matchwinner in skill and temperament; the decisive decision-maker at the crucial period and the critical passage; a player of immense power, the more impressive for it being veiled by the certainty of his timing, and an almost aesthetic sense of his elegance of movement; in everything there was innate balance, and unhurried speed, and safe hands. Also [unlike his brother, Ian], he set his face against the permissive in a looked-up-to international sportsman; he spurned "sledging", sloppy-dressing, and general bad manners, and he strove to maintain the high standards he set.'

That could, word for word, serve well enough as an all-hail and farewell to Michael Lynagh when the time comes.

While on the subject, young Lynagh's other sporting hero, and one he dotingly continues in awe of to this day, is the American champion golfer Jack Nicklaus. Many years ago, Alistair Cooke wrote this of Nicklaus's predecessor in golf's all-time hall of fame, Bobby Jones – and it surely applies to Nicklaus too: 'What we talk about here is not the hero as golfer, but that something which the people hungered for and found; the best performer in the world who was also the hero as human being, the gentle, wholly self-sufficient male, Jefferson's lost paragon: "the wise innocent".' It surely applies, as well, to Michael Lynagh as rugby's third World Cup approaches, when he will still be in the prime of his wisdom and his early thirties – and his 'wise innocence'.

Once young Michael had begun to take his school rugby more seriously than his cricket and golf, the word was around Australian rugby circles like a bush fire. In no time he was in the all-Australian age-level teams. One afternoon, when the Wallaby under-seventeens were practising for a match at the Coogee Oval, an interested touchline bystander, name of Bob Dwyer, asked the coach, Jeff Sayle, 'Who's that little kid with the fair hair?' Replied Sayle, 'Don't knock him, he's the star.' Dwyer insisted he was not so much knocking as knocked out by the obvious and innate precociousness of the talent. It was Dwyer, of course, as the Wallabies' coach, who was to be guide, friend and adviser in the days of glory to come.

Filling out rapidly as he moved at eighteen from school to Queensland University, the boy was at once, as a fresher, organizing the varsity XV to such a striking extent that within three matches he was in the Queensland state side – at fly-half, with the celebrated Paul McLean at full-back.

Spotting the talent, McLean clucked around the boy, generously passing on all he knew about the intricacies of

240

fly-half play and the techniques, and whens and where-fores of kicking. It was in that first state season of his that Lynagh's nickname 'Noddy' was writ indelibly in the legend – such was the intense and concentrated nodding of his head when in an earnest coaching seminar with McLean. (Another affectionate name he answers to with the Wallabies' champion side is 'the One O'Clock Gun' – when he fires, the whole team fires.)

What an apprenticeship and education, for after McLean's tutelage at Queensland, it was straight into the national side's yellow-ochre as inside-centre to Mark Ella. As the good Australian writer Wayne Smith observes, 'Where McLean taught him tactics and disciplines, Ella imbued him with the magic and artistry of the game. And in many respects, Lynagh emerged as the synthesis of the two.'

Unquestionably what he learned from Ella was the utter mastery of – and absolute necessity for – the quickfire fingertip pass, inside or outside, to the full-pelt, support-ing colleague. Lynagh, as Ella did, lies so flat and close that the pass itself regularly breaches the gain-line – and the Wallabies are on an irresistible stampede once again. Moreover, as each year passed since that bigtime entrance at Twickenham in 1984 so, as regular as succeeding Easters and Christmas, he inexorably continued to festoon his game with ever more rounded qualities of nous and vision in attack and defence. Ditto his kicking from hand. His competitiveness was as upright and clean-cut as his tackling was low and clean-cut scything. And his support play was a joy – as you asked yourself with Ella, how many times had Lynagh scored the try. having in-stigated the move five passes back? Or seven, or eight?

All topped, of course, by his priceless place-kicking. Oddly – or understandably more like, if you think about it – as his all-round fly-half game burgeoned and bloomed into such brilliant colours, so Lynagh's place-kicking showed signs of just slightly slipping standards. He kicked very poorly in the Bledisloe Cup matches against New Zealand which served as a warm-up rehearsal for the

1991 World Cup. In that competition, he was seldom unerringly on target as his team had come to expect (the balls the sponsors foisted on the tournament did not suit him, he pointed out – but not in a whingeing way: he just went out to practise with them some more).

Yet the figures show that in the thirteen international matches from his disastrous Bledisloe Cup day in Auckland in 1991 (when he kicked only one goal in seven attempts), till he went off with a dislocated shoulder against Ireland in Dublin at the end of 1992, his kicking success rate dropped below 50 per cent for the first time in his career – with exact precision, for in precisely 100 shots he goaled only 48.

Even so, that Dublin game on All Saints Day (Australia 42, Ireland 17) still left Lynagh far and away the game's most prodigious and prolific points scorer, with an astonishing 760 points in fifty-nine matches, haring away with disdain since the day, years before, he had overtaken Hugo Porta's 530. (Porta, by the way, remains Lynagh's most difficult and respected opponent at fly – 'he was hard even to get near', he says; 'Hugo "played" you like a matador, and when he was going well, which was always, you could only keep doing your best, and sit back and admire him through gritted teeth').

The value – spiritually as well as actually – at which the Wallabies priced their gem was illustrated after his injury at Dublin in the middle of that short tour to Ireland and Wales in 1992. After Dublin, the team played four more weeks, ending with matches on successive Saturdays against Wales and the Barbarians. From Ireland, Lynagh flew back to Australia for an operation on his shoulder – only to return immediately for the final ten days of the tour, 'just because he is such an invaluable influence around the changing room with his strength of purpose and knowledge and tactical brain and general heroic good-eggery,' said the coach, Dwyer. 'Anyway,' he added, 'Michael wanted to come back, it's his team.'

Dwyer is a revelation, and the whole of world rugby was truly blessed when he arrived out of Randwick almost in the very same months that the global game was still in deep mourning at the death of coaching's luminous visionary from Wales (though unhonoured as a prophet in his own loopy land), the onliest Carwyn James.

Dwyer was a Randwick wing-forward who 'fell' into coaching his club at the instigation, and inspiration, of the club's grand old man and outrageously good Wallaby centre of the 1930s, Cyril Towers. Thus Ella and his brothers 'fell' into Dwyer's lap at Randwick. What more could a coach ask? Well, only one's own challenging and daring originality, and a flair for, and joy in, paring a presumably simple game down to even more basic tenets – which latter, it so happens, has been confusing so-called coaches for a century. For Dwyer's stark philosophy is that he strives to put the winning of a game in his team's hands and not throw the onus on the opposition to avoid losing it – in other words, to pressurize the opposition into mistakes with the ball in hand, rather than giving the ball, or kicking it, to the opposition and then trying to pressure them into mistakes. (Whenever Dwyer voices these riveting philosophies, my mind always goes back to that memorable day in the Malone clubhouse when Ella, the 'child', preached to the coaches in their temple.)

The Australian coach is a delightful man, erudite, companionable, and as honestly made and straight as a Roman road. He does not suffer idiots (except, for some reason, in this particular case), and when I asked him which of the two fly-halves was the better, he said that, truly, he could not split the difference or the two. I somehow presumed that, even unconsciously, he would choose the Randwick boy from the shacks – and not irrespective of that sort of social-history romance, but because Ella's neon-flashing coruscations and almost (no, certainly) revolutionary's, slipper-soft talents would reflect themselves more brightly on the ultimate game which Dwyer himself was aiming for.

We were in Dublin Airport, plane-waiting after the Australians' stupendously organized victory against the All Blacks in the 1991 World Cup semi-finals. He just could not answer the question – except to make it a dead-heat between Ella and Lynagh. Knowing him, even slightly, I was certain Dwyer was not being diplomatic towards his present fly-half. He was just saying it, as ever, as he saw it:

'Mark had quite wonderful handling skills, mesmerizing sometimes. But just watch Lynagh's. You cannot possibly say Lynagh's handling is not on the same level of sheer brilliance, can you? At running "angles" and a sort-of "shuffling" subtlety, Mark was above anyone who can ever have played the game, except perhaps Barry John. But our "Noddy" Lynagh's running is of a different calibre and momentum, and you cannot tell me that it's not so effective, can you? In defence, it's probably far more direct and potent. In attack-support as well – different, but both crucially outstanding. Never bettered, I would say. And if, as you romantics insist – and, I suppose, so do I, yes – Mark had that indefinable dusting with "glittery fairy-powder", then his intuitive kicking to redefine and announce our next area of attack (I'm not talking about potting at penalty goals) puts Michael ahead. So, sorry, pal, it's neck-and-neck, a nose-to-nose draw between Ella and Lynagh.'

I took it all down in a notebook. We broke up to wander round to other pals in the departure lounge. Just before the flight was finally called, I caught Bob's eye. I went over. 'Tell you something for nothing,' he said, 'if Michael had not scored that try last week [the dramatic quarter-final last-minuter against Ireland at Lansdowne Road], I would have told you that the only major and radical difference between the two of them was and is that Mark, bless the old boy, could "smell" a try up to ten passes and two rucks before we scored it. And once I could sense him "smelling" that try, we seldom failed to nail it down. Some real sort of innate sporting genius, don't you think?'

Then he added: 'But it might be even less than a dead-level draw between the two now, because Lynagh's try against Ireland last week might not only remain the grandest of all grand things he has ever done in rugby – it showed that he can "smell" a try, and score it, with an even more powerful sense of smell than Ella had.' And he smiled, with his always challenging inscrutability, through his top-lip Kaiser's busby – and went to catch his aeroplane to London, where he and his were to win the World Cup. I smiled too, and followed on into the Smoking seats. And reflected with pleasure (dammit, even as a second-generation colonial who supports Ireland at everything, even tennis) on Michael Lynagh's sense of 'smell' eight days before in the old rickety arena, much beloved, alongside the railway line.

What had happened is this. Unfancied Ireland had played a tremendous match with their traditional jingle-jangling, out-of-my-way donnybrook fire in their bellies and claws as sharp as Kilkenny cats. Early on, Lynagh had taken over as captain when Farr-Jones wrenched his knee. As the merry old ding-dong wore on, it looked as if the Wallabies' class at keeping the ferments and fervours of the home side at arm's length had seen them narrowly through, into the semi-final against the All Blacks. With six minutes left, Australia led by 15–12 and looked safe, for while the Irish continued with their huff and puff, they seemed fast running out of the latter. Oh, yeah ... suddenly Jack Clarke popped the ball to Gordon Hamilton, who turned a foot into a yard, saw the line, and pinned back his ears and went for it – with all Ireland, half Boston, and sweet Molly Malone on his shoulders and whipping him home. He made it, and the old place went even crazier when Ralph Keyes, veteran Munster fly-half who had been mucked around for years by the selectors, strolled up and calmly plonked the conversion over the bar and, he thought, into history. 18–15, and surely the favourites were done for?

Lynagh kicked off. Too deep. Ireland's Rob Saunders had ample time to find touch, but muffed it. The Wallabies' full-back, Marty Roebuck, drilled the ball back. Brian Robinson flapped at it, total panic ... no green man could hoick the ball off the island. The

Wallabies thundered in and, after a devilish scrap, won the ball . . . bing, bang, bong, along the line – and Lynagh himself goes over and triumphantly into the semi-final.

Lynagh recalls it: 'As soon as they scored, the first thing I did was ask the ref, "How long?" He said, "About four minutes after the conversion." I called the guys together on the line and said, "We've just got to keep calm. Just get us down their end and we will score, I promise." That's just what we did. Once we had composed ourselves in their twenty-two, I called a simple "play" we had practised loads of times – in it, Tim [the inside-centre, Horan] sends a cut-out pass to Marty [Roebuck], and Jason rockets into the line outside Marty, hence to Campo, who scores. Easy. In the event it worked perfectly – till Jason was badly obstructed, then Campo was collared. But as he fell, Campo was able to pop the ball up – and I just happened to be there, and went over. Great.'

Says Dwyer: 'It could well have been Michael's finest moment in rugby. In the stand, my legs turned to jelly when Ireland scored, and they were still like old rope fully an hour later. But not Michael's. He could have panicked and said to the boys on the line, "We've botched it up, dammit. Let's pull a trick or something and go for a field goal, it's our last hope." Instead he calmly says, "We need to get down there, so I'll kick-off deep, you pressure them to give us our ball back, then you forwards give it to us backs – and we'll score the try." It was an utter triumph of composure and grace under intense pressure – and it must never be forgotten when people ask you "who was better than who?" and all that evaluation poppycock.'

But, soon afterwards, the estimable Dwyer answered – or, fascinatingly, tried to – the question himself. He wrote the best memoir of its type I have read, *The Winning Way*, with the leading Sydney sportswriter Phil Derriman. Phil had to ask the burning question of the man who had worked so intimately with them both – Lynagh or Ella? 'Exactly equal in general play, with Lynagh superior in kicking.'

By the time Australia were passing round the World

Cup at Twickenham a fortnight after that Dublin palpitator, Lynagh's eight points which had helped sink England in a thrilling final (Australia 12, England 6) had stretched his world record to 689 points. Over twelve months later, by the New Year of 1993, his tally stood at 760 in fifty-nine matches – a strike-rate average of 12.8 points per match. Many more points, sure, but not as good as a rival, kicking fly-half, Grant Fox of New Zealand, whose 571 points in forty matches gave him a top fly-halves' average of 14.2 per match. But surprisingly, Lynagh, for all his admitted loss of kicking form through the World Cup and after, had an average still ahead of the perceived kicking ace of them all, the South African Naas Botha, who had only played in twenty-five Tests because of his country's banishment, and whose tally stood, as 1993 began, at 279, average 11.1 per Test. (The averages of other fly-halves, past or present, read at that point – Camberabero and Porta, an identical 10.0 each in 33 Tests; Campbell 8.3 in 29; Romeu 7.7 in 34; Ward 6.9 in 19; and Bennett 5.6 in 33. Of course, no end of full-back kickers intersperse those figures.)

I first saw the astonishing Grant James Fox kick the French to death in two successive international matches against France, in Nantes and Paris, in 1990. Another 28 points for his kitty to sustain, exactly, his average. But what surprised me on those first two sightings was the New Zealand fly-half's most telling efficiency with the ball in his hands. Nothing in the least bit fancy, mind, no fly-half play of the Welsh chapel-dazzler kind or Irish flamboyance. Just a superior, chieftain's level of maturity under pressure, a totally assured inner calm of which way to go, which option to take, whether to feed the line or set his pack back on the prowl, to kick long rakers or short stingers. It was a complete display, and a pleasure to watch. Especially from a man they say has little more to offer than the kick of a Mevagissey mule.

That is the trouble with being very good at one thing: people think it is your only thing. True, Fox's kicking has been phenomenal since he became a regular All Black just before 1987's inaugural World Cup (in which his 126 points in just six matches helped secure the trophy more than somewhat). Fastest in history to 100 points; to 200 points; to 300; to 400. Incredible. It seems like only yesterday that he overtook the All Blacks record of that grand old hoofer, the solemn full-back Don Clarke, whose tally of 207 points had stood for years. Now this unassuming, well-mannered young man has trebled the Don's double century: in 1993 he topped the 600 as he punished the British Lions to defeat and distraction.

When Fox took over in 1987 from the inventive, far more silky and less pragmatic Wayne Smith, he said he had to learn sixty-two different calls for the myriad of ploys and alternatives the All Blacks had rehearsed for any given moment. As his confidence has grown – and as new men take the places of the old guard to leave him, by the match almost, ever more the relied-on commanding officer – he has pared down the frills.

'Now we just have about thirty-three calls to choose from. The only trouble is, sometimes I toss one out which is used by Auckland or my University club side, one that isn't on the All Blacks' list. Still, it confuses the opposition even more, with a bit of luck.

'No worries, really, because the great thing with All Black tradition is to rely on basics. Everything I do is geared to keeping the forwards moving, get as many men in position to outnumber the opposition when we're attacking and outnumber them when we're defending. That's what my calls are all about, no more, no less.'

It is much to do with concentration, he says, and by lunchtime, having found himself a quiet corner away from the pre-match hum, he will be 'visualizing' each of his calls, every conceivable possibility for any square yard of the field. The din, the tensions, the dangers weighed up, and the momentary chink of opportunity.

'It must be second nature, programmed, literally not a moment to reflect – well, say three seconds at the most, to tell the chaps what's on,' he reckons. 'Very seldom more than three seconds.'

Decisions, decisions. All those and goalkicking too. And as quietly unobtrusive as the man himself. Over the bar they sail, almost unnoticed by anyone except the frantic bloke on the scoreboard. Not the great howitzer thumps of a Paul Thorburn; nor the amiable bar-creepers of Michael Kiernan; nor the agricultural, timeless inevitability of a caress by Dusty Hare; nor the precision-tooled, torpedo job of a Bob Hiller. No elastic-legged Moulin Rouge follow-through like little Phil Bennett, nor the casually joyous 'corner-kick' of Barry John. Fox comes up, minimum of fuss, takes aim, and over she goes while everyone's nose is still in the programme seeing who scored the try.

All he alters, and that only fractionally, is the angle on the divot: sitting back towards him a half-inch for the shorties; dead upright for the mid-iron pot; and the ball just slightly tilted towards the posts when the right foot is prepared to let rip to give it a belt, as if off the tee on a par-five. The metaphor fits. He knows that goalkicking is like golf: for all the club-waggling favourite routines, perfect timing is the essence.

And when he is not kicking, Fox calls his shots, shovels or shoes the ball on, so his centres are never short of opportunities for a spearing thrust, nor his wingers for a dash. It is the way the All Blacks play; and so it has ever been – nothing flash or glam at first five-eighths but, invariably, teak-tough centres good on the ball, and wing-men fast, direct, and ditto. Fox fits the bill perfectly for a Kiwi first five. His field-kicking is a stupendous bonus.

A mighty different kettle of kicker is Naas Botha. He is one heck of a hoofer, but an unhappy one to be derided, as he is, by half the game for the single-minded, metronome swing of his boot. As I say, it is a surprise his Test kicking average is not higher, such is his reputation. But then it is not so much his points-scoring place-kicking that is so famed as his kicking out of hand with punt or drop. As with his compatriot of over half a century ago, Bennie Osler, it is uncanny that the very mention of the name of Botha comes heaped with implied criticism of his reliance on his feet in a handling game. Yet kicking is part – very much part – of rugby, and so Naas Botha deserves his due. Osler might have been better than him – who knows? – but for sure no-one has been better than the two South Africans who learned to fly the ball such vast distances through the thin air of the High Veldt at altitude.

Botha's first, and last, match at Twickenham was at the end of 1992. He was thirty-five. The Springboks, their banishment over, had forgotten too much in the meanwhile, as the rest of the game had progressed into far more polished areas. England beat them by a record margin. But Botha put on a stupendous show of punting on a filthy day, and a drop-goal on the turn was an act the Magic Circle might have bought for its Christmas concert. The chief sports correspondent of *The Times*, David Miller, was there. He is not a regular rugby man, and has no entrenched axe to grind about over-kicking fly-halves, so his memorable piece the following morning is, in fairness and justice to Botha's supreme single talent, all the more worthy of the archives and posterity:

'Anyone who had missed seeing Botha 12 years ago, as I had, should be grateful for a last glimpse of a special performer. The difficulty of handling and kicking a rugby ball is part of the game's fascination, something that hardly one per cent of all those who play ever truly master. Imagine trying to hit a tennis or cricket ball that was triangular. Botha, marvellously proportioned physically and with that elusive secret of timing, makes his skills appear utterly natural to a degree that can unhinge the opposition in split seconds. He can swerve the ball off the outside of the foot and do things with it few can aspire to.

'His kicking on Saturday, even in greasy conditions, was a marvel, rifling the ball 50 and 60 yards to stem English attacks and send them lumbering backwards. Rob Andrew is an accomplished kicker, too, though his technique has a studied, mathematical calculation. Botha's art is altogether more spontaneous, and the nonchalance with which he spun away from onrushing forwards to send a dropped goal soaring between the posts after 25 minutes was a wonderful demonstration of his technique.'

I had first set eyes on Botha, remember, over a dozen years before, on the last Lions tour of the Republic before the apartheid portcullis clanged shut on it. He was twenty-two, a beautifully built athlete at 5 ft 10 in. and twelve stones, handsomely blond and magnificently balanced. Straight from the Hendrik Verwoerd School, he had been chosen to lead the line for Northern Transvaal, at nineteen, all of three years earlier. He was obviously going to play in the Tests, and the Lions could not wait to get a look at him. I was sitting next to Carwyn James, who was sending a regular column to my own paper, the *Guardian*, and Carwyn was next to Barry John. Within five minutes of Botha kicking off for Northern Transvaal, Carwyn was sighing, his head in his hands – and this is what he cabled off to the *Guardian* that evening:

'Another forgotten art was in evidence throughout the match – Botha's inability and that of his threequarters to pass the ball at speed. Theirs were pathetic attempts at an art which is absolutely basic to the game of Rugby Football. For that reason alone I was delighted to see the Lions giving a cocky, swankpot team the lesson of their lives. Rugby is not about a big dominating pack winning possession at will and plying their halves with kickable ball. Week after week we had heard of the victories gained by Northern Transvaal, with perhaps a try or maybe two, but mainly through the boot of Botha, who usually manages a hat-trick of dropped goals. In South Africa Botha is the new golden boy. By world standards he is a very ordinary outside-half.'

Later on in the tour Carwyn was asked to give a coaching seminar to the boys of Windhoek High School. In his record of the tour, *Injured Pride*, which he shared with Chris Rea, Carwyn recalled:

'It was a course for sixteen-year-olds and under; I talked to them at length about the approach to the game, emphasizing over and over again that Rugby is a running and a handling game, and that they should not emulate a Naas

Botha. I qualified my remarks about the young Naas Botha who, four years earlier, had impressed the 1976 All Blacks, and whom J. J. Stewart, the coach, regarded as a better player than Gerald Bosch, the Springboks' outside-half. Botha then had yet to start worrying about winning matches at any price. I mentioned to the lads of Windhoek that at the start of one season at Llandovery College, in the pre-dispensation law period, I insisted that no player should ever kick the ball in any of their matches. It was one of the finest seasons we ever had. I then asked the Windhoek boys to play a practice match before I took the coaching session. The headmaster was amazed, and a little thrilled, that not a single boy kicked the ball in thirty minutes, not even the lad who had confided that he wanted to be a Naas Botha.'

Over a dozen years later, and poor, loved Carwyn dead and buried, I went to Bordeaux Airport to greet Naas Botha and his new Springbok team – let out of jail and into Europe to resume their business with a short thirteen-match tour, beginning in France (where they were to win a Test and lose one) and ending with the match against England at Twickenham. They brought with them Hennie le Roux, a fly-half of gleaming talent and promise. But the young man would have to wait to display his charms on the international stage – but Springboks management, as it ever has, knows pragmatic reasons over and above any winning asset of swerving, sidestepping gaiety. At thirty-five and almost ten years older than his rival at out-half, Naas Botha remains the man to kick his side from seemingly anywhere on the field to within inches of an opponent's corner-flag and then, from any resulting penalty, to bisect the 'H' unerringly.

No matter that Botha has only a passing acquaintance-ship with his inside-centre – sorry, rephrase that: no passing acquaintanceship – the fellow must be the dead-liest and most destructively accurate kicker from both hand and turf that the game has ever seen.

He is no muscle-bound man for such a mulish hoofer – although his feet, when you see them flip-flopping in sandals across marble hotel foyers, seem inordinately large. His wheat-stook mop of hair and unmuddied pristine-Persil shorts – he is no hurly-burly tackler – make him a distinctive pin-up. But his permanent frown is that of a put-upon politician. Which, in a way, he is.

Throughout, and in spite of, South Africa's sporting bondage, he had remained the totem of the Springbok in exile. What feats he might have done this past fifteen years? But outside Northern Transvaal there is resentment of his star status and undirtied knees. The non-Transvaal press continued its bitter sniping against the guy. Botha resigned once and threatened to on another occasion in just the first twelve weeks the Springboks were back in the fold.

In no time, as the French tour fell into a leaden stride for the unaccustomed tourists, Botha was having to cover his back, especially the vulnerable slots immediately below the shoulder-blades – for the daggers were winging in: 'Naas Botha, who for more than a decade has been Springbok and South African rugby's most potent weapon and prolific points scorer, has now become its Achilles' heel,' Chris Swanepoel wrote in the Johannesburg-based newspaper *Citizen*. Even though the veteran fly-half was a superb tactician and kicker, he was effective only when his forwards dominated possession.

'Botha without the ball is as toothless as an old hag,' Swanepoel added. 'For Botha to be effective and kick a team to victory, a good percentage of line-out possession on the opponents' throw-in is vital. Nothing after three games in France has suggested that the present crop of forwards can win most of their own throw-ins, let alone their opponents'.'

At which the 'toothless old hag' shrugged – threw a toothy-bright, wide, Maclean's-ad smile (his first and last of the trip that I witnessed) and said the critics knew not a fig about either rugby or life, and most certainly less about the former. 'That's nothing', he said, 'to what the so-called journalists from the Cape or Natal are calling me – and have done almost since I was a boy. I just look at it as jealousy, or traditional provincial rivalry. It's the same in the team. I'm Northern Transvaal, and half the Springboks' side have no time for me. I know it. In our isolation we have become introverted and inward-looking. We had only provincial rivalries and hatreds to bite on. Because of the Currie Cup [provincial competition], rugby in South Africa has developed a tribal structure. There are players in the squad who left Northern Transvaal because of me. There are those who did not want to play with me. Suddenly, they found themselves having to play with me.

'So at once they have been asked to change their perceptions, to like and look up to their captain, Naas Botha. Well, they can't – and I understand it, because it's against human nature to suddenly be told to like a guy they have hated for seven years or more. That's why this Springboks is not one team – it's thirty individuals split up into pockets of tribal rivalry. When guys in the team go out together, it will be a group from Natal together, or a group from Western Province. Okay, it's natural in a way for friends to stay together, but for a Springbok team it's bad. It shows our allegiances are still formed by bitter provincialism.'

Botha's golden reputation has been based solely on his near genius at kicking. An apocryphal yarn has it that, on the flight over to France in 1992, an air-hostess asked him to pass a cup across to Danie Gerber, who was in an inside, window seat. Botha did – and Gerber remarked it was the only decent pass he'd ever received from the fly-half in his life.

As for his tackling: David Campese, the mischievous Wallaby, laughed at Botha for being the only player he has ever seen who wears a rugby jersey with special inbuilt shoulder-pads – yet has never been known to tackle. David Sole, the former Scottish stalwart and captain, played with Botha for a World XV against New Zealand in 1992.

'I'm rather ashamed to admit that once we had seen Naas playing we took to calling him the traffic policeman in view of his eagerness to wave the opposition through,' Sole wrote. 'The England centre Jerry Guscott, who was also in the World XV, says that Naas is the only fly-half he has ever seen pulling people out of rucks to stand in front of him so that he doesn't have to make the tackle! Naas may be a legend back home on the veldt but, in my opinion and certainly on the evidence of his performances in the World squad, he has a long way to go before he has mastered the skills that we would expect of an international fly-half these days.'

Botha pooh-poohs such criticism. 'They must have been reading the papers again,' he says. He is his own man, that's for sure – just like, when the apartheid revulsion was at its most bitter and the Springboks could not get a game with anyone, he went and played six games of grid-iron (only as a kicker) for Dallas Cowboys.

The week before his astonishing kicking display at Twickenham I read to him a newspaper cutting. He listened silently, nodding at the vindication. This is what I read out:

'In the art of attacking tactical kicks he was undoubtedly a master. Like a conjurer pulling things out of a hat he had a variety of these in his repertoire. Invariably, at the start of a game, he employed his "high skier" which was apt to unnerve any but the bravest full-backs. He had an uncanny skill in being able to place his punts just where he wanted them, and his diagonal kicks for the wings were designed to bring the opposition under pressure and his wings into a scoring position. As a line-kicker one has not seen his equal. If his three-quarters must have cursed him at times, his forwards had reason to bless him. He could always be relied on to keep them going forward, and he had a way of imparting screw so that the ball curved into touch at the end of its flight. This was often demonstrated when he took a penalty from a position close to the touchline that provided no angle.'

'Nice,' said Naas. 'Did you write that?'

'No,' I said, 'but I will tell you who did. It was written by your famous old journalist from the *Cape Argus*,

255

"Ace" Parker, many, many years ago. And he was writing about – yes, Bennie Osler! You see, Naas, there's nothing new at all under the cold wintery suns of rugby.'

A week later, having taken his drop-goal tally to an astonishing 18 in just twenty-eight Tests (one more than Rob Andrew in fifty-two), he announced his retirement, sounding not unlike Richard ('you won't have me to push around any more') Nixon: 'Some people will be glad to see the back of me but at least I retire with my head held high. I never gave less than 100 per cent. I sacrificed everything for rugby, and it was worth it.'

And he was gone. Still without a smile. Come to think of it, when did you last see a Springbok smile? A real, big, broad, happy-to-be-alive sunburst job. I mean a real whopper – like their forefathers' smiles. For is it not ninety years since an obviously hopeful and smiling cove, Field General Maritz, of the Transvaal Scouts, sent that invitation for a short Boer War ceasefire and a game of rugby to the Hon. Major Edwards of the British Army? That's nothing; in 1991 South African rugby celebrated the centenary of the first Test Match at Cape Town, when W. E. Maclagan's team from Britain were beaten. Smiles that night in Newlands, that's for sure.

14

Enchanting the Gods

There were probably even wider smiles up at altitude on the Veld fully 104 years later – and so was most of rugby grinning with a shared emotion at the end of 1995's staunchly fought World Cup final in Johannesburg when President Nelson Mandela handed the prize to the South African captain François Pienaar. During the game's two previous World Cups, in 1987 and 1991, Mandela had been still incarcerated in prison – as he would have been for the six before those, had they been staged – but now on an Ellis Park occasion festooned with symbolism the President presented the Cup while touchingly wearing a replica of Pienaar's No. 6 Springbok shirt of myrtle-green with yellow piping, the very livery which, before the former Republic's dramatic conversion to democracy, had been the wretched metaphor itself of apartheid's white supremacy. If it was the dignity (not to mention the defence) of back-row forward Pienaar which had been the capstan around which the Springboks' defiant triumph had been coiled that day, it was Naas Botha's heir at No. 10 Joel Stransky who had settled the thing in the dying minutes of extra-time with a nervelessly struck drop-goal.

If he was to be only briefly a luminous star on the main stage, Stransky's acute and vivid play from first match to that epic last all through the 1995 tournament ensures his glowing place in this legend. Meanwhile, two men with a far longer pedigree for the pantheon, had been forced to make their exit curtain-calls imminently before the World Cup had been settled by the South African fly-half. And of course, a year before those finals, the All Black Grant Fox had also tiptoed from the arena as surreptitiously as he had come to it – but now England's Rob Andrew and the Australian maestro Michael Lynagh also took their leave from international rugby.

Two Saturdays before Stranksy's resounding drop at Ellis Park had bisected the H and then sailed on around the world, Andrew had also swung his boot from infield at the very last and with a similarly daring flamboyance: in Cape Town, England's quarter-final against Australia (and Lynagh) stood at 22–22 with 82 minutes already gone when Martin Bayfield's expert lineout catch, a skilful forward drive and feed to scrum-half Dewi Morris allowed Andrew the sliver of daylight he needed to swing his boot from all of 45 yards and though Lynagh's desperate, diving chargedown was only a fingernail away, the ball flew gloriously on and upwards to win the match. It was Lynagh's last Test, and just a week later – same old stadium, brand new phenomenom – Andrew also knew his time was up as England were thunderously ransacked by Jonah Lomu and his New Zealanders in the semi-final. With his immaculate kicking – 645 points in 46 Tests – Fox had averaged 14 points a match. The figures of Andrew and Lynagh tell a more subtle tale:

Andrew, 70 Tests, 396 points (2 tries, 33 conversions, 86 penalty goals, 21 drop goals).

Lynagh, 72 Tests, 911 points (17 tries, 140 conversions, 176 penalty goals, 9 drop goals).

In almost the same number of matches, they spectacularly show a difference in their two styles, or more particularly the styles of the two sides for which they played. While aware that Andrew was not always England's kicker – during his long tenure they fielded a number of full-back hoofers – his two tries to Lynagh's 17 is graphic evidence of Australia's more flexible friendliness for 15-man rugby. Also, Lynagh's 140 conversions to

Andrew's 33 display an Australian predeliction to tries. And do Rob's more than double tally of drop-goals mean that when England were in striking distance of an opponent's line, the captain cautiously would prefer to call for a booted 3-pointer rather than daring for a 7-point converted try?

Within weeks of the 1995 World Cup, the dauntless Andrew became the first English Test player publicly to turn professional when he took a large salary to become Director of Rugby at the 'sister' club of the Newcastle United soccer team. To be sure, by the end of that August of 1995, at the International Rugby Board's meeting in Paris – and a century almost to the day since 'northern' rugby league had broken away – the game announced itself 'open and professional'. The precipitate, unplanned, decision caused fevered and sometimes seemingly fatal ructions which tore at the very fabric, culture, and administration of the British game – but for all that chaos, it happily allowed the likes of Lynagh (with the London club Saracens) and Stransky (Leicester) to grace the English league for an enlightening season or two with their sublime and definitive talents in the No. 10 shirt.

For his first two seasons in the celebrated green-and-pink of Leicester's Tigers, mind you, Stransky had to wear the letter J – for Joel? for Jewel? – on his back, for the club continued as long as they could to defy Twickenham's ruling on the numbering (as opposed to bizarre and antique lettering) on their shirts. In each of those two years, Stransky was the leading scorer in the English First Division. But it was not his dead-eyed kicking – unerring from the ground and richly varied out of hand – which so warmed those two bleak and argumentative English rugby winters, but his full repertoire of arts: his calm, the intuitively timed pirouettes and darts close to his forwards or, as a breathtaking surprise, his sparing but cruel scalpel-slash which would gapingly open up midfield. There was much of Jack Kyle's glory about Stransky at his best. The South African's masterclass in the mud for Leicester, week in, week out, rounded off the education of

England's young centre prospect outside him, Will Greenwood, and proved the re-making of the hitherto languishing flanker inside him, Neil Back. When Lynagh bade farewell after just as many command performances for Saracens in the spring of 1998, the Australian said simply, 'Thoroughbred rugby is in good hands as long as Joel stays playing somewhere; he is a true great and right up there with Hugo Porta and Mark Ella as the top three Number Tens I have encountered in my whole career'.

Born in Pietermaritzburg in 1967, Stransky was already past his mid-twenties and still officially uncapped by the time South Africa was readmitted to the world's confraternity. He had numbingly experienced the extent of his country's banishment when he was only 16. 'I toured Britain with Maritzburg College and even after we had arrived three separate school opponents in England suddenly cancelled their fixtures with us.' The unbeaten 1974 Lions to South Africa had defied the boycott and Stranksy remembers how, even as a seven-year-old, he had identified on television at home with the quicksilver genius of Welshman Phil Bennett. 'Around that time, of course, they kept replaying over and over the Barbarians seven-man try at Cardiff, and I used to run outside and practise those three Bennett sidesteps which began it – Wow, man!'

As a kicker, he says, he is basically self taught, 'although after he sees me on television my good old maths teacher at school, in his mid-eighties now, still telephones me with valuable hints about basic technique and "body shape"'. He is not one, he says, for 'all this modern psycho-visualization stuff, you know, go into a trance and imagine the ball going through the poles even before you've kicked it'. Practise and routine are his two staples – 'place it, four steps back at an angle, settle, a tiny half-step . . . and then just run up and hit it'. And drop kicks? 'Just instinct, bonuses taken on the hoof if the opportunity suddenly arises.'

When it did at Ellis Park that June afternoon in 1995 when the soft-voiced, scholarly Stranksy untapped a tumult of delirium around a land already intoxicated by its so recent conversion to democracy:

'It was 9–9 at the end of 80 minutes. The intensity of extra-time was almost unbearable. The All Blacks took a 12–9 lead. Somehow we dug even deeper. With a penalty I levelled to 12–12. They continued to throw everything at us. Our defence was unbelievable. Two minutes before the end of normal time, I had sensed a chance for a forward drive from a lineout which might have given me a last glimmer for a drop at goal, but François (captain Pienaar) had ignored me and called something else for the back-row. Now with extra-time draining away and the New Zealanders, who'd been in these pressure-cookers before, still pounding us, we once again cleared our lines and suddenly were awarded a scrum inside their half. The intensity was massive as the two packs squared-up for what might have been the final scrum. Again I muttered to François that a good push to hold them in and it might be in my range for a drop. But François shakes his head and calls a totally different back-row move. What?! I couldn't believe it. I was furious. So was Joost (scrum-half Van der Westhuizen), but he just gave me a nudge and a wink and tells Rudi (No. 8 Straeuli) they would get the ball to me; Rudi nods agreement that we should rebelliously ignore the captain's call and attempt to go for the last-gasp drop. I just needed for them to hold the ball in, and the All Black flankers off, for that momentary calming space in which to settle my aim.

'The packs go down. The whole stadium is in a taut frenzy, so is the whole country. Joost puts the ball in; a quick heel, a massive heave, and good Rudolf does his stuff in the middle of the back-row. Then . . . Joost to me and, steady as she goes, head down, I just swing my leg . . .'

And sweet as a little brown nut, from far away, the ball sails – swirls even, with a garnish of swagger and certainty – over the bar and, almost, the towering posts, and unquestionably over the rainbow and into everlasting fame. Joy unconfined. 'Half of me didn't know where to look. Certainly not at François. The three of us had ignored, over-ruled, our great captain's call . . . Not that I've ever heard, from that day to this, one serious or solitary word of complaint from François about disobeying orders.'

With Straeuli, Stransky's partner in that ravishingly mutinous crime, was scrum-half Van der Westhuizen, who was to continue to be one of the most priceless diamonds of the game's history as the century ran its course. Just as Lynagh had, successively, supportive scrum-half partners in the foraging George Gregan and the tactically pluperfect Farr-Jones, so was Stransky blessed in Tests to have inside him the combative, cleft-jawed magnificence of Van der Westhuizen. 'It was a privilege to partner Joost,' says Stransky, 'he has strength and speed, daring and vision, all with a gymnast's athleticism. Has any scrum-half in the century had more?'

Stransky played only 15 Tests (176 points), his move to Leicester to all intents ruling him out of Springbok selection. It was ageing Henry Honiball, two years older than Stransky, who seemed at last to emerge from a flurry of seemingly sharper rivals and a scrapbook of terrible early notices, to be the probable Springbok banker at No. 10 for 1999. Henry was always an upright high-stepper, a patrician High Church fly. Confident at last, he played the 1998 Tri-Nations tournament with a beautiful precision and even élan. He is also from Natal, a farmer of dairy cattle and beef from Bergville, some 130-miles from Durban. Oddly enough, in that Tri-Nations' competition, in which New Zealand collectively played more poorly than they can have done in memory, much of the blame was heaped on another fly-half born in Natal. Andrew Mehrtens was only 18 months when his parents, who had been on an extended stay with relatives in South Africa, returned to Canterbury, New Zealand, and it was fully 20 years till the young man returned – as the rookie All Black for the 1995 World Cup. In spite of his callow years, his tactical nous marshalled the compelling verve of his team right up to the final, and he was comfortably the tournament's most impressive fly after Lynagh and Stransky. On the eve of the final, Mehrtens, choirboy innocence had him enthusing: 'Pressure? What pressure? Test rugby is an enjoyment for me, a thrill and excitement, and if it is pressure on my shoulders then I reckon it makes me feel great, mighty good.' He was too young to twig fear then; but in the intervening seasons deep furrows came to that boyhood brow and although Mehrtens kept returning to the All Blacks those pressures he once hadn't noticed were palpably weighing heavy under the consistent challenge for his shirt from the livelier, younger, and admittedly chancier, 'running' fly from Auckland, Carlos Spencer.

Mehrtens had, of course, played only one Test (and kicked a debutant's record 28 points against Canada) the month before storming, unafraid, to that World Cup so, with a new one imminent, there remained time for the All Blacks to steady the ship and either find, or settle on, their favoured man. But it was unusual to see New Zealand fret so long over such a crucial position – especially as Australia, after a similar string of failed auditions as South Africa, were looking increasingly content with the steadily serious progress and chutzpah of their converted fullback in the scrum-cap Steve Larkham. To fill the places of Lynagh and Stransky with, respectively, Larkham and Honiball was a significant bonus in team building for both Australia and South Africa although, mind you, Stransky might not have so spectacularly played his way into the legend by settling the 1995 World Cup had France had a satisfactory fly-half. If they had done so, the Gauls could readily have won the thing, but coach Pierre Berbizier persisted in choosing the inert and indecisive Christophe Deylaud, a soft-shoe shuffling 30-year-old they called 'The Tramp'. Mind you, it was not so much Charlie Chaplin that his generally bewildered play caricatured but the even sadder faced Hollywood comic Buster Keaton. Certainly, the unfortunate Deylaud was no remote general for a side otherwise bristling with potential and know-how both fore and aft which, as it was, came within four points and a disputed try of beating South Africa in the semi-final at a waterlogged Durban and then, with classy veteran Franck Mesnel at last being given the No. 10 shirt, haughtily defeating England in the third place play-off. Berbizier's stubborness over Deylaud defied reason – outstanding in the centre for France had been Thierry Lacroix, a natural-born fly, and with such seasoned outside-halves to call on as Alain Penaud, Christophe Lamaison, and David Aucagne, it was a blunder of serious proportion. Thereafter with those being chopped and changed almost by the match, it looked, to be sure, that the new regime of Jean-Claude Skrela, who took over as coach from Berbizier, also had a blind spot about fly-halves – till the crucial season of 1997–98, that is, when a 23-year-old sprite who had begun his career as a precocious centre suddenly burst on the sombrely grey European game with an engaging charm and colourful fluttering of wings.

Thomas Castaignède was a bundle of mischief, a darting catch-me-if-you-dare. A Toulousain who played for Castres, his merry jigs cut a joyous swathe through the winter's Championship in which France were unbeaten. He orchestrated the 51–0 rout of Wales in the final match at Wembley. The grandeur of the Slam indeed, and the venerable old stadium cannot often have been the stage for such singular coruscations in a team game through all its 75-year-old history. 'Such a magically historic stadium inspired me to put on a face of fun and self-belief – but that, anyway, is simply my rugby philosophy,' said Castaignède. His seething Welsh markers were bewildered by a kaleidoscope of attacking patterns, precise transfers long, short and outrageous, and a murderously sadistic awareness of when to go for the metaphorical jugular. For *The Times*, the onliest Gerald Davies was again next to me in the pressbox. Gerald, of course, had played outside Mike Gibson, Barry John, and Phil Bennett, yet here he was inspired next day to write of 'true genius', serenading the diminutive Frenchboy 'for providing a complete performance of fly-half artistry that surely cannot have been bettered by anyone, anywhere, any time. Each occasion he held the ball, the Welsh defence held its breath ... whether a man marked him mattered not at all; he showed them the ball and raced away on whichever angle he chose. He departed the field to a standing ovation; not just from the French, but from the vast Welsh throng, too, and even amid their deep despondency was recognised this rarest of talents.'

As for Davies's own native No. 10 of the legend, the 1990s continued to be hauntingly barren. Max Boyce's factory simply seemed to have closed its lift-shafts and all was now, in Alan Watkins's words 'cosmic confusion', although this time a confusion *not* succeeded 'by the emergence again of a great outside-half'. In fact, you might not only have suggested, but been spot-on, that over the eight years which took in the first two World Cups of the 1990s, the best two Welsh No. 10s were the bonnily engaging good-egg and worldwide rugby gypsy, Gareth Rees (captain and beloved totem of Canada, but whose family roots are in Maesteg), and the commandingly calm Paul Turner, Swindon-bred to a soccer family who was grudgingly capped twice at the turn of the decade, the first Newbridge back to be so, and then was cruelly ignored as he shone in English club rugby, yet another Welsh prophet without honour. Banished by the Welsh selectors, Turner was nevertheless seriously considered for two British Lions' tours; his maturity on the ball, classic tutorials almost, would have readily coped with such elevation – but, alas, it was left to historians to summon remembrance of the Old Cranleighan Jeff Reynolds, who won three 'second choice' caps for England in the 1937–38 season, at once went with the Lions to South Africa and played with such verve and panache to be hailed as 'the Prince of Flies' throughout the world game – but realized that such a message could not possibly go down with his Twickenham selectors for England so, having fallen for a South African girl, he never bothered to return home, but married instead and became a famous African hotelier.

The Welsh fly-half who did become, if not the prince then certainly the series-winning hero for the Lions in South Africa in 1997 did so, wouldn't you know, as a full-back. The single-minded all-in-a-day's-work Neil Jenkins of Pontypridd emphatically kept the seemingly over-whelmed Lions in with a chance in what was their ultimately victorious Test series against the Springboks. But only with his meticulously accurate and unafraid goalkicking, and no matter that his singular and tottering approach, having placed the ball, had him resembling a drunken matelot on a storm-tossed deck.

By the time Jenkins had passed 50 international caps he had smithereened Wales's previous points record with more than 500. As well as full-back, he was capped in the centre, but he was mostly at fly-half – and each time he aroused a discordant brouhaha of ayes and noes around the Principality, east and west, which cannot have been matched since the 'class wars' of some three score years before when half the little nation yearned for Willie Davies and the other lot for Cliff Jones. That the cour-ageous but athletically and aesthetically ungainly Jenkins was one heck of a rugby player was never in doubt, but rugby's aesthetes flatly refused to so much as look at his credentials as a fly-half of the regal Welsh lineage. Especially after France's Castaignède had made such a monkey of him at Wembley – and for a season or so before that, particularly when it looked just possible, from Trebanos deep in the Swansea Valley, that Wales had unearthed at last a true gem from the heartland, for at first it looked as if the spindly man-child Arwel Thomas had all the makings of true heir.

But the sandbagging intensity of international marking too often juddered the development of Thomas just as, a few years before, it had consigned to the fastness of Llanelli another slightly built fly of delicate skills, Colin Stephens. The sturdier and laid-back Mark Ring displayed glimpses of engaging swank behind a usually beaten pack, but while the country wept for a successor to the regal line which had ended when Jonathan Davies travelled north with, as the west Walian academic Siân Nicholas had it, 'his unsettling combination of tactical maturity and impish optimism', the national side had to 'make do' with the sandy-haired 'scruff', Jenkins of Pontypridd, one tough boyo, body and soul. As his compatriot the barrister-historian Tim Williams counselled for the defence: 'What Neil Jenkins has – say it loud, say it proud – is the right stuff. The fact that there is even a question mark about him in Wales says more about the abject state of the game in his homeland than it does about him . . . He represents the welcome triumph of character, determination and application over mere personality in a culture which worships the latter and finds the former concepts pedestrian and actually rather plebeian.'

As they ever did in those dingy taprooms and pub parlours of the Principality when the differing merits of Llewellyn Lloyd or 'Dancing' Dick Jones had been under discussion 100 years before, the fevered pros and cons continued to swirl around Jenkins' credentials as a natural-born No. 10 . . . At the very same time, in Scotland, no rugby follower in their right mind would argue that their glistening talent Gregor Townsend could have, as the Edinburgh critic Norman Mair wrote, 'reached for the Number Ten jersey in any changing-room on this sceptered isle without a single murmer of protest' – yet till he tried his luck in France at Toulouse in the 1998–99 season both for his country and his club (Northampton) Townsend had more often than not found himself a victim of his own cutting-edge variety, versatility and, to be sure, generosity, by agreeing to play in the centre. For Scotland, with its limited resources, the tactic at least allowed the now veteran Chalmers to whittle a few more notches onto his distinguished fly-half career, but when the British Lions chose Townsend as its senior No. 10 for the 1997 tour of South Africa it seemed bizarre in the extreme because the Lions' coach was the very same director of rugby at Northampton (Ian McGeechan, 12 times a fly for Scotland and 19 times a centre), who had almost permanently selected Townsend as club centre, outside England's Paul Grayson at fly. If not as waspish or imaginative a playmaker as Townsend, as he vied for the all-white shirt with the South African-born all-rounder Mike Catt, the orderly, unfazed Grayson quietly impressed as a most accomplished footballer and goal-kicker in the timeless English tradition which ran back from Andrew all the way to Davies and Stoop.

Of course, the royal succession had been established in prehistory well before those two – indeed the very day it was first exported to the wider world can be precisely logged as 27 January 1893, when the news came through that the James brothers had 'gone north' for £2 a week and jobs in a warehouse. But the two bold little copper-ladlers, the 'pocket-halves' and the 'curly-haired marmosets', had, between them, turn and turnabout, deftly 'invented' the singular skills and differences of scrum-half and fly-half play. They founded a feast – on instinct and without giving a thought.

Easily enough, anyway, in the century since then, for them to have unleashed and let rip the glamorous innovators like Willie Trew, or HM Consul Percy Bush; Louis Magee, the Dublin vet in his string gloves, or the dashing Maclear in his white ones. Then there was the courage of Darkie Peters; and Stoop, pukka public schoolboy devoted to the fly-half's possibilities – so the Admiralty man from the *Iron Duke* could develop them wondrously. Then Herbert Waddell took it from there; though not Bennie Osler, who began his own thing – and sixty years later, as we have seen, a compatriot's boot finished the job for him. The parade marches on . . . Nicholls and Lawton, Du Manoir and Spong . . . are you, boyo, for Cliff Jones, or are you for Davies?

Dr Jack, missionary in more ways than one; Cliff, with his gleam and his beam; Sharp and Hawthorne and Kirton . . . the leprechaun dancers Ollie and Tony . . . and Bennett's hopscotch jigs. Not to mention Camberabero's 'panache'; or Castaignède's brazen and boyish charms.

Was Barry really the king of them all? Perhaps. Mark Ella was the prince for sure. But where does that leave the very regal Rutherford? Each to their time and – as Naas Botha would insist – his context. If the modern era's emperor, Michael Lynagh, had not dared his crusade in Dublin that day, which of Grant Fox or Rob Andrew would have laid their hands on the golden cup and drunk deep?

Four years later, both Lynagh and Andrew had the prize dashed from them in a vibrant World Cup tournament under the southern skies, when such new luminaries as the All Blacks, Jonah Lomu, Christian Cullen, and Jeff Wilson, cut a dash, along with Andre Jourbert and Joost Van der Westhuizen for the winners. And who will similarly settle the thing, as Joel Stransky did in front of his new president in 1995, for the enchantment and satisfaction of the gods, the next time it is played for? For sure, it will be a fly-half (or a ruddy 'first-five'!). Because as long as life and the good game go on – be assured, so will the rich and royal line continue of those good fellows who strut their stuff in the livery numbered '10'.

Appendix

A century of fly-halves

These lists are arranged by country and show, chronologically to January 1993, all fly-halves and their international caps. Opposing teams are abbreviated as follows:

A = Australia
Arg = Argentina
Bh = Barbarians
BI = British Isles
C = Canada
CV = New Zealand Cavaliers
Cz = Czechoslovakia
E = England
F = France
Fj = Fiji
G = Germany
I = Ireland
It = Italy
J = Japan
K = New Zealand Kiwis
M = Maoris
NZ = New Zealand
P = President's XV
R = Romania
S = Scotland
SA = South Africa
S Am = South America
Tg = Tonga
US = United States
W = Wales
Wld = World
WS = Western Samoa
Z = Zimbabwe
(R) = Replacement

If the player in question did not take part in a full series, figures after the name of the opposing team show which Test matches he played in. Not all listed appearances were necessarily at fly-half, especially in the early days of 'left-right' formation at half-back. These tables list those who won caps *mostly* at fly-half. For instance, in the case of Ireland's C. M. H. Gibson, it is simply noted that he won 81 caps, but only 25 at fly-half, whereas his compatriot S. O. Campbell's full 22 appearances are listed, although in fact he was picked four times at centre threequarter.

AUSTRALIA
C. H. HODGENS 1910 NZ 1, 2, 3
W. G. TASKER 1913 NZ 1, 2, 3, 1914 NZ 1, 2, 3
T. LAWTON 1925 NZ, 1927, I, W, S, 1928 E, F, 1929 NZ 1, 2, 3, 1930 BI, 1932 NZ 1, 2
J. C. STEGGALL 1931 M, NZ, 1932 NZ 1, 2, 3, 1933 SA 1, 2, 3, 4, 5
R. R. BILLMANN 1933 SA 1, 2, 3, 4
L. S. LEWIS 1934 NZ 1, 2, 1936 NZ 2, 1938 NZ 1
V. S. RICHARDS 1936 NZ 1, 2, (R), M, 1937 SA 1, 1938 NZ 1
J. F. CREMIN 1946 NZ 1, 2, 1947 NZ 1
D. P. BANNON 1946 M

270

N. A. EMERY 1947 NZ 2, S, I, W, 1948 E, F, 1949 M 2, 3, NZ 1, 2

E. G. BROAD 1949 M 1

H. J. SOLOMON 1949 M 3, NZ 2, 1950 BI 1, 2, 1951 NZ 1, 2, 1952 Fj 1, 2, NZ 1, 2, 1953 SA 1, 2, 3, 1955 NZ 1

M. J. TATE 1951 NZ 3, 1952 Fj 1, 2, NZ 1, 2, 1953 SA 1, 1954 Fj 1, 2

S. W. BROWN 1953 SA 2, 3, 4

G. W. G. DAVIS 1955 NZ 2, 3

A. G. R. SHEIL 1956 SA 1

A. J. SUMMONS 1958 W, I, E, S, M 2, NZ 1, 2, 3

R. M. HARVEY 1958 F, M 3

B. G. WELLS 1958 M 1

J. H. DOWSE 1961 Fj 1, 2, SA 1, 2

H. F. ROBERTS 1961 Fj 1, 3, SA 2, F

N. J. D. STOREY 1962 NZ 1

P. F. HAWTHORNE 1962 NZ 3, 4, 5, 1963 E, SA 1, 2, 3, 4, 1964 NZ 1, 2, 3, 1965 SA 1, 2, 1966 BI 1, 2, W, 1967 E, I 1, F, I 2, NZ

P. R. GIBBS 1966 S

J. P. BALLESTY 1968 NZ 1, 2, F, I, S, 1969 W, SA 2, 3, 4

R. G. ROSENBLUM 1969 SA 1, 3, 1970 S

G. C. RICHARDSON 1971 SA 1, 2, 3, 1972 NZ 2, 3, Fj, 1973 Tg 1, 2, W

R. L. FAIRFAX 1971 F 1, 2, 1972 F 1, 2, NZ 1, Fj, 1973 W, E

P. G. ROWLES 1972 Fj, 1973 E

P. E. McLEAN 36 caps, 17 at fly-half

K. J. WRIGHT 1975 E 1, 2, J 1, 1976 US, F 1, 2, 1978 NZ 1, 2, 3

J. C. HINDMARSH 9 caps, 3 at fly-half

T. C. MELROSE 1978 NZ 2, 1979 I 1, 2, NZ, Arg 1, 2

M. G. ELLA 1980 NZ 1, 2, 3, 1981 F 2, S, 1982 E, S 1, NZ 1, 2, 3, 1983 US, Arg 1, 2, NZ, It, F 1, 2, 1984 Fj, NZ 1, 2, 3, E, I, W, S

M. P. LYNAGH 1984 Fj, E, I, W, S, 1985 C 1, 2, NZ, 1986 It, F, Arg 1, 2, 1988 E 1, 2, NZ 1, 3 (R), E, S, It, 1989 BI 1, 2, 3, NZ F 1, 2, 1990 F 1, 2, 3, US, NZ 1, 2, 3, 1991 W, E, NZ 1, 2, [Arg, WS, W, I, NZ, E], 1992 v SA 2, NZ 3, I

D. KNOX 1985 Fj 1, 2, 1990 US (R)

P. KAHL (Q) 1992 SA, W

ENGLAND

E. W. TAYLOR 1892 I, 1893 I, 1894 W, I, S, 1895 W, I, S, 1896 W, I, 1897 W, I, S, 1899 I

C. M. WELLS 1893 S, 1894 W, S, 1896 S, 1897 W, S

R. H. B. CATTELL 1895 W, I, S, 1896 W, I, S, 1900 W

S. NORTHMORE 1897 I

H. MYERS 1898 I

G. T. UNWIN 1898 S

R. O'H. LIVESAY 1898 W, 1899 W

R. O. SCHWARZ 1899 S, 1901 W, I

J. C. MARQUIS 1900 I, S

B. OUGHTRED 1901 S, 1902 W, I, S, 1903 W, I

J. E. RAPHAEL 1902 W, I, S, 1905 W, S, NZ, 1906 W, S, F

W. V. BUTCHER 1903 S, 1904 W, I, S, 1905 W, I, S

P. S. HANCOCK 1904 W, I, S

A. D. STOOP 1905 S, 1906 S, F, SA, 1907 F, W, 1910 W, I, S, 1911 W, F, I, S, 1912 W, S

D. R. GENT 1905 NZ, 1906 W, I, 1910 W, I

J. PETERS 1906 S, F, 1907 I, S, 1908 W

T. G. WEDGE 1907 F, 1909 W

G. V. PORTUS 1908 F, I

J. DAVEY 1908 S, 1909 W

A. H. ASHCROFT 1909 A

F. HUTCHISON 1909 F, I, S

H. COVERDALE 1910 F, 1912 I, F, 1920 W

W. J. A. DAVIES 1913 SA, W, F, I, S, 1914 I, S, F, 1920 F, I, S, 1921 W, I, S, F, 1922 I, F, S, 1923 W, I, S, F

F. M. TAYLOR 1914 W

E. MYERS 1920 I, S, 1921 W, I, 1922 W, I, F, S, 1923 W, I, S, F, 1924 W, I, F, S, 1925 S, F

V. G. DAVIES 1922 W, 1925 NZ

H. J. KITTERMASTER 1925 NZ, W, I, 1926 W, I, F, S

H. C. C. LAIRD 1927 W, I, S, 1928 A, W, I, F, S, 1929 W, I

C. C. BISHOP 1927 F

S. S. C. MEIKLE 1929 S

R. S. SPONG 1929 F, 1930 W, I, F, S, 1931 F, 1932 SA, W

T. J. M. BARRINGTON 1931 W, I

T. C. KNOWLES 1931 S

J. A. TALLENT 1931 S, F, 1932 SA, W, 1935 I

W. ELLIOT 1932 I, S, 1933, W, I, S, 1934 W, I

C. F. SLOW 1934 S

P. L. CANDLER 1935 W, 1936 NZ, W, I, S, 1937 W, I, S, 1938 W, S

J. R. AUTY 1935 S

T. A. KEMP 1937 W, I, 1939 S, 1948 A, W

F. J. REYNOLDS 1937 S, 1938 I, S

G. A. WALKER 1939 W, I

N. M. HALL 1947 W, I, S, F, 1949 W, I, 1952 SA, W, S, I, F, 1953 W, I, F, S, 1955 W, I

I. PREECE 1948 I, S, F, 1949 F, S, 1950 W, I, F, S, 1951 W, I, F

E.. M. P. HARDY 1951 I, F, S

M. REGAN 1953 W, I, F, S, 1954 W, NZ, I, S, F, 1956 I, S, F

D. G. S. BAKER 1955 W, I, F, S

M. J. K. SMITH 1956 W

R. M. BARTLETT 1957 W, I, F, S, 1958 I, F, S

J. P. HORROCKS-TAYLOR 1958 W, A, 1961 S, 1962 S, 1963 NZ 1, 2, A, 1964 NZ, W

A. B. W. RISMAN 1959 W, I, F, S, 1961 SA, W, I, F

R. A. W. SHARP 1960 W, I, F, S, 1961 I, F, 1962 W, I, F, 1963 W, I, F, S, 1967 A

M. P. WESTON 1960 W, I, F, S, 1961 SA, W, I, F, S, 1962 W, I, F, 1963 W, I, F, S, NZ 1, 2, A, 1964 NZ, W, I, F, S, 1965 F, S, 1966 S, 1968 F, S

T. J. BROPHY 1964 I, F, S, 1965 W, I, 1966 W, I, F

J. F. FINLAN 1967 I, F, S, W, NZ, 1968 W, I, 1969 I, F, S, W, 1970 F, 1973 NZ 1

I. R. SHACKLETON 1969 SA, 1970 I, W, S

A. R. COWMAN 1971 S, (2 [1C]) P, 1973 W, I

A. G. B. OL.D 1972 W, I, F, S, SA, 1973 NZ 2, A, 1974 S, I, F, W,

1975 I, A, 2, 1976 S, I, 1978 F

M. J. COOPER 1973 F, S, NZ 2 (R), 1975 F, W, 1976 A, W, 1977 S, I, F, W

W. N. BENNETT 1975 S, A, 1, 1976 S (R), 1979 S, I, F, W

C. G. WILLIAMS 1976 F

J. P. HORTON 1978 W, S, I, NZ, 1980 I, F, W, S, 1981 W, 1983 S, I, 1984 SA 1, 2

L. CUSWORTH 1979 NZ, 1982 F, W, 1983 F, W, NZ, 1984 S, I, F, W, 1988 F, W

S. BARNES 1984 A, 1985 R (R), NZ 1, 2, 1986 S (R), F (R), 1987 I (R), 1988 Fj

C. R. ANDREW 1985 R, F, S, I, W, 1986 W, S, I, F, 1987 I, F, W, [J (R), US], 1988 S, I, 1, 2, A 1, 2, Fj, A, 1989 S, I, F, W, R, Fj, 1990 I, F, W, S, Arg 3, 1991 W, S, I, F, Fj, A, [NZ, It, US, F, S, A], 1992 S, I, F, W, 1992 v C, SA

FRANCE

E. BILLAC 1920 S, E, W, I, US, 1921 S, W, 1922 W, 1923 E

A BOUSQUET 1921 E, I, 1924 R

J. PASCOT 1922 S, E, I, 1923 S, 1926 I, 1927 G 2

C. LACAZEDIEU 1923 W, I, 1928 A, I, 1929 S

C. MAGNANOU 1923 E, 1925 W, E, 1926 S, 1929 S, W, 1930 S, I, E, W

H. GALAU 1924 S, I, E, W, US

Y. LeP. DU MANOIR 1925 I, NZ, S, W, E, 1926 S, 1927 I, S

V. GRAULE 1926 I, E, W, 1927 S, W, 1931 G

J. SOURGENS 1926 M

R. GRACIET 1926 I, W, 1927 S, G, I, 1929 E, 1930 W

A. VERGER 1927 W, E, G 1, 1928 I, E, G, W

H. HAGET 1928 S, 1930 G

R. SARRADE 1929 I

A. CUTZACH 1929 G

I. SERVOLE 1931 I, S, W, E, G, 1934 G, 1935 G

A. BARBAZANGES 1932 G, 1933 G

J. DAGUERRE 1933 G

J. DESCLAUX 1934 G, 1935 G, 1936

G 1, 2, 1937 G, It, 1938 G 1, R, G 2, 1945 B 1

G. LAVAIL 1937 G, 1940 B

J. CHASSAGNE 1938 G 1

G. VASSAL 1938 R, G 2

A.-J. ALVAREZ 1945 B 2, 1946 B, I, K, W, 1947 S, I, W, E, 1948 I, A, S, W, E, 1949 I, E, W, 1951 S, E, W

M.-M. TERREAU 1945 W, 1946 B, I, K, W, 1947 S, I, W, 3, 1948 I, A, W, E, 1949 S, Arg 1, 2, 1951 S

L. BORDENAVE 1948 A, S, W, E, 1949 S

P. DIZABO 1948 A, S, E, 1949 S, I, E, W, Arg 2, 1950 S, I, 1960 Arg 1, 2, 3

J. PILON 1949 E, 1950 E

P. LAUGA 1950 S, I, E, W

F. FOURNET 1950 W

J. CARABIGNAC 1951 S, I, 1952 SA, W, E, 1953 S, I

R. FURCADE 1952 S

A. LABUZUY 1952 I, 1954 S, W, 1956 E, 1958 A, W, I, 1959 S, E, It, W

M. LECOINTRE 1952 It

R. MARTINE 1952 S, I, It, 1953 It, 1954 S, I, NZ, W, E, It, Arg 2, 1955 S, I, W, 1958 A, W, It, I, SA 1, 2, 1960 S, E, Arg 3, 1961 S, It

L. BIDART 1953 W

A. HAGET 1953 E, 1954 I, NZ, E, Arg 2, 1955 E, W, It, 1957 I, E, It, R 1, 1958 It, SA 2

R. BASAURI 1954 Arg 1

J. BOUQUET 1954 S, 1955 E, 1956 S, I, W, It, E, Cz, 1957 S, E, W, R 2, 1958 S, E, 1959 S, It, W, I, 1960 S, E, W, I, R, 1961 S, SA, E, W, It, I, R, 1962 S, E, W, I

P. ALBALADEJO 1954 E, It, 1960 W, I, It, R, 1961 S, SA, E, W, I, NZ 1, 2, A, 1962 S, E, W, I, 1963 S, I, E, W, It, 1964 S, NZ, W, It, I, SA, Fj

C. VIGNES 1957 R 1, 2, 1958 S, E

C. MANTOULAN 1959 I

G. CAMBERABERO 1961 NZ 3, 1962 R, 1964 R, 1967 A, E, It, W, I, SA 1, 3, 4, 1968 S, E, W

S. PLANTEY 1961 A, 1962 It

C. LACAZE 1961 NZ 2, 3, A, R, 1962 E, W, I, It, 1963 W, R, 1964

S, NZ, E, 1965 It, R, 1966 S, I, E, W, It, R, 1967 S, E, SA 1, 2, 3, R, 1968 S, E, W, Cz, NZ 1, 1969 E

J. GACHASSIN 1961 S, I, 1963 R, 1964 S, NZ, E, W, It, I, SA, Fj, R, 1965 S, I, E, W, It, R, 1966 S, I, E, W, 1967 S, A, It, W, I, NZ, 1968 I, E, 1969 S, I

J. C. HIQUET 1964 E

J. P. CAPDOUZE 1964 SA, Fj, R, 1965 S, I, E

J. C. ROQUES 1966 S, I, It, R

J. L. DEHEZ 1967 SA 2, 1969 R

J. MASO 24 caps, 4 at fly-half

J. BOUJET 1968 NZ 2, A (R)

L. PARIES 1968 SA 2, R, 1970 S, I, W, 1975 E, S, I

J. L. BEROT 1968 NZ 3, A, 1969 S, I, 1970 E, R, 1971 S, I, E, W, SA 1, 2, A 1, 2, R, 1972 S, I 1, E, W, A 1, 1974 I

A. MAROT 1969 R, 1970 S, I, W, 1971 SA 1, 1972 I 2, 1976 A 1

H. CABROL 1972 A 1 (R), A 2, 1973 J, 1974 SA 2

J. P. ROMEU 1972 R, 1973 S, NZ, E, W, I, R, 1974 W, E, S, Arg 1, 2, R, SA 1, 2, (R), 1975 W, SA 2, ARG 1, 2, R, 1976 S, I, W, E, US, 1977 W, E, S, I, Arg 1, 2, NZ 1, 2, R

J. P. PESTEIL 1975 SA 1, 1976 A 2, R

B. VIVIES 1978 E, S, I, W, 1980 SA, R, 1981 S, A 1, 1983 A 1 (R)

A. CAUSSADE 1978 R, 1979 I, W, E, NZ 1, 2, R, 1980 W, E, S, 1981 S (R), I

P. PEDEUTOUR 1980 I

G. LAPORTE 1981 I, W, E, R, NZ 1, 2 1986 S, I, W, E, R 1, Arg 1, A (R), 1987 [R, Z (R), Fj]

M. SALLEFRANQUE 1981 A 2, 1982 W, E, S

J. P. LESCARBOURA 1982 W, E, S, I, 1983 A 1, 2, R, 1984 I, W, E, S, NZ 1, 2, R, 1985 E, S, I, W, Arg 1, 2, 1986 Arg 2, A, NZ 1, R 2, NZ 2, 1988 S, W, 1990 R

D. CAMBERABERO 1982 R, Arg 1, 2, 1983 E, W, 1987 [R (R), Z, Fj (R), A, NZ], 1988 I, 1989 B, A 1, 1990 W, S, I, R, A 1, 2, 3, NZ 1, 2,

273

1991 S, I, W 1, E, R, US 1, 2, W 2, [R, Fj, C]

C. DELAGE 1983 S, I

F. MESNEL 1986 NZ 2 (R), 3, 1987 W, E, S, I, [S, Z, Fj, A, NZ], R, 1988 E, Arg 1, 2, 3, 4, R, 1989 I, W, E, S, NZ 1, A 1, 2, 1990 E, S, I, A 2, 3, NZ 1, 2, 1991 S, I, W 1, E, R, US 1, 2, W 2 [R, Fj, C, E], 1992 W, E, S, I

T. LACROIX 1989 A 1 (R), 2, 1991 W 1 (R), 2 (R), [R, C (R), E]

A. PENAUD 1992 W, E, S, I, v SA 2

IRELAND

W. S. BROWN 1893 S, W, 1894 E, S, W

A. M. MAGEE 1895 E, S, W, 1896 E, S, W, 1897 E, S, 1898 E, S, W, 1899 E, S, W, 1900 E, S, W, 1901 E, S, W, 1902 E, S, W, 1903 E, S, W, 1904 W

T. T. H. ROBINSON 1904 E, S, 1905 E, S, W, NZ, 1906 SA, 1907 E, S, W

B. MACLEAR 11 caps 3 at fly-half, v E, S, W, 1906

E. D. CADDELL 1904 S, 1905 E, S, W, NZ 1906 E, S, W, SA, 1907 E, S, 1908 S, W

H. R. ASTON 1908 E, W

G. PINION 1909 E, S, W, F

R. A. LLOYD 1910 E, S, 1911, E, S, W, F, 1912 F, E, S, W, SA, 1913 E, S, W, F, 1914 F, E, 1920 E, F

A. N. McCLINTON 1910 W, F

H. W. JACK 1914 S, W, 1921 W

W. DUGGAN 1920 S, W

J. R. WHEELER 1922 E, S, W, F, 1924 E

W. H. HALL 1923 E, S, W, F, 1924 F, S

F. S. HEWITT 1924 W, NZ, 1925 F, E, S, 1926 E, 1927 E, S, W

E. O'D. DAVY 1925 W, 1926 F, E, S, W, 1927 F, E, S, W, A, 1928 F, E, S, W, 1929 F, E, S, W, 1930 F, E, S, W, 1931 F, E, S, W, SA, 1932 E, S, W, 1933 E, W, S, 1934 E

P. F. MURRAY 1927 F, 1929 F, E, S, 1930 F, E, S, W, 1931 F, E, S, W, SA, 1932 E, S, W, 1933 E, W, S

L. B. McMAHON 1931 E, SA, 1933 E, 1934 E, 1936 E, S, W, 1937 E, S, W, 1938 E, S

J. L. REID 1934 S, W

A. H. BAILEY 1934 W, 1935 E, S, W, NZ, 1936 E, S, W, 1937 E, S, W, 1938 E, S

V. A. HEWITT 1935 S, W, NZ, 1936 E, S, W

G. E. CROMEY 1937 E, S, W, 1938 E, S, W, 1939 E, S, W

J. W. KYLE 1947 F, E, S, W, A, 1948 F, E, S, W, 1949 F, E, S, W, 1950 F, E, S, W, 1951 F, E, S, W, SA, 1952 F, S, W, E, 1953 F, E, S, W, 1954 NZ, F, 1955 F, E, W, 1956 F, E, S, W, 1957 F, E, S, W, 1958 A, E, S

W. J. HEWITT 1954 E, 1956 S, 1959 W, 1961 SA

S. KELLY 1954 S, W, 1955 S, 1960 W, F

M. A. F. ENGLISH 1958 W, F, 1959 E, S, F, 1960 E, S, 1961 S, W, F, 1962 F, W, 1963 E, S, W, NZ

D. C. GLASS 1958 F, 1960 W, 1961 W, SA

W. K. ARMSTRONG 1960 SA, 1961 E

F. G. GILPIN 1962 E, S, F

G. G. HARDY 1962 S

J. B. MURRAY 1963 F

C. M. H. GIBSON 81 caps, 25 at fly-half

W. M. McCOMBE 1968 F, 1975 E, S, F, W

B. J. McGANN 1969 F, E, S, W, 1970 SA, F, E, S, W, 1971 F, E, S, W, 1972 F 1, E, F 2, 1973 NZ, E, S, W, 1976 F, W, E, S, NZ

M. A. M. QUINN 1973 F, 1974 F, W, E, S, P, NZ, 1977 S, F, 1981 SA 2

S. O. CAMPBELL 1976 A, 1979 A 1, 2, 1980 E, S, F, W, 1981 F, W, E, S, SA 1, 1982 W, E, S, F, 1983 S, F, W, E, 1984 F, W

A. J. P. WARD 1978 S, F, W, E, NZ, 1979 F, W, E, S, 1981 W, E, S, A, 1983 E (R), 1984 E, S, 1986 S, 1987 [C, Tg]

P. M. DEAN 1981 SA 1, 2, A, 1982 W, E, S, F, 1984 A, 1985 S, F, W, E, 1986 F, W, R, 1987 E, S, F, W,

274

[W, A], 1988 S, F, W, E 1, 2, WS, It, 1989 F, W, E, S

R. P. KEYES 1986 E, 1991 [Z, J, S, A], 1992 W, E, S

B. A. SMITH 1989 NZ, 1990 S, F, W, Arg, 1991 F, W, E, S

P. RUSSELL 1990 E, v A 1992

D. R. McALEESE 1992 F

NEW ZEALAND 'FLY-HALVES'

Into the 1990s, New Zealand continued to list their teams with three 'half-backs' – a scrum-half and two 'five-eighths', a 'first' and 'second'. Which of the latter played 'first' or 'second five' at any given match is difficult to establish from the ancient records.

SCOTLAND

J. W. SIMPSON 1893 I, E, 1894 W, I, E, 1895 W, I, E, 1896 W, I, 1897 E, 1899 W, E

J. T. MABON 1898 I, E, 1899 I, 1900 I

J. I. GILLESPIE 1899 E, 1900 W, E, 1901 W, I, E, 1902 W, I, 1904 I, E

F. H. FASSON 1900 W, 1901 W, I, 1902 W, E

R. M. NEILL 1901 E, 1902 I

J. KNOX 1903 W, I, E

E. D. SIMSON 1902 E, 1903 W, I, E, 1904 W, I, E, 1905 W, I, E, NZ, 1906 W, I, E, 1907 W, I, E

L. L. GREIG 1905 NZ, 1906 SA, 1907 W, 1908 W, I

P. MUNRO 1905 W, I, E, NZ, 1906 W, I, E, SA, 1907 I, E, 1911 F, W, I

J. ROBERTSON 1908 E

G. CUNNINGHAM 1908 W, I, 1909 W, E, 1910 F, I, E, 1911 E

J. M. TENNENT 1909 W, I, E, 1910 F, W, E

J. Y. M. HENDERSON 1911 E

A. W. GUNN 1912 F, W, I, SA, 1913 F

J. L. BOYD 1912 E, SA

J. H. BRUCE-LOCKHART 1913 W, 1920 F

T. C. BOWIE 1913 I, E, 1914 I, E

A. T. SLOAN 1914 W, 1920 F, W, I, E, 1921 F, W, I, E

A. S. HAMILTON 1914 W, 1920 F

E. C. FAHMY 1920 F, W, I, E

R. L. H. DONALD 1921 W, I, E

J. C. DYKES 1922 F, E, 1924 I, 1925 F, W, I, 1926 F, W, I, E, 1927 F, W, I, E, A, 1928 F, I, 1929 F, W, I

G. P. S. MACPHERSON 1922 F, W, I, E, 1924 W, E, 1925 F, W, E, 1927 F, W, I, E, 1928 F, W, E, 1929 I, E, 1930 F, W, I, E, 1931 W, E, 1932 SA, E

S. B. McQUEEN 1923 F, W, I, E

H. WADDELL 1924 F, W, I, E, 1925 I, E, 1926 F, W, I, E, 1927 F, W, I, E, 1930 W

H. D. GREENLEES 1927 A, 1928 F, W, 1929 I, E, 1930 E

H. LIND 1928 I, 1931 F, W, I, E, 1932 SA, W, E, 1933 W, E, I, 1934 W, I, E, 1935 I, 1936 E

A. H. BROWN 1928 E, 1929 F, W

W. D. EMSLIE 1930 F, 1932 I

T. M. HART 1930 W, I

K. L. T. JACKSON 1933 W, E, I, 1934 W

J. L. COTTER 1934 I, E

R. W. SHAW 1934 W, I, E, 1935 W, I, E, NZ, 1936 W, I, E, 1937 W, I, E, 1938 W, I, E, 1939 W, I, E

C. F. GRIEVE 1935 W, 1936 E

W. A. ROSS 1937 W, E

R. B. BRUCE-LOCKHART 1937 I, 1939 I, E

I. J. M. LUMSDEN 1947 F, W, A, 1949 F, W, I, E

W. H. MUNRO 1947 I, E

C. R. BRUCE 1947 F, W, I, E, 1949 F, W, I, E

D. P. HEPBURN 1947 A, 1948 F, W, I, E, 1949 F, W, I, E

L. BRUCE-LOCKHART 1948 E, 1950 F, W, 1953 I, E

A. CAMERON 1948 W, 1950 I, E, 1951 F, W, I, E, SA, 1953 I, E, 1955 F, W, I, E, 1956 F, W, I

J. N. G. DAVIDSON 1952 F, W, I, E, 1953 F, W, 1954 F

G. T. ROSS 1954 NZ, I, E, W

J. T. DOCHERTY 1955 F, W, 1956 E, 1958 F, W, A, I, E

275

M. L. GRANT 1955 F, 1956 F, W, 1957 F

T. McLUNG 1956 I, E, 1957 W, I, E, 1959 F, W, I, 1960 W

J. M. MAXWELL 1957 I

G. H. WADDELL 1957 E, 1958 F, W, A, I, E, 1959 F, W, I, E, 1960 I, E, SA, 1961 F, 1962 F, W, I, E

I. H. P. LAUGHLAND 1959 F, 1960 F, W, I, E, 1961 SA, W, I, E, 1962 F, W, I, E, 1963 F, W, I, 1964 F, NZ, W, I, E, 1965 F, W, I, E, SA, 1966 F, W, I, E, 1967 E

G. SHARP 1960 F, 1964 F, NZ, W

K. J. F. SCOTLAND 27 caps, only 2 at fly-half, v I, E, 1963

D. H. CHISHOLM 1964 I, E, 1965 E, SA, 1966 F, I, E, A, 1967 F, W, NZ, 1968 F, W, I

B. M. SIMMERS 1965 F, W, 1966 A, 1967 F, W, I, 1971 F (R)

J. W. C. TURNER 1966 W, A, 1967 F, W, I, E, NZ, 1968 F, W, I, E, A, 1969 F, 1970 E, A, 1971 F, W, I, E, (2 [1 C])

I. ROBERTSON 1968 E, 1969 E, SA, 1970 F, W, I, E, A

C. M. TELFER 1968 A, 1969 F, W, I, E, 1972 F, W, E, 1973 W, I, E, P, 1974 W, E, I, 1975 A, 1976 F

I. R. McGEECHAN 31 caps, 12 at fly-half

R. WILSON 1976 E, I, 1977 E, I, F, 1978 I, F, 1981 R, 1983 I

R. W. BREAKEY 1978 E

J. Y. RUTHERFORD 1979 W, E, I, F, NZ, 1980 I, F, E, 1981 F, W, E, I, NZ 1, 2, A, 1982 E, I, F, W, A 1, 2, 1983 E, NZ, 1984 W, E, I, F, R, 1985 I, F, W, E, 1986 F, W, E, I, R, 1987 I, F, W, E, [F]

B. M. GOSSMAN 1980 W, 1983 F, W

D. S. WYLLIE 1984 A, 1985 W (R), E, 1987 I, F, [F, Z, R, NZ], 1989 R, 1991 R, [J (R), Z]

R. I. CRAMB 1987 [R (R)], 1988 I, F, A

C. M. CHALMERS 1989 W, E, I, F, Fj, 1990 I, F, W, E, NZ 1, 2, Arg, 1991 F, W, E, I, R, [J, Z (R), I, WS, E, NZ], 1992 E, I, F, W, v NZ 2

SOUTH AFRICA

F. P. LUYT 1910 BI 1, 2, 3, 1912–13 S, I, W, E

J. H. IMMELMAN 1912–13 F

W. D. TOWNSEND 1921 NZ 1

C. DU P. MEYER 1921 NZ 1, 2, 3

B. L. OSLER 1924 BI 1, 2, 3, 4, 1928 NZ 1, 2, 3, 4 1931–2 W, I, E, S, 1933 A 1, 2, 3, 4, 5

T. A. HARRIS 1937 NZ 2, 3, 1938 BI 1, 2, 3

J. D. BREWIS 1949 NZ 1, 2, 3, 4, 1951–2 S, I, W, E, F, 1953 A 1

A. I. KIRKPATRICK 1953 A 2, 1956 NZ 2, 1958 F 1, 1960 S, NZ 1, 2, 3, 4, 1960–1 W, I, E, S, F

I. J. RENS 1953 A 3, 4

C. A. UYLATE 1955 BI 1, 2, 3, 4, 1956 NZ 1, 2, 3

B. D. PFAFF 1956 A 1

B. F. HOWE 1956 NZ 1, 4

D. A. STEWART 1960 S, 1960–1 E, S, F, 1961 1, 1963 A 1, 3, 4, 1964 W, F, 1965 I

K. OXLEE 1960 NZ 1, 2, 3, 4, 1960–1 W, I, S, 1961 A 1, 2, 1962 BI 1, 2, 3, 4, 1963 A 1, 2, 4, 1964 W, 1965 NZ 1, 2

C. F. NIMB 1961 I

N. M. RILEY 1963 A 3

M. J. LAWLESS 1964 F, 1969–70 E (R), I, W

J. H. BARNARD 1965 S, A 1, 2, NZ 3, 4

P. J. VISAGIE 1967 F 1, 2, 3, 4, 1968 BI 1, 2, 3, 4, F 1, 2, 1969 A 1, 2, 3, 4, 1969–70 S, E, 1970 NZ 1, 2, 3, 4, 1971 F 1, 2, A 1, 2, 3

D. S. L. SNYMAN 1972 E, 1974 BI 1, 2, (R), F 1, 2, 1975 F 1, 2, 1976 NZ 2, 3, 1977 Wld

G. R. BOSCH 1974 BI 2, F 1, 2, 1975 F 1, 2, 1976 NZ 1, 2, 3, 4

R. BLAIR 1977 Wld

H. E. BOTHA 1980 S Am 1, 2, BI 1, 2, 3, 4, S Am 3, 4, F, 1981 I 1, 2, NZ 1, 2, 3, US, 1982 S Am 1, 2, 1986 CV 1, 2, 3, 4 1989 Wld 1, 2, 1992 v NZ, A, F 2, E

E. G. TOBIAS 1981 I 1, 2, 1984 E 1, 2, S Am 1, 2

WALES

E. JAMES 1890 S, 1891 I, 1892 S, I, 1899 E

D. JAMES 1891 I, 1892 S, I, 1899 E

R. B. SWEET-ESCOTT 1891 S, 1894 I, 1895 I

H. P. PHILLIPS 1892 E, 1893 E, SI, I, 1894 E, S

S. H. BIGGS 1895 E, S, 1896 S, 1897 E, 1898 I, E, 1899 S, I, 1900 I

D. MORGAN 1895 I, 1896 E

G. I. LLOYD 1896 I, 1899 S, I, 1900 E, S, 1901 E, S, 1902 S, I, 1903 E, S, I

W. J. TREW 1900 E, S, I, 1901 E, S, 1903 S, 1905 S, 1906 S, 1907 E, S, 1908 E, S, F, I, A, 1909 E, S, F, I, 1910 F, E, S, 1911 E, S, F, I, 1912 S, 1913 S, F

R. JONES 1901 I, 1902 E, 1904 E, S, I, 1905 E, 1908 F, I, A, 1909 E, S, F, I, 1910 F, E

P. F. BUSH 1905 NZ, 1906 E, SA, 1907 I, 1908 E, S, 1910 S, I

R. A. GIBBS 1906 S, I, 1907 E, S, 1908 E, S, F, I, 1910 F, E, S, I, 1911 E, S, F, I

J. M. C. LEWIS 1912 E, 1913 S, F, I, 1914 E, S, F, I, 1921 E, S

W. J. MARTIN 1912 I, F, 1919 NZ, A

H. W. THOMAS 1912 SA 1913 E

J. J. WETTER 1914 S, F, I, 1920 E, S, F, I, 1921 E, 1924 I, NZ

W. BOWEN 1921 S, F, 1922 E, S, I, F

W. J. DELAHAY 1922 E, S, I, F, 1923 E, S, F, I, 1924 NZ, 1925 E, S, F, I, 1926 E, S, I, F, 1927 S

D. E. JOHN 1923 F, I, 1928 E, S, I

A. OWEN 1924 E

V. M. GRIFFITHS 1924 S, I, F

E. WILLIAMS 1924 NZ, 1925 F

W. J. HOPKINS 1925 E, S

R. JONES 1926 E, S, F

W. H. LEWIS 1926 I, 1927 E, F, I, A, 1928 F

E. G. RICHARDS 1927 S

W. ROBERTS 1929 E

F. L. WILLIAMS 1929 S, F, I, 1930 E, S, I, F, 1931 F, I, SA, 1932 E, S, I, 1933 I

H. M. BOWCOTT 1929 S, F, I, 1930 E, 1931 F, S, 1933 E, I

A. R. RALPH 1931 F, I, SA, 1932 E, S, I

R. R. MORRIS 1933 S, 1937 S

C. W. JONES 1934 E, S, I, 1935 E, S, I, NZ, 1936 E, S, I, 1938 E, S, I

W. T. H. DAVIES 1936 I, 1937 E, I, 1939 E, S, I

B. L. WILLIAMS 22 caps, one at fly-half v E 1947

G. DAVIES 1947 S, A, 1948 E, S, F, I, 1949 E, S, F, 1951 E, S

W. B. CLEAVER 1947 E, S, F, I, A, 1948 E, S, F, I, 1949 I, 1950 E, S, I, F

C. I. MORGAN 1951 I, F, SA, 1952 E, S, I, 1953 S, I, F, NZ, 1954 E, I, S, 1955 E, S, I, F, 1956 E, S, I, F, 1957 E, S, I, F, 1958 E, S, I, F

A. G. THOMAS 13 caps, one at fly-half v F 1952

R. BURNETT 1953 E

G. JOHN 1954 E, F

C. R. JAMES 1958 A, F

C. ASHTON 1959 E, S, I, 1960 E, S, I, 1962 I

M. C. THOMAS 27 caps, one at fly-half v F 1959

B. RICHARDS 1960 F

K. H. L. RICHARDS 1960 SA, 1961 E, S, I, F

A. REES 1962 E, S, F

D. WATKINS 1963 E, S, I, F, NZ, 1964 E, S, I, F, SA, 1965 E, S, I, F, 1966 E, S, I, F, 1967 I, F, E

B. JOHN 1966 A, 1967 S, NZ, 1968 E, S, I, F, 1969 S, I, F, E, NZ 1, 2, A, 1970 SA, S, E, I, 1971 E, S, I, F, 1972 E, S, F

P. BENNETT 1969 F (R), 1970 SA, S, F, 1972 S (R), NZ, 1973 E, S, I, F, A, 1974 S, I, F, E, 1975 S (R) I, 1976 E, S, I, F, 1977 I, F, E, S, 1978 E, S, I, F

J. D. BEVAN 1975 F, E, S, A

W. G. DAVIES 1978 A 1, 2, NZ, 1979 S, I, F, E, 1980 F, E, S, NZ, 1981 E, S, A, 1982 I, F, E, S, 1985 S, I, F

P. J. MORGAN 1980 S (R), I, NZ (R), one at fly-half v I 1980, 1981 I

M. DACEY 1983 E, S, I, F, R, 1984 S,

277

I, F, E, A, 1986 Fj, Tg, WS, 1987 F
(R), [Tg]
J. DAVIES 1985 E, Fj, 1986 E, S, I, F,
Fj, Tg, WS, 1987 F, E, S, I, [I, Tg
(R), C, E, NZ, A], 1988 E, S, I, F,
NZ 1, 2, WS, R
B. BOWEN 23 caps, 4 at fly-half
P. TURNER 1989 I (R), F, E
A. DAVIES 1990 Bb (R), 1991 A
N. R. JENKINS 1991 E, S, I, F 1,
1992 I, F, E, S
C. J. STEPHENS 1992 I, F, E, A

BRITISH ISLES

Test appearances by fly-halves up to
mid-1993.
(Figures denote which Test match of
series was played)

1910 to South Africa
J. A. SPOORS 1, 3, C. H. PILLMAN
2

1924 to South Africa
H. WADDELL 1, 2, 4, W.
CUNNINGHAM 3

1930 to New Zealand and Australia
R. S. SPONG 1, 2, 3, 4–1

1938 to South Africa
F. J. REYNOLDS 1, 2 G. CROMEY 3

1950 to New Zealand and Australia
J. W. KYLE 1, 2, 3, 4–1, 2

1955 to South Africa
C. I. MORGAN 1, 2, 3, 4

1959 to Australia and New Zealand
A. B. W. RISMAN 1, 2–1, 4, M. J.
PRICE 2, J. P. HORROCKS-
TAYLOR 3

1962 to South Africa
G. H. WADDELL 1, 2, R. A. W.
SHARP 3, 4

1966 to Australia and New Zealand
D. WATKINS 1, 2–1, 2, 3, 4

1968 to South Africa
B. JOHN 1, C. M. H. GIBSON 2, 3, 4

1971 to New Zealand
B. JOHN 1, 2, 3, 4

1974 to South Africa
P. BENNETT 1, 2, 3, 4

1977 to New Zealand
P. BENNETT 1, 2, 3, 4

1980 to South Africa
A. J. P. WARD 1, W. G. DAVIES 2, S.
O. CAMPBELL 3, 4

1983 to New Zealand
S. O. CAMPBELL 1, 2, 3, 4

1989 to Australia
C. M. CHALMERS 1, C. R.
ANDREW 2, 3

1993 to New Zealand
C. R. ANDREW 1, 2, 3

Index

281

CHARLTON: The Autobiography
by Jack Charlton

'I know who you are: you're The Boss.'
The words of His Holiness John Paul II, on meeting Jack Charlton and his Republic of Ireland team before the 1990 World Cup finals.

Indeed, Jack Charlton is The Boss – a man whose strength of character has driven him to achievements beyond the scope of his own natural talents or those of the teams who have played under him.

His book tells of his childhood in a Northumberland mining village and how he escaped a life down the mine by joining Leeds where he played for twenty years. As a player he also touched the pinnacle in England's legendary 1966 World Cup winning team. As a manager he dragged the Republic of Ireland team from the backwaters of international football to compete with the world's best. As a man, he is noted for his forthright personality – one whose views are as honest as they are respected. This is his story, the story of a man who specializes in the improbable.

'A tough, uncompromising book . . . A great read and an intriguing insight into Big Jack'
Frances Edmonds, *Daily Telegraph*

'Big Jack is a universally popular figure in football. The autobiography captures why'
Independent

0 552 14519 X

SUMMERS WILL NEVER BE THE SAME
A Tribute to Brian Johnston
Edited by Christopher Martin-Jenkins & Pat Gibson

'I understand there are some men who do not like cricket, but I would not like my daughter to marry one'
Brian Johnston

Brian Johnston, who died in January 1994, was one of the best loved figures on radio. His unique broadcasting style won him a special place in the hearts of listeners everywhere.

Although 'Johnners' became known as the voice of cricket, he was also a national figure as the presenter of *Down Your Way*. His many other broadcasting credits include presenting for television the Queen's Coronation and the Boat Race.

Most of all, Johnners will be remembered for his schoolboy humour. Specially revised and updated for the paperback edition, this volume of tributes includes anecdotes and memoirs from over sixty colleagues and friends – including John Major, Sir Colin Cowdrey, Richie Benaud, John Paul Getty, Lord Whitelaw, Tim Rice, Lord Carrington and Jonathan Agnew – as well as short extracts from Johnners's own publications and transcripts of some of his most famous broadcasts.

0 552 99631 9

SEVE: The Biography
by Lauren St John

'One of the most comprehensive analyses of any golfer in recent times'
Sunday Telegraph

In 1976, aged nineteen, Seve Ballesteros became a star in the eyes of the public when he narrowly failed to win the Open despite having led for three rounds. Since then he has confirmed his early promise and gone on to win countless tournaments and a host of majors. Dark, handsome and talented, Ballesteros has the capacity to excite the imagination in a way that no other player does. No-one can match his fire, his brilliance or his charisma. He is volatile and outspoken but also generous and passionately loyal.

In retracing his life from childhood right up to the present day as Captain of Europe's Ryder Cup team, Lauren St John has compiled a detailed portrait of Seve Ballesteros which will provide all followers of golf with a fascinating insight into this captivating champion. *Seve: The Biography* is the definitive account of the greatest and most charismatic player of the current age.

'A searching and highly readable examination . . . One of the bravest hearts the game has ever seen'
Observer

'Has passages of such lyrical and descriptive beauty that you are convinced the writer not only has a love for her subject but is held in thrall by the game of golf'
Scotland on Sunday

0 552 14588 2

A SELECTED LIST OF RELATED TITLES
AVAILABLE FROM CORGI AND PARTRIDGE

25272 3	MICHAEL SCHUMACHER (Hardback)	*James Allen*	£16.99
14519 X	JACK CHARLTON: THE AUTOBIOGRAPHY	*Jack Charlton*	£5.99
14003 1	CLOUGH THE AUTOBIOGRAPHY	*Brian Clough*	£5.99
25262 6	HANDS AND HEELS (Hardback)	*Richard Dunwoody*	£20.00
13937 8	THE FIRST FIFTY – MUNRO–BAGGING WITHOUT A BEARD		
		Muriel Gray	£9.99
13754 5	AYRTON SENNA: THE HARD EDGE OF GENIUS		
		Christopher Hilton	£7.99
14494 0	AN EVENING WITH JOHNNERS	*ed. Brian Johnston*	£6.99
25263 4	COMING TO THE LAST: A TRIBUTE TO PETER O'SULLEVAN		
	(Hardback)	*Sean Magee*	£12.99
99631 9	SUMMERS WILL NEVER BE THE SAME		
		Christopher Martin-Jenkins & Pat Gibson	£6.99
25268 5	THRUST: THE REMARKABLE STORY OF ONE MAN'S QUEST FOR		
	SPEED (Hardback)	*Richard Noble*	£20.00
25254 5	JENNY PITMAN: THE AUTOBIOGRAPHY (Hardback)		
		Jenny Pitman	£17.99
25230 8	STEVEN REDGRAVE'S COMPLETE BOOK OF ROWING (Hardback)		
		Steven Redgrave	£17.99
25196 4	COMPLETE BOOK OF MINI RUGBY (Hardback)		
		Don Rutherford	£8.99
25261 8	GREG NORMAN: THE BIOGRAPHY (Hardback)		
		Lauren St John	£16.99
25228 6	OUT OF BOUNDS (Hardback)	*Lauren St John*	£16.99
14588 2	SEVE: BIOGRAPHY OF SEVE BALLESTEROS		
		Lauren St John	£7.99
14552 1	DICKIE: A TRIBUTE TO UMPIRE HAROLD BIRD		
		ed. Brian Scovell	£6.99